A. P Huguenet, C Hossfeld

Hossfeld's new practical method for learning the French language

A. P Huguenet, C Hossfeld

Hossfeld's new practical method for learning the French language

ISBN/EAN: 9783337085827

Printed in Europe, USA, Canada, Australia, Japan

Cover: Foto ©Paul-Georg Meister /pixelio.de

More available books at **www.hansebooks.com**

HOSSFELD'S EDUCATIONAL WORKS.

SPANISH.

	s.	d.
English-Spanish Grammar, by Hossfeld's New Method, arranged for Classes, Schools, and Private Lessons	3	0
Spanish-English Grammar, by Hossfeld's New Method	4	0
Key to above	2	0
Conjugation of the Spanish Regular and Irregular Verbs	0	6
English-Spanish Commercial Correspondent	2	0
German-Spanish Commercial Correspondent	2	0
French-Spanish Commercial Correspondent	2	0
Spanish-English and English-Spanish Dictionary (New Edition)	3	6
Ditto, by Velasquez	6	0
Ditto, by Velasquez (Large Edition)	24	0
Hossfeld's Spanish Reader	2	0
German-Spanish Reader	2	0
Hossfeld's Spanish Dialogues	1	6
Don Quixote, in Spanish	5	0
Gil Blas, in Spanish	2	0

ITALIAN.

	s.	d.
English-Italian Grammar, by Hossfeld's New Method, arranged for Classes, Schools, and Private Lessons	3	0
Italian Composition and Idioms	2	6
Conjugation of Italian Regular and Irregular Verbs	0	6
English-Italian and Italian-English Dictionary, by Meizi (2 vols.)	7	6
Ditto, by Millhouse (2 vols.)	12	0
Ditto, by Hossfeld	2	0
Italian Reader, by Dr. C. Scotti	2	0

PORTUGUESE.

	s.	d.
Grammar, by Grauert	5	0

DUTCH.

	s.	d.
English-Dutch and Dutch-English Dictionary	4	6

RUSSIAN.

	s.	d.
English-Russian and Russian-English Dictionary	4	6
Hints on Language, by R. I. Isnard	1	0

HIRSCHFELD BROS.,
22 AND 24, BREAMS BUILDINGS, FETTER LANE, LONDON, E.C.

HOSSFELD'S EDUCATIONAL WORKS.

FRENCH.

	s.	d.
English-French Grammar, by Hossfeld's New Method, arranged for Classes, Schools, and Private Lessons	3	0
Elementary French Grammar	1	0
Advanced French Grammar	2	6
French Composition and Idioms	2	6
Conjugation of French Regular and Irregular Verbs	0	6
Polyglot Correspondent (English, French, German, Spanish)	3	6
English-French Commercial Correspondent	2	0
French-English Commercial Correspondent	2	0
English-French Dictionary	1	0
French-English Dictionary	1	0
The Two Dictionaries in one volume	2	0
Manual of French Conversation	1	6
100 Passages for Translation into English and German	2	0
100 Passages for Translation into German and French	2	0
Molière, Les Fourberies De Scapin	1	0

GERMAN.

	s.	d.
English-German Grammar, by Hossfeld's New Method, arranged for Classes, Schools, and Private Lessons	3	0
Mengel's German Exercises and Idioms	2	6
Conjugation of German Regular and Irregular Verbs	0	6
Hossfeld's German Reader	2	0
English-German Commercial Correspondent	2	0
French-German Commercial Correspondent	2	0
English-German Dictionary	1	0
German-English Dictionary	1	0
The Two Dictionaries in one volume	2	0
Select German Stories	1	6

SWEDISH.

	s.	d.
English-Swedish and Swedish-English Dictionary	4	6

DANO-NORWEGIAN.

	s.	d.
English-Dano-Norwegian and Dano-Norwegian-English Dictionary	4	6

HIRSCHFELD BROS.
22 AND 24, BREAMS BUILDINGS, FETTER LANE, LONDON. E.C.

FRENCH GRAMMAR.

HOSSFELD'S NEW METHOD.

INVALUABLE TO STUDENTS OF MODERN LANGUAGES.

HINTS ON LANGUAGE

As a means of Mental Discipline,
And on the Importance of the Study of Modern Languages,
By Prof. R. J. Isnard.

PRICE ONE SHILLING.

HIRSCHFELD BROS.,
BREAMS BUILDINGS, FETTER LANE, LONDON, E.C.

HOSSFELD'S

NEW PRACTICAL METHOD

FOR LEARNING THE

FRENCH LANGUAGE

BY

A. P. HUGUENET,

Officier d'Académie, Université de France;
Membre de la Société Nationale des Professeurs de Français en Angleterre.
Instructor Royal Naval College, Greenwich;
Examiner at Queen's College, London, &c. ;
Occasional Examiner to Her Majesty's Civil Service Commissioners.

NEW AND REVISED EDITION.

London:

HIRSCHFELD BROTHERS,
BREAMS BUILDINGS, FETTER LANE, E.C.

1892.

ENTERED AT
STATIONERS' HALL.

ALL
RIGHTS RESERVED.

CONTENTS.

	page
Preface	3
French alphabet	5
Accents and signs	5
Pronunciation of the vowels	6
Reading of words with vowels	7
Compound vowels.—Diphthongs	8
Pronunciation of the nasal sounds	8
Reading of words with compound vowels and diphthongs	9
Reading of words with nasal sounds	9
Pronunciation of the liquid sounds	10
Pronunciation of the consonants	10
Reading of words with liquid sounds	11
Reading of words with consonants	11
Linking of two words	14
Reading exercise on the linking of words	15
General exceptions to the rules of pronunciation	16
Division of syllables	18
Punctuation	18
Parts of speech	18
Numbers	19
Genders	19
The article and the noun.—Definite article	20

	page
Formation of the plural of nouns	20
Indefinite article	28
Partitive article	32
Words which are the same or nearly the same in English and French	36
The adjective	40
Qualifying adjectives.—Formation of the feminine	40
„ „ Formation of the plural	48
Degrees of comparison	48
Place of adjectives	52
Determinative adjectives.—Cardinal numeral adjectives	56
Ordinal numeral adjectives	60
Demonstrative adjectives	64
Possessive adjectives	68
Indefinite adjectives	68
The pronoun.—Personal pronouns	72
Demonstrative pronouns	80
Possessive pronouns	88
Relative and interrogative pronouns	92
Indefinite pronouns	96
Verbs	104
Adverbs.—Adverbs of manner	108
Adverbs of time	112
Adverbs of place	112
Adverbs of order	112
Adverbs of quantity	112
Adverbs of comparison	112
Adverbs of affirmation, negation and doubt	112
Adverbs of interrogation	112
Prepositions	116
Conjunctions	120
Government of conjunctions	120
Interjections	128
Remarks on verbs	132
Words with aspirated *h*	136

	page
Twenty Dialogues ... ... 141 to	160
A meeting, *une rencontre*	141
About the way, or road, *au sujet du chemin* ...	142
Visit, *visite*	143
Railway journey, *voyage en chemin de fer*	144
,, ,, ,, ,, ...	145
Sea journey, *traversée*	146
At a town, *dans une ville*.	147
Letting apartments, *location d'appartements* ...	148
With a servant, *avec un domestique*	149
Meals, *repas*	150
To write a letter, *pour écrire une lettre*	151
At a money-changer's, *chez un changeur*	152
Buying, *achats*	153
Carriages, *voitures*	154
At table, *à table*	155
A walk, *une promenade*	156
With a doctor, *avec un docteur*	157
Paris Museums, *Musées de Paris*	158
The Streets of Paris, *les rues de Paris*	159
How to progress in French, *comment faire des progrès en Français*	160
Syntax	162
Construction of affirmative sentences	166
Interrogative sentences	170
Negative sentences	178
Syntax of the article	186
Syntax of the noun.—Rules how to ascertain the gender of French nouns by their signification	194
Rules to ascertain the gender of French nouns by their endings	198
Gender of several nouns	206
Nouns which are of different gender according to their signification	214
Feminine of some nouns	218
Remarks on the number of nouns	222
Plural of compound nouns	226

	page
Syntax of the qualifying adjective.—Agreement of adjectives with nouns or pronouns	230
Place of adjectives	238
Adjectives of dimensions	242
Syntax of the determinative adjectives.—Possessive adjectives	246
Indefinite adjectives	250
Syntax of the pronoun.—Personal pronouns	254
Demonstrative pronouns	266
Indefinite pronouns	270
Syntax of the verb.—Subject of the verb	274
Complements of the verb	282
Use of the auxiliary verbs	286
Use of the tenses and moods	286
Syntax of the participles.—Present participle	298
Past participle	298

Instructions, how to correspond in French with the aid of HOSSFELD's Commercial Correspondent ... 321—336

The verb ... ... (supplement) 1.—36

INDEX

A

	PAGE
Acute accent	
Adjectives (qualifying)	40, 44, 48
Adjectives (place of)	52, 238
Adjectives (complements of)	242
Adverbs	108, 112
Affirmation, negation and doubt (adverbs of)	112
Affirmative sentences (construction of)	166
Agreement of adjectives with nouns or pronouns	230, 234
Agreement of participles	298, 302
Apostrophe	5
Article (definite)	20, 24
Article (indefinite)	28
Article (partitive)	32
Article (syntax of the)	186
Attribute	162
Au, à la, à l', aux, to the	24
Aucun, nul, no, none	68, 96, 250
Avoir l'air, to look	242
Auxiliary verbs (use of)	286

C

Ce, cet, cette, ces, this, that, these, those	64, 80, 84
Ce, ceci, celui-ci, celui-là, ceux-ci, ceux-là, &c., this, that, these, those	80, 84, 266
Chacun, everyone	96, 270
Chaque, every, each	68
Cedilla	5
Circumflex accent	5
Collective nouns	278
Commercial correspondence	231, 336
Comparison (adverbs of)	112

	PAGE
Comparison (degrees of)	48, 52
Compound adjectives	234
Compound vowels (pronunciation of)	8
Compound nouns (plural of)	226
Complements of the verb	282
Conjunctions	120, 124, 128
Conjunctive personal pronouns	72, 76, 254
Conversations	22, 26, 30
(and on the 3rd page of each lesson)	

D

Demonstrative adjectives	64
Demonstrative pronouns	80, 84
Dialogues (twenty on subjects of every day life)	140
Diæresis	5
Dimensions (adjectives of)	242
Dipthongs (pronunciation of)	8
Disjunctive personal pronouns	72, 76, 254
Dont, of whom, of which	92
Du, de la, de l', des, of the	24, 32

E

Elle, elles, she, they	72
En, of him, of her, of it, of them, in, by, thence	72, 76, 246, 262
Endings of French verbs (supplement)	35
Est-ce que, is it that	174
Eux, they, them	72
Exercises	21, 25, 29
(and on the 2nd page of each lesson)	

F

Feminine of adjectives	40, 48
Feminine of some nouns	218
Feu, late	230

G

Genders	19
Genders (how to ascertain by the signification)	194, 198

	PAGE
Genders (how to ascertain by the endings)	198, 202
General collective nouns	278
Government of verbs (supplement)	32
Grave accent	5
Gens, people	210

H

H (aspirated)	136
Hyphen	5

I

Il, ils, he, they	72
Imperfect, past definite, past indefinite (use of the)	290
Indefinite adjectives	68
Indefinite adjectives (syntax of)	250
Indefinite pronouns	96, 100
Indefinite pronouns (syntax of)	270
Interjections	128
Interrogation (adverbs of)	112
Interrogative pronouns	92
Interrogative sentences	174
Irregular verbs, first group (supplement)	24
Irregular verbs, second group (supplement)	26

J

Je, I	72

L

Le, la, l', les, the	20, 24
Le, la, l', les, him, her, it, them	72, 76, 258
Lequel, laquelle, lesquels, lesquelles, which	92
Leur, leurs, their	68, 246, 278
Leur, to them	72
Lui, leur, he, to him, to her, to them	72, 76, 262
Le mien, le tien, le sien, &c., mine, thine, his, hers, its, &c.	88
Le peu de, the few, the want of	278
Linking of words	14
Liquid sounds (pronunciation of)	10

	PAGE
L'un, l'autre, l'un l'autre, l'un et l'autre, l'un ou l'autre, ni l'un ni l'autre, the one, the other, each other, both, either, neither	96, 270

M

Manner (adverbs of)	108
Me, me, to me	72
Même, same, even, self	250
Moi, I, me	72
Mon, ma, mes, my	68
Moods (use of)	294

N

Nasal sounds (pronunciation of)	8
Ne, ne...pas, non, not, no	178, 182
Negative sentences	178
Ni, neither, nor	274
Nu, demi, bare, half	230
Nous, we, us	72
Nouns (plural of)	20, 24, 28
Nouns (syntax of)	194
Nouns (genders of several)	206, 210, 214
Nouns (remarks on the number of several)	222
Nouns (of foreign origin)	222
Numeral adjectives (cardinal)	56
Numeral adjectives (ordinal)	60
Numbers	19

O

On, one, we, they, people	96, 100
Order (adverbs of)	112
Ou, or	274

P

Participle (syntax of the)	298
Partitive collective nouns	278
Past participles (agreement of)	298, 302
Period	162

	PAGE
Personal pronouns	72, 76
Personal pronouns (syntax of)	254
Personne, nobody, anybody	96, 270
Place (adverbs of)	112
Possessive adjectives	68
Possessive adjectives (syntax of)	246
Possessive pronouns	88
Plural of nouns	20, 24, 28
Plural of adjectives	48
Plusieurs, several	68
Prepositions	116
Pronunciations (exceptions to the rules of)	16, 17
Propositions	162
Proper nouns	222
Punctuation	18

Q

Qualifying adjectives	40, 44, 48
Qualifying adjectives (syntax of)	230
Quantity (adverbs of)	112
Que, that	128
Quel, which, what	68
Quelconque, whatever	68
Quiconque, whoever	96
Quelque, some, any	68
Quelque, however	250
Quel que, whoever, whatever	250
Quelqu'un, somebody, anybody	96
Questions on grammar	22, 26, 30
(and on the 3rd page of each lesson)	
Qui, que, quoi, who, whom, what	92
Qui est-ce qui, qui est-ce que, &c., who, whom, &c.	174

R

Reading exercises	23, 27, 31
(and on the 4th page of each lesson)	
Relative pronouns	92
Rien, nothing, anything	96, 270

S

	PAGE
Se, soi, himself, herself, themselves, one's self	72, 76, 262
Son, sa, ses, leur, leurs, his, her, its, their	68, 246, 278
Speech (parts of)	18, 19
Subject of the verb	162, 274
Syllables (division of)	18
Syntax	162

T

Te, thee, to thee	72
Tel, such	68
Tenses (use of)	286, 290
Toi, thou, the	72
Time (adverbs of)	112
Tout, all, every, whole, quite	68, 96, 250
Tu, thou	72

U

Un, une, a, an, one	28, 56

V

Verbs	104
Verbs (remarks on)	132
Verbs (syntax of)	274
Verbs (Supplement; *see* special index)	
Vocabularies	21, 25, 29
(and on the 2nd page of each lesson)	
Vous, you	72
Vowels (pronunciation of)	6

W

Words which are the same or nearly the same in English and French	36

Y

Y, to, it, there, thither	72, 76, 262

INDEX

TO THE PIECES OF PROSE AND POETRY TO BE FOUND IN THIS VOLUME.

PROSE.

	PAGE
Les jardins de Babylone, *Rollin*	245, 249
Histoire d'une servante (Extrait de l'), *Lamartine*	253, 257
Immortalité de l'âme, *Jean Jacques Rousseau*	261
Combat de Télémaque, *Fénelon*	265
Etudes de la nature (Extrait des), *Bernardin de St. Pierre*	269
La conscience, *Châteaubriand*	273
Lettre à sa fille, *Madame de Sévigné*	277
Lettre à Madame Dupuy, *Voltaire*	281, 285
Adieux de Fontainebleau, *Napoléon I.*	289
Un réveille-matin, *Xavier de Maistre*	293
Les Romains conquérants, *Montesquieu*	297
Comment il faut causer, *La Bruyère*	301
Prononciation de l'U, *Molière*	305
Conseils sur l'art d'écrire, *Voltaire*	306
Pourquoi l'homme naît plus faible que les animaux, *Saintine*	306
La bosse de l'art militaire, *Tœpffer*	307
L'incendie de St. Sylvain, *Jules Sandeau*	308

POÉSIES.

L'huître et les plaideurs, *Boileau*	311
La laitière et le pot au lait, *La Fontaine*	311
Le singe qui montre la lanterne magique, *Florian*	312
La jeune captive, *André Chénier*	313
Derniers moments d'un jeune poète, *Gilbert*	315
A une fleur, *Alfred de Musset*	316
Hymne, *Victor Hugo*	317
La feuille, *Arnault*	318
Image de la vie, *Madame Tastu*	318
Chœur d'Athalie, *Racine père*	318
Preuves de l'existence de Dieu, *Racine fils*	319

Signs and Abbreviations.

In the first 19 Reading Exercises, nasal and liquid sounds are indicated by italics, and the linking of words is indicated thus ‿

m., masculine.

f., feminine.

p. or *pl.*, *plu.* or *plur.*, plural.

p. d., past definite.

i. or *imp.*, imperfect.

sing., singular.

PREFACE.

Notwithstanding the great success of the different works for the study of the French language, published by HIRSCHFELD BROS., it has been found that no one of them entirely meets the requirements of teaching in schools, and we have been frequently asked to publish another book on HOSSFELD's method which would be at the same time a Grammar, a Book of Exercises, a Manual of Conversation and a Reading-book, giving more development to the grammatical part and lengthening the exercises.

The present publication will be found to meet this acknowledged want.

The book is divided into 66 lessons, each of which consists of 4 pages:

The *first page* is devoted to Grammar;

The *second* contains Exercises on Verbs and on the Rules on the opposite page;

The *third* gives Questions on the same Rules destined for pupils who are preparing for an examination at which they will have to answer similar questions; and also Conversations in which these rules are illustrated;

The *fourth* page consists always of a Reading Exercise, which must not only be read aloud, but also translated with the help of the indications given either between the lines, or at the bottom of the page.

THE FRENCH ALPHABET.

The French Alphabet consists of 26 letters:

A	a	ah	J	j	zhee	S	s	ess
B	b	beh	K	k	kah	T	t	teh
C	c	ceh	L	l	ell	U	u	ü (†)
D	d	deh	M	m	emm	V	v	veh
E	e	eh	N	n	enn	W	w	dooble veh
F	f	eff	O	o	oh	X	x	iks
G	g	zheh	P	p	peh	Y	y	ee greck
H	h	ash	Q	q	kü (†)	Z	z	zed
I	i	ee	R	r	err			

NOTE.—The letters *k* and *w* are very seldom used, and only occur in words of foreign origin.

The simple Vowels are: *a, e, i, o, u* and *y*; and the remaining letters are Consonants.

Accents and Signs.

Accents in French are signs placed over a vowel to give it a different sound from its ordinary pronunciation, sometimes merely to indicate the difference between two words of the same spelling but different in their meanings.

There are three accents:

the acute (´) which can only be applied to *e*: *é*.
the grave (`) which can be applied to *a, e, u*: *à, è, ù*.
the circumflex (^) which can be applied to all the vowels: *a, e, i, o, u*: *â, ê, î, ô, û*.

The cedilla (¸) is a sign placed under *c*: (*ç*) before *a, o, u*, to indicate that this consonant must be pronounced like *s*.

The diæresis (¨) is placed over *e* and *i*: *ë, ï*, to indicate that these vowels must be pronounced separately from a preceding vowel, and over *e* (mute) to indicate that the *u* which precedes it must be pronounced: *haïr, aiguë*.

The apostrophe (') is used to indicate the elision of the vowel *e*, and also that of *a* in the article *la* before a vowel, and of the *i* of *si* before *il* or *ils*: *l', s'il*.

The hyphen (-) is used to connect words.

(*) It is quite impossible to indicate the correct pronunciation of *u* by any spelling.

Pronunciation of the Vowels.

Note.—In pronouncing a French word, the emphasis or stress is always upon the last syllable pronounced, but the emphasis is very slight. The consonants in the examples are pronounced as in English. In French, consonants at the end of words are not sounded, except *c, f, l, r*, which are generally pronounced.

a sounds like *a* in *at*; as in,
 la, fatal, papa, bal, mal

e (unaccented) at the end of a syllable (*) sounds like *e* in *her*; as in, le, me, te, cela, repas, arsenal

e (unaccented) at the end of a word of more than one syllable is always silent; as in,
 cabale, rame, malade, tasse, salade, avare

é (acute accent) sounds almost like *ey* in *abbey*; as in,
 métal, répété, sérénade, armée, marée

e (unaccented) sounds like *é* in the end syllables *ed, ez*, and in *er*, if the final consonant is mute; as in,
 pied, assez, nez, armer, parler

è (grave accent) sounds like *e* in *where*; as in,
 mètre, remède, frère, élève, carène, nèfle

e (unaccented) sounds like *è* in a syllable terminated by one or more consonants (*); as in,
 esclave, fer, préfet, tablette, belle

ê (circumflex accent) sounds like *ay* in *hay*; as in,
 tête, frêle, fenêtre, rêve, crême

i & **y** sound like the English *e* in *equal*; as in,
 il, mine, victime, flétrir, myrte

o sounds like the *o* in *cross*; as in,
 corset, mol, col, botte, dormir, donner

u having no equivalent in English must be heard from the master. In order to get at the sound pronounce the *ee* in *been* with rounded lips as in whistling; as in,
 bulbe, cumul, futur, butte, brutal, rupture

u is silent after *q* and between *g e* and *g i* (not before *ë* or *ï*); as in, quart, qui, guérir, guide

Note: All vowels have a short sound, except in the following principal cases, when the sound becomes long:
 1. if they have the circumflex accent; as in,
  pâle, tête, île, ôter, flûte
 2. if followed by *rr*, a final *s* or *se*, a final *r* or *re*; as in,
  barre, terre, ses, dos, base, brise, rose, muse, finir, avare, frère, lire, pore, pure
 3. if followed by an *e* mute; as in, armée, vie, rue

(*) viz.: Division of syllables on page 18.

Reading of Words with Vowels.

Malade	rupture	pêle-mêle	matinal(*)	alité	écume
ill	rupture	pell-mell	early	laid up	foam
salade	une	âne	pelure	sérénade	morbide	élève
salad	a	ass	peel	serenade	morbid	pupil
ballade	café	verre	marmelade	lunette	morale	perle
ballad	coffee	glass	marmalade	eye-glass	morals	pearl
si	fortune	prune	urbanité	livre	carnaval	futur	il
if	fortune	plum	urbanity	book	carnival	future	he
regard	fibre	régal	alêne	universel	rude	canal
look	fibre	feast	awl	universal	rude	canal
ridicule	calamité	bal	navire	crêpe	mortalité	mer
ridicule	calamity	ball	ship	crape	mortality	sea
rival	maritime	maturité	cataracte	colonel	elle
rival	maritime	maturity	cataract	colonel	she
répète	col	amical	abbé	minéral	mal	divinité	me
repeats	collar	amicable	abbot	mineral	evil	divinity	me
il jette	pâle	que	docilité	nèfle	miracle	dos	terre
he throws	pale	that	docility	medlar	miracle	back	earth
amiral	redevenir	mol	vulgarité	balustrade	guerre
admiral	to become again	soft	vulgarity	balustrade	war
colosse	quatre	utilité	paternel	nul	relatif	or
colossus	four	utility	paternal	null	relative	gold
fermer	guinée	idole	répété	réalité	carpe	flûte
to shut	guinea	idol	repeated	reality	carp	flute
mercure	pied	forme	avenir	véritable	frêle
mercury	foot	form	future	veritable	slender
ver	lune	if	rareté	arme	tabernacle	dîner	vérité
worm	moon	yew	rarity	arm	tabernacle	dinner	truth
avarice	vertical	crépuscule	fanatisme	mur	il va
avarice	vertical	twilight	fanaticism	wall	he goes
barre	pyramide	table	morose	plume	calme	assez
bar	pyramid	table	morose	feather	calm	enough
dûreté	tu lis	trône	éternité	pur	âme	futilité
hardness	thou readest	throne	eternity	pure	soul	futility
porosité	culture	pâte	rhume	rapacité	verdure
porosity	culture	paste	cough	rapacity	verdure
urne	fil	amabilité	tulle	manifeste	canapé	énormité
urn	thread	amiability	net	ma nifesto	couch	enormity

(*) As final consonants are seldom pronounced, we have printed in Italics those which must be sounded.

Compound Vowels.

ai, ei are pronounced like *ai* in *hair*:
    clair, plaine, gai, laine, neige, pleine, reine

au, eau are pronounced like *o* in *note*:
    aube, aurore, beau, cadeau, peau, plateau, veau

eu, œu are pronounced somewhat like *u* in *but*:
    Dieu, peuple, fleur, vœu, sœur, œuvre

ou is pronounced like *oo* in *wood*:
    goutte, poule, route, boule, louve, sou, fou

Diphthongs.

ay is pronounced like the French *ai-i*:
    balayer, essayer, ayant, pays, payer

oi is pronounced like the two English interjections *oh* and *ah* joined together:
    roi, miroir, bois, boire

ui is pronounced by giving to the two vowels their natural sound, but pronouncing them as a single syllable:
    lui, puis, fuire, nuire, nuit, cuit

oy, uy are pronounced like the French *oi-i* and *ui-i*:
    foyer, royal, écuyer, fuyard

Pronunciation of the nasal sounds.

A NASAL SOUND(*) arises when a simple or compound vowel is followed by *m* or *n*; but no nasal sound is produced if the *m* or *n* is followed by another vowel or another *m* or *n*.

aim, ain, ein, im, in, ym sound nearly like *an* in *pang*:
    faim, main, ceindre, impérial, vin, nymphe

am, an, em, en sound nearly like *aun* in *aunt*:
    amputer, dans, embellir, en, enfant

om, on sound somewhat like *on* in *long*:
    plomb, bonbon, fond, garçon, non

um, un sound somewhat like *un* in *lung*:
    humble, parfum, brun, un, lundi

The nasal sound *en* in the end syllables *ien*, **yen** has the sound of the nasal sound *ain*:
    bien, rien, citoyen, moyen

oin is pronounced like *o-ain*:
    besoin, coin, foin, joindre

(*) Similar nasal sounds are found in the English words: *aunt, long, pang, lung*. In order to get the pronunciation of the French nasal sounds, *an, on, ain, un* are pronounced nearly as in the above words but without sounding the *g*.

Reading of words with compound vowels and diphthongs.

Baie	peine	aurore	pays	feu	.eu	fou	foyer
bay	pain	aurora	country	fire	vow	mad	hearth
appuyer	reine	paysanne	sœur	roi	clou	tournée	
to support	queen	peasant (f.)	sister	king	nail	circuit	
essuyer	seize	aumône	balayer	Dieu	œuvre	royal	
to wipe	sixteen	alms	to sweep	God	work	royal	
maître	fou	baleine	eau	cœur	boutoir	boyaux	
master	fool	whale	water	heart	snout	bowels	
fuyard	beauté	bœuf	écumoire	ouverture	vous		
fugitive	beauty	ox	skimmer	opening	you		
plaire	taureau	ivoire	poudre	yeux	palais	aile	
to please	bull	ivory	powder	eyes	palace	wing	
mœurs	loi	moineau	couteau	bateau	voleur	œuf	
manners	law	sparrow	knife	boat	thief	egg	
soie	coudoyer	foule	peau	beurre	fuseau	noyer	
silk	to elbow	crowd	skin	butter	distaff	to drown	
tuyau	mémoire	croûte	oiseau	peuple	bois	poule	
tube	memory	crust	bird	people	wood	hen	

Reading of words with nasal sounds.

Ambulant	emballer	ciment	bimbelot	quinze
ambulatory	to pack up	cement	toy	fifteen
lymphatique	daim	bain	ceindre	criant	conscience
lymphatic	deer	bath	to gird	crying	conscience
France	ancien	combat	bonbon	humble	brun
France	ancient	combat	sugar-plum	humble	brown
besoin	fonte	enfant	cendre	grimper	dinde	essaim
want	casting	child	ashes	to climb	turkey-hen	swarm
crainte	dépeindre	fiancée	ancienne	comte	parfum
fear	to describe	betrothed	ancient	count	perfume
aucun	fantaisie	membre	denrée	allemand	nymphe
no one	fantasy	member	provisions	German	nymph
faim	gain	étreinte	friand	expérience	citoyen
hunger	profit	grasp	dainty	experience	citizen
moyen	rompre	citron	défunt	foin	son	gant
means	to break	lemon	deceased	hay	sound	glove
remplacer	enchanter	imparfait	incandescent	feinte
to replace	to enchant	imperfect	white-hot	pretence

Pronunciation of the liquid sounds.

il and ill if preceded by a simple or compound vowel, have a liquid sound and are pronounced like *ee-y* in the middle and *ee* at the end of words; the vowels preceding *il* or *ill* keep their usual pronunciation, except *e*, which i pronounced like è:

bail, caillou, bataille, soleil, meilleur, bouteille, fauteuil, feuillet, feuille, fenouil, bouillir, patrouille

œ and *ue* before *il* and *ill* have the sound of the French *eu*:
œil, œillet, cercueil

ill not preceded by a vowel has also a liquid sound, as in *billet, famille*, except in words which commence with *ill, mill, vill*, and a few others, *illégale, mille, millimètre, ville, village, piller, fille, grille, habiller, mantille*.

Pronunciation of the Consonants.

CONSONANTS are generally pronounced as in English, but, as a rule, are not sounded at the end of words. *c, f, l, r*, however, when they occur as last letters of a word, are pronounced. But *r* is not pronounced in words of more than one syllable ending in *er*.

REMARKS ON THE PRONUNCIATION OF CONSONANTS.

c   is pronounced like *k;* but like *ss* before *e* and *i*, and also before *a, o, u*, when the cedilla is placed underneath:
duc, ceci, cela, cidre, ça, déçu, façade, reçois

cc is pronounced like *ks* before *e* and *i*, and like *k* before *a, o, u* or a consonant:
accéder, accident, vaccine, accorder, accréditer, accumuler

ch is pronounced like *sh:*
chasse, chat, charade, cheval, biche, château
but is pronounced like *k* before *r*, and in the greater number of words derived from the Greek:
chrôme, chronique, choral, chaos, écho

g   is pronounced like *g* in gallop; but it is pronounced like *s* in *pleasure* before *e, i* and *y*:
gorge, galop, gelée, genou, girafe, gymnase.

Reading of words with liquid sounds.

Bataille	cerfeuil	carillon	œil	bouillir	canaille
Battle	chervil	chime	eye	to boil	rabble

bouteille	deuil	mantille	aillade	brouillard	citrouille
bottle	mourning	mantilla	garlic-sauce	fog	pumpkin

ferrailleur	caillot	corbeille	écureuil	drille	œillet
fighter	clot of blood	basket	squirrel	fellow	eyelet-hole

quenouille	éventail	merveille	fauteuil	famille	fouiller
distaff	fan	marvel	arm-chair	family	to search

douillet	taille	soleil	feuille	fille	grenouille	travail
soft	waist	sun	leaf	daughter	frog	work

vermeil	seuil	papillon	rouille	gargouille	abeille
rosy	threshold	butterfly	rust	gutter-spout	bee

pareil	veille	bétail	railler	maille	raillerie	réveil
alike	eve	cattle	to banter	stitch	raillery	awaking

andouille	treille	soupirail	détaillant	treuil	funérailles
twist	vine	air-hole	retailer	windlass	funeral

écueil	tenailles	cercueil	écaille	éveillé
rock	tongs	coffin	scale	awakened

Reading of words with consonants.

Cheval(*)	botte	bal	cabale	chrôme	cela	duo
horse	boot	ball	cabal	chrome	that	duke

chair	sec	célèbre	chalet	chronique	cadre	celle
flesh	dry	celebrated	cottage	chronicle	frame	this

échec	chaleur	calice	accélérer	accaparer	accorder
check	heat	chalice	to accelerate	to forestall	to grant

dormir	badaud	fable	beaucoup	gelée	galop
to sleep	cockney	fable	much	frost	gallop

mois	habile	face	petit	genou	riche	darder	bord
month	clever	face	little	knee	rich	to dart	edge

facteur	ceci	germer	gymnase	aigre	fortune
postman	this	to germinate	gymnasium	sour	fortune

cerf	lire	papa	poli	laborieux	passer	nager	palais
stag	to read	papa	polite	industrious	to pass	to swim	palace

cavalerie	demande	bananier	chat	chameau	dromadaire
cavalry	demand	banana-tree	cat	camel	dromedary

badinage	canon	canif	fatalité	furie	Chine	comète
frolic	cannon	penknife	fatality	fury	China	comet

(*) No further indications will be given when final consonants must be pronounced.

Pronunciation of the Consonants *(continued)*.

gn is pronounced somewhat nasal and very much the same as *ni* in the English word *companion:*
    signe, agneau, campagne, gagner, Boulogne

h is generally silent, but if aspirated (usually indicated in dictionaries by 'h) its sound is but faintly heard:
    homme, hôte, heureux, 'héros, 'haricot

j is always pronounced like *s* in *pleasure:*
    jambon, jardin, je, jubilé, jaune, jeudi

p is generally silent before *t:*
    baptême, baptiser, sculpture.

ph is pronounced like *f:*
    phrase, physique, philosophe

qu is pronounced like *k:*
    quatre, requête, liquide, quai

r is harder than in English, principally at the beginning of words, and when followed by another *r:*
    reproche, râle, brigade, drame, serre, horrible

it is silent at the end of words of more than one syllable ending in *er:*
    abuser, goûter, charger, premier, mensonger

s is pronounced hard at the beginning of words, and between a vowel and a consonant:
    sable, serpe, passage, estime, reste, narcisse, masse

It is pronounced soft like *z* between two vowels, except when it is the first letter of the second word in compound words:
    visage, ruse, asile, visible, phase; but *belle-sœur, parasol, entre-sol, demi-siècle*

sc is pronounced like *ss* before *e* and *i*, and like *sk* before *a, o, u,* or a consonant:
    sceau, scélérat, sciage, scission; scapulaire, scolastique, sculpture, scrupuleux

Reading of words with consonants.

lire	papa	poli	laborieux	honnête	mal	nous	nager
to read	papa	polite	laborious	honest	evil	we	to swim
palais	baptême	phare	quatre	acoustique			mercredi
palace	baptism	light-house	four	acoustics			Wednesday
jaconas	coup	baptiser	quiétude		église		ans
jaconet	blow	to baptise	quietude		church		years
laisser	laver	quitter	arroser	radis	rire	mère	car
to leave	to wash	to leave	to water	radish	to laugh	mother	for
mer	sable	visage	belle-sœur		pas	bras	sceau
sea	sand	face	sister-in-law		step	arm	seal
scrofuleux	reproche	marine	cher	cocher		ruse	frimas
scrofulous	reproach	navy	dear	coachman		cunning	rime
baratte	cirque	charrette	barbe	choc	ciseau		machine
churn	circus	cart	beard	shock	chisel		machine
nicher	papier	drap	compter		pharmacie		barrique
to nestle	paper	cloth	to reckon		chemistry		cask
jardinier	nomade	parade	galop	gâteau		phrase	onze
gardener	wandering	parade	gallop	cake		phrase	eleven
esclave	sculpture	prière	former	fleur	passage		table
slave	sculpture	prayer	to form	flower	passage		table
sol	cygne	'héros	quatorze	que	erreur		amusement
soil	swan	hero	fourteen	that	error		amusement
pur	quarante	sur	signe	paresse	muse		humeur
pure	forty	upon	sign	laziness	muse		humour
'hideux	bois	poésie	mur	campagne	souvent		qualificatif
hideous	wood	poetry	wall	country	often		qualificative
soigneux	jaune	histoire	quoique	salut	fer		digne
careful	yellow	history	though	salute	iron		worthy
qui	été	quel	quoi	peu	heure	habitant	qualité
who	summer	which	what	little	hour	inhabitant	quality
prier	magnifique	'hagard	quel	je	plaigne		'hache
to pray	magnificent	haggard	which	I	may pity		axe
assurance	habit	querelle	honneur		'honte		reçu
assurance	coat	quarrel	honour		shame		received
épargne	homme	dose	'hauteur		phrase	sel	'haine
saving	man	dose	height		phrase	salt	hatred
usage	jus	dignité	'haïr	humble	Afrique.		
custom	juice	dignity	to hate	humble	Africa		

Pronunciation of the Consonants *(concluded)*.

t is pronounced like *s* in the end syllable *tie* preceded by a vowel:

diplomatie, minutie, prophétie

also in the middle of words in the syllable *ti* followed by a vowel:

partiel, ambitieux, nation, martial, béotien, impatience, factieux

But *t* has its natural sound in the syllables and endings *stion, xtion, tié, tier, tière, tième*, and in the endings *tions* and *tiez* of the tenses of verbs in *ter*:

question, mixtion, amitié, portier, litière, giletière, septième, nous portions, vous portiez

th is pronounced like a single *t*:

théâtre, théologie, thyrse

x has the sound of *gs* at the beginning and in the middle of words:

exercer, examiner, Xénophon, exemple

it is pronounced like *k* when before *ce* and *ci*:

excéder, excellence, excepter, exciper, exciter

Linking of two words.

The linking of two words is the pronouncing of the last consonant of a word with the first syllable of the next word when it begins with a vowel or mute *h*. Linking only takes place between words closely connected by their meaning, as articles and nouns, adjectives and nouns, personal pronouns and verbs; Ex.: *les⁀amis, deux⁀beaux⁀oiseaux, ils⁀ont parlé.*

In linking *d* is pronounced like *t*, *f* like *v*, *s* and *x* like *z*: Ex.: *le grand⁀enfant, le mauvais⁀homme, neuf⁀ans, dix⁀oiseaux.*

READING OF WORDS WITH CONSONANTS.

jet	façade	aristocratie	laitier	homme	septième	théâtre
throw	front	aristocracy	milkman	man	seventh	theatre
tacher	distrait	que	démocratie	portier	cafetière	
to stain	distracted	that	democracy	porter	coffee-pot	
jeune	théière	taffetas	plat	lit	séditieux	
young	tea-pot	taffeta	dish	bed	seditious	
valet	troisième	excéder	beaux	assez	zèle	
servant	third	to exceed	fine	enough	zeal	
vassal	chaque	zénith	chez	velours	exercer	quinze
vassal	every	zenith	at	velvet	to exercise	fifteen
maison	excepter	doux	zéphir	nez	Athénien	
house	to except	sweet	zephyr	nose	Athenian	
impartial	radieux	isolement	salade	musicien	sultan	
impartial	radiant	loneliness	salad	musician	sultan	
rat	ambitieux	imposant	misérable	collection	supériorité	
rat	ambitious	imposing	miserable	collection	superiority	
physique	expédition	radeau	réussir	escalade	flux	
physics	expedition	raft	to succeed	scaling	flow	
rassemblement	hypocrite	opposition	crise	majesté		
gathering	hypocrite	opposition	crisis	majesty		

Reading exercise on the linking of words.

Nous‿avons. Trois‿oiseaux. Un petit‿homme.
We have. Three birds. A little man.

Ils‿eurent. Vous‿avez. Des‿habits‿usés. Les‿états.
They had. You have. Some coats worn out. The states.

Nous‿attendons‿Alfred. Ils‿ont. Six‿heures. Est‿elle
We expect Alfred. They have. Six hours. Is she

chez‿elle? Comment vous‿appelez-vous? Deux‿amis.
at home. How do you call yourself? Two friends.

Il‿est‿ici. Mes‿enfants. Nos‿ennemis. Elles‿entrèrent.
He is here. My children. Our enemies. They entered.

Un grand‿ami. Il a neuf‿ans. Avez-vous‿un mauvais‿
A good friend. He has nine years. Have you a bad

ouvrier?
workman

General Exceptions to the Rules of Pronunciation.

(For reference only.)

1. A is silent in—*août, Saône, toast* (*st* pronounced.)
2. B *(final)* is sounded in—*club, nabab, rob.*
3. C *(final)* is silent in—*accroc, banc, blanc, clerc, cric, croc, échecs, escroc, estomac, flanc, franc, lacs, marc, porc, raccroc, tabac, tronc.* Also in the singular present of the verbs *vaincre* and *convaincre*; as in *je vaincs, il convainc,* etc.
4. C & CH sound like *g* in—*second, drachme.*
5. D is sounded in—*sud, Talmud.*
6. E is silent between *g* and *a* or *o*, when it serves to give the *g* the soft sound; as in *vengeance, pigeon,* etc.
7. E sounds like *è*, if the first letter of a word, and followed by a double consonant; and in all words beginning with *dess*, as in *effacer, essarter, desscher,* etc., also in the word *et* (and).
8. E sounds like *a* at the beginning of the adverbial termination *emment*, as in *prudemment,* etc.; *e* has also the sound of *a* in the words *femme, solennel,* and their derivatives.
9. F *(final)* is silent in—*bœufs, cerf, cerf-volant, chef-d'œuvre, clef,* (or *clé*), *nerfs, œufs.*
10. G *(final)* is sounded in—*grog, zigzag.*
11. G is silent in—*doigt, legs, signet, vingt.*
12. GN is pronounced hard *g-n* in—*agnat, cognat, gnôme, gnômon, igné, ignition, ignicole, imprégnation, inexpugnable, stagnant, stagnation.*
13. L is silent in—*baril, chenil, coutil, fusil, gentil, outil, persil, sourcil.*
14. M is silent in—*damner, condamner, automne.*
15. P is sounded in—*cap, cep, croup, group, hanap, jalap, julep, salep;* also in *septembre, septuple.*
16. P is silent in—*corps, temps, printemps.*
17. R is sounded in the end syllable *er* (*e* pronounced *è*) of the following words of more than one syllable:—*amer, belvéder, cancer, cuiller, cutter, enfer, fier, frater, hier, hiver, magister, outremer, pater,* and in proper names.
18. R is silent in—*monsieur, messieurs.*
19. S *(final)* is sounded in—*atlas, biceps, bis, cassis, chorus, fils* (pronounce *fiss*), *gratis, jadis, lis, mais, mars, mœurs, oasis, obus, omnibus, ours, papyrus, prospectus, rébus, tournevis, typhus, vis,* and in all nouns in *us* derived from the Latin.
20. T *(final)* is sounded in—*abject, aconit, brut, Christ, chut, contact, correct, cobalt, déficit, district, direct, dot, est* (east), *exact, fat, incorrect, indirect, infect, intellect, lest, mat, net, ouest, post, prétérit, rit, strict, suspect, test, transit.*
21. T in *tie* sounds like *t* in—*épizootie, rôtie, sotie.*
22. T in *ti* sounds like *t* in—*chrétien, entretien, maintien, soutien;* and in *bestial, bestiaire, vestiaire, galimatias,* and their derivatives.
23. T in *tier* sounds like *s* in all the tenses of verbs in *tier* (except *châtier*); as in *balbutier, balbutiant, nous balbutions,* etc.

24. **ST** is silent in—*est* (is) and *Jésus Christ*, but is pronounced in *Christ*.
25. **TH** is silent in—*asthme, asthmatique, isthme.*
26. **U** after *qu*, or *gu*, is sounded in—*équestre, équidistant, équilatéral, équitation, liquéfier, questeur, quintuple,—arguer, aiguille, guise, inextinguible, linguistique,* and in all words derived from the adjective *aigu;* as, *aiguiser, etc.*
27. **U** in *qua* sounds like the French *ou* in—*aquarelle, aquatique, équateur, équation, quatuor, quaternaire, quinquagénaire,* and their derivatives; and in all words beginning with *quadr;* as, *quadrupède.*
28. **X** *(final)* is sounded in—*Aix, index, lynx, préfix, silex, sphynx.*
29. **X** sounds like *z* in—*deuxième, dixième, sixième.*
30. **X** sounds like *ss* in—*Auxonne, Bruxelles, Cadix, soixante.*
31. **Z** is sounded in—*gaz,* and in words of foreign origin—*Rodez, Suez, Cortez, Fernandez.*

---

32. **EU** sounds like the French *u* in the tenses of the verb *avoir;* as in, *j'eus, eu, que j'eusse.*
3. **OE & OÊ** sound like (the French) *oi* in—*moelle, poêle.*
34. **OI** sounds like *o* in—*encoignure, oignon, empoigner, poignard, poignet.*

---

35. **ILL** is not liquid but fully sounded in—*Achille, codicille, distiller, imbécillité, Lille, osciller, pupille, scintiller, titiller, tranquille, vaciller.*
36. **IL** is liquid in—*avril, babil, péril, grésil, gentilhomme,* and sometimes in *cil* and *gril.*

---

37. **AM, EM, IM, UM** at the end of words are not nasal, and the *m* is sounded; as in—*Abraham, album, etc.*
but they remain nasal in—*Adam, dam, quidam, parfum.*
38. **EMM** at the beginning of words is nasal and sounds like *en-m;* as in *emménager, emmener, etc.*
39. **ENT** in the 3rd person plural of verbs is silent; as in—*ils parlent, elles parleraient.*
40. **EN** is nasal in—*enivrer, ennoblir, enorgueillir, ennui* (and its derivatives).
41. **EN** sounds like *ain* (nasal) in—*Benjamin, examen, mentor, memento.*
42. **EN** sounds like *enn* in—*abdomen, amen, Eden, gluten, gramen, Hymen, lichen.*
43. **IEN** (not *ienn*) in the tenses of the verbs *venir* and *tenir*, and their derivatives sounds like *i-ain* (nasal); as in—*je viens, nous tiendrons, etc.*
44. **AEN & AON** sound like *an* (nasal) in—*Caen, faon, paon, taon,* (sometimes pronounced *ton*).

NOTE: The nasal sound is generally written with *m* before *p* and *b*; as in, *empire, rompre, impérial.* Consonants at the end of foreign proper names are generally pronounced, as in—*Alep, Bagdad, Périclès.*

Division of Syllables.

In French words are divided into syllables according to the following principal rules:
1. A consonant between two vowels commences the new syllable; as,
i-nu-ti-le, a-mi, pè-re, a-ca-dé-mie
2. When there are two consonants between two vowels one of them belongs to the first and the other to the second syllable; as,
ex-cep-ter, e-xer-cer, col-lec-tion, in-cor-po-ra-tion
3. Consonants however followed by *l* or *r* are not added to the first syllable but commence the second; thus,
ta-bleau, fa-ble, li-vre, œu-vre

Punctuation.

The signs of punctuation are the same as in English, viz: (,) *virgule*, comma; (.) *point*, period; (;) *point-et-virgule*, semi-colon; (:) *deux points*, colon; (!) *point d'exclamation*, note of exclamation; (?) *point d'interrogation*, note of interrogation.

Parts of Speech.

The French language contains ten parts of speech. Six are flexible: *le substantif* or *nom*, the noun; *l'article*, the article; *l'adjectif*, the adjective; *le pronom*, the pronoun; *le verbe*, the verb; and *le participe*, the participle. Four are inflexible: *l'adverbe*, the adverb; *la préposition*, the preposition; *la conjonction*, the conjunction; and *l'interjection*, the interjection.

Definition of the Parts of Speech.

The ARTICLE (*l'article*) is a word used before nouns to limit or define their application; as,
the man, l'*homme*; *the* house, la *maison*
a man, un *homme*; *a* house, une *maison*

The NOUN (*le nom*) is the name of anything which exists, or which we can conceive to exist, whether material or immaterial; as, man, *homme*; house, *maison*; virtue, *vertu*

The ADJECTIVE (*l'adjectif*) is a word added to a noun to qualify or determine it; there are two kinds of adjectives in French:—1. *the qualifying adjective* as in English; as,
a good boy, *un bon garçon*; the *young* girl, *la jeune fille*

2. the *determinative adjective*, in English ordinarily called pronoun; as, *this* boy, *ce garçon*; *which* girl, *quelle fille*; *my* son, *mon fils*

A Pronoun *(un pronom)* is a word used instead of a noun; as, *He* (John) is rich, il *(Jean) est riche; this* is good, ceci *est bon*

The Verb *(le verbe)* is a word by which we affirm—1. What anybody or anything does; 2. What is done to him or to it; 3. In what state he or it exists; as,
    the man *works, l'homme* travaille; the boy *was punished,* le garçon fut puni; the child *sleeps, l'enfant* dort

The Participle *(le participe)* is so called because it partakes of the nature of the verb from which it is derived, and assumes in part the nature of an adjective; as,
    a son *protecting* his mother, *un fils* protégeant *sa mère;* a *burnt* house, *une maison* incendiée; your letter is badly *written, votre lettre est mal* écrite

An Adverb *(un adverbe)* is a word which modifies a verb, an adverb, or an adjective; as,
    he wrote *well, il écrivait* bien; he will be here *soon, il sera* bientôt *ici;* my sister is *as* pretty, *ma sœur est* aussi *jolie*

The Preposition *(la préposition)* serves to show the relation of a noun or pronoun to some other word in the sentence; as,
    the book is *on* the table, *le livre est* sur *la table;* he sat *behind* me, *il était assis* derrière *moi*

A Conjunction *(une conjonction)* is a word which serves to connect the different parts of an extended sentence; as,
    John *and* Jacob went out yesterday, *Jean* et *Jacob sortirent hier;* I cannot come, *because* I am ill, *je ne puis pas venir,* parceque *je suis malade*

The Interjection *(l'interjection)* is a word which expresses any sudden desire or violent emotion; as,
    Hush! *paix! chut!* ah! *ah!* alas! *hélas!* bravo! *fort bien!*

Numbers.

There are two numbers in French the *singular* and the *plural;* the singular refers to one person or thing, the plural to more than one.

Genders.

There are but two genders in French, the *masculine* and the *feminine;* therefore things which are *neuter* in English are in French either masculine or feminine.

Rules to ascertain the gender of inanimate objects will be given later on; but we advise students never to learn a noun without placing either the definite or indefinite article before it, as this is by far the best plan for fixing the proper gender in the memory.

FIRST LESSON.   *Première Leçon*

The ARTICLE and the NOUN.

The Definite Article *the* is translated:

le before a masculine singular noun beginning with a consonant; as,—*le frère*, the brother; *le livre*, the book.

la before a feminine singular noun beginning with a consonant; as,—*la sœur*, the sister; *la porte*, the door.

l' before masculine or feminine nouns in the singular, when they begin with a vowel or *h* mute; as,—
l'oncle, the uncle; *l'hôtel*,(m.*) the hotel; *l'église*, (f.*) the church; *l'hôtesse*, the landlady.

les before masculine or feminine nouns in the plural; as,
les frères, the brothers; *les sœurs*, the sisters;
les hôtels (*m.*), the hotels; *les églises* (*f.*), the churches.

FORMATION OF THE PLURAL OF NOUNS.

1.—The plural of nouns is formed by adding *s* to the singular;
as,—*le livre*, the book, *les livres*, the books; *le chat*, the cat, *les chats*, the cats; *la sœur*, the sister, *les sœurs*, the sisters; *la maison*, the house, *les maisons*, the houses.

2.—Nouns ending in *s*, *x*, *z* do not change in the plural; as,
le bras, the arm, *les bras*, the arms; *la voix*, the voice, *les voix*, the voices; *le nez*, the nose, *les nez*, the noses.

The Verbs being of the utmost importance we shall add a portion of them to each lesson, independently of the other rules.

The auxiliary verb *avoir*, to have.

SINGULAR.	*Indicative Present.*	SINGULAR.
1st Person j'ai,(**) *I have*		ai-je, *have I?*(†)
2nd ,, tu as, *thou hast*		as-tu, *hast thou?*
3rd ,, { il a, (*m.*) *he has* / elle a, (*f.*) *she has*		a-t-il, *has he?* / a-t-elle, *has she?*
PLURAL.		PLURAL.
1st Person nous avons, *we have*		avons-nous, *have we?*
2nd ,, vous avez, *you have*		avez-vous, *have you?*
3rd ,, { ils ont,(*m.*) } *they* / { elles ont,(*f.*) } *have*		ont-ils, } *have they?* / ont-elles,

---

(*) We indicate the gender of nouns either by placing *le* before or *m.* (masculine) after a masculine noun, *la* before or *f.* (feminine) after a feminine noun.

(**) *je, ne, me, que, ce, se,* etc. before a vowel become *j', n', m', qu', c', s',* etc.

(†) In the interrogative form the pronoun is placed after the verb and a hyphen inserted; if the 3rd person singular ends in a vowel, for euphony's sake, a *t* placed between two hyphens is inserted (-t-).

The Vocabulary

is to be learned by heart as these words will not be given again

and, *et* (*)
arm, *bras m.*(**)
book, *livre m.*
brother, *frère m.*
cat, *chat m.*
church, *église f.*
dog, *chien m.*
door, *porte f.*(**)

hand, *main f.*
herring, *'hareng m.*(†)
hotel, *hôtel m.*
house, *maison f.*
landlady, *hôtesse f.*
madam, *madame f.*
mouse, *souris f.*
no, *non*

nose, *nez m.*
price, prize, *prix m.*
sir, *monsieur m.*(*)
sister, *sœur f.*
uncle, *oncle m.*
voice, *voix f.*
who, whom, *qui*
yes, *oui*

Exercise No. 1.

Translate the Singular and Plural of the following nouns and articles.

1. The brother, the brothers,—the dog, the dogs,—the nail (*clou m.*), the nails,—the sister, the sisters,—the cow (*vache f.*), the cows,—the hand, the hands,—the child (*enfant m.*), the children,—the hotel, the hotels,—the church, the churches,—the story (*histoire f.*), the stories,—the mouth (*mois m.*), the months,—the mouse, the mice,—the price, the prices,—the nut (*noix f.*), the nuts,—the nose, the noses,—the book, the books,—the landlady, the landladies,—the herring, the herrings,—the voice, the voices,—the cat, the cats,—the fan (*éventail m.*), the fans,—the arm, the arms,—the door, the doors,—the uncle, the uncles,—the coat (*habit m.*), the coats.

He has,—have we?—have I?—you have,—have they (*f.*)?—thou hast,—has she?—they have,—we have,—has he?—have you?—I have,—have they?—she has,—they (*f.*) have.

2. Les frères et les sœurs. Le chat et la souris. L'hôtesse a le chien. Ils ont entendu[1] la voix. Avez-vous lu[2] le livre? Nous avons les maisons. J'ai vu[3] l'église. A-t-il vu[3] l'hôtel? Qui a les harengs? Le bras et la main. L'oncle a donné[4] le prix. Elle a deux[5] hôtels. La maison a deux[5] portes.

The cats and the mice. Have we the books? He has two[5] uncles. The arms and the hands. Who has seen[3] the hotels? Have you the dogs? The sister has given[4] the prizes. Who has seen[3] the churches? Has she the herring? The landlady has two[5] houses. Who has heard[1] the voices? The brother has the hotel. Has he the dog? Yes, he has the dog. Have you seen[3] the cat, sir? No, madam.

(*) Pronounce *et—é*; *monsieur—me-si-eu*

(**) Students should always place the article before a noun they are learning, this being the best way to remember the proper gender: *le bras, la porte,* etc.

(†) The *h* when aspirated, i.e. to be pronounced, is indicated by an apostrophe ('h) and in this case *le* or *la* must be used and not *l'*.

1 *entendu*, heard 2 *lu*, read 3 *vu*, seen 4 *donné*, given 5 *deux*, two

Questions on Grammar.

1. How is the definite article *the* rendered in French?
2. When is *le* used, when *la*, when *l'*, and when *les*?
3. How is *the* translated before *'h* (aspirated)?
4. What is the gender of a noun preceded by *le*, what when preceded by *la*?
5. What is the first and general rule for the formation of the plural of nouns?
6. Which nouns do not change in the plural?
7. When is the *e* of *je* elided and an apostrophe placed instead?
8. What is the place of the pronoun subject in the interrogative form of verbs in French?
9. When is a *t* between two hyphens inserted after the verb?

Conversation.

Good morning, } sir. Good day,	Bonjour, monsieur.
Good evening, madam.	Bonsoir, madame.
Thanks, (thank you).	Merci (je vous remercie).
Have you the book, madam?	Avez-vous le livre, madame?
No, sir, his *(sa)* sister has the book.	Non, monsieur, sa sœur a le livre.
Has he seen *(vu)* his *(son)* uncle?	A-t-il vu son oncle?
Yes, sir.	Oui, monsieur.
Has she the cat?	A-t-elle le chat?
No, madam, she has the dog.	Non, madame, elle a le chien.
What *(que)* have they in *(dans)* their *(leurs)* hands?	Qu'ont-ils dans leurs mains?
They have four *(quatre)* herrings.	Ils ont quatre harengs.
Who has bought *(acheté)* the hotel?	Qui a acheté l'hôtel?
His *(son)* brother has bought the hotel.	Son frère a acheté l'hôtel.
Has the dog (translate: the dog has he) the mouse?	Le chien a-t-il la souris?
No, it is *(c'est)* the cat which *(qui)* has the mouse.	Non, c'est le chat qui a la souris.
Have you heard *(entendu)* the voice?	Avez-vous entendu la voix?
Yes, I have heard the voice.	Oui, j'ai entendu la voix.
Has the church (translate: the church has she) two doors?	L'église a-t-elle deux portes?
No, the church has three doors, and the house has two doors.	Non, l'église a trois portes, et la maison a deux portes.
Has he paid *(payé)* the price asked *(demandé)* for *(pour)* the dog?	A-t-il payé le prix demandé pour le chien?
Yes, he has paid the price.	Oui, il a payé le prix.

Reading Exercise (*) No. 1.

Tout commencement est(24†)difficile. Qu'avez-vous dans
All   commencement is   difficult.   What have you in

votre main? J'ai un journal français. Qu'est-ce? A
your hand I have a newspaper French. What is that To

qui appartient(43†)cela? Sont-ils riches? Etes-vous pauvre?
whom belongs   that Are they   rich   Are you   poor

Il fait froid. Fait-il chaud? Qui est là? Bonjour.
It makes cold Makes it warm Who is there Good day

Bonsoir. Bonne nuit. Où étiez-vous hier(17)? J'étais à la
Good evening Good night Where were you yesterday I was at the

campagne. Je n'ai pas d'argent. Où est-il? Notre chat
country   I „ have not of money Where is he Our cat

a pris une souris. Parlez-vous français? Oui, un peu.
has caught a mouse Speak you   French   Yes a little

Pouvez-vous me comprendre? Pas du tout. Que désirez-
Can you me understand   Not at all   What wish

vous? Veuillez me donner mon chapeau? Je vous
you   Will   me give my hat   I   you

remercie. Sortirez-vous cette après-midi? Non; je
thank   Will go out you this afternoon   No I

resterai chez moi. Le temps(16) est trop froid. Aujourd'hui
shall remain at me The weather is too cold   To-day

il fait très chaud. Quelle heure est-il? Il est dix heures.
It makes very warm   What hour is it   It is ten hours

Pourquoi venez-vous si tard? J'ai manqué le train. Mon
Why   come you so late I have missed the train My

frère était aujourd'hui au théâtre. Veuillez prendre un
brother was   to-day   at the theatre   Will   take   a

siège. N'oubliez pas de venir ce soir. Demain soir
seat. „ Forget   not to come this evening To-morrow evening

nous irons au concert. Avez-vous déjà dîné? Non, nous
we shall go to the concert   Have you already dined   No we

ne dînons pas avant six heures. A demain.
„ dine not before six hours. To to-morrow

(*) In order to assist the student in practising these exercises nasal and liquid sounds are printed in italics, and the linking is indicated by a curved line.

(†) The figure in parenthesis indicates the group amongst which the word is included on pages 16 and 17.

Second Lesson. *Deuxième Leçon.*

The Article and the Noun *(continued)*.

The article is frequently preceded by prepositions as in English; but the articles *le* and *les*, can never be preceded by *de*, (of *or* from), or *à* (to *or* at), and the following contractions are used:

du instead of *de le* } before a masculine singular noun be-
au   „   „   *à le* } ginning with a consonant; as—

du frère, of the brother.   *au frère*, to the brother.
du livre, of the book.   *au livre*, to the book.

des instead of *de les* } before masculine and feminine
aux   „   „   *à les* } nouns in the plural; as,—

des frères, of the brothers.   *aux frères*, to the brothers.
des sœurs, of the sisters.   *aux sœurs*, to the sisters.
des oncles, of the uncles.   *aux oncles*, to the uncles.
des hôtesses, of the landladies. *aux hôtesses*, to the landladies.

Observation: *la* and *l'* are never contracted; as—

de la sœur, of the sister.   *à la sœur*, to the sister.
de l'oncle, of the uncle.   *à l'oncle*, to the uncle.

The form of the English Possessive: *the father's hat, the girl's bonnets, Charles' book, etc.*, must be altered when translating into French thus: *the hat of the father*, le chapeau du père; *the bonnets of the girl*, les chapeaux de la fille; *the book of Charles*, le livre de Charles etc.

Formation of the Plural of Nouns *(continued)*.

3.—Nouns ending in *au* and *eu* take *x* in the plural instead of *s*; as,— *le chapeau*, the hat, *les chapeaux*, the hats.
le neveu, the nephew, *les neveux*, the nephews.

4.—Nouns ending in *al* change this termination into *aux*;
as,— *le cheval*, the horse, *les chevaux*, the horses.
l'animal, the animal, *les animaux*, the animals.

The auxiliary verb *être*, to be.
Indicative Present.

je suis, *I am*	suis-je, *am I?*
tu es, *thou art*	es-tu, *art thou?*
il, elle est, *he, she is*	est-il, est-elle, *is he, is she?*
nous sommes, *we are*	sommes-nous, *are we?*
vous êtes, *you are*	êtes-vous, *are you?*
ils, elles sont, *they are*	sont-ils (elles), *are they?*

Interrogative sentences, as: *Has the aunt read the book? Are the soldiers in the house?* etc., must be changed in form, when translating into French, thus: The aunt *has she* read the book, *la tante a-t-elle lu le livre?* the soldiers *are they* in the house, *les soldats sont-ils dans la maison?*

animal, *animal m.*	hat (bonnet), *chapeau*	officer, *officier m.*
aunt, *tante f.*	horse, *cheval m.* [*m.*	on, *sur*
bird, *oiseau m.*	in, *dans*	room, *chambre f*
chair, *chaise f.*	knife, *couteau m.*	soldier, *soldat m.*
curtain, *rideau m.*	nephew, *neveu m.*	street, *rue f.*
fire, *feu m.*	newspaper, *journal m.*	table, *table f.*
general, *général m.*	niece, *nièce f.*	where, *où.*

Exercise No. 2.

1. Of the soldier, to the soldier,—of the dog, to the dog,—of the arms, to the arms,—of the rooms, to the rooms,—of the hotels, to the hotels,—of the churches, to the churches,—of the table, at(*)the table, of the hotel, at the hotel,—of the church, to the church,—the brother's book,—the aunt's cat,—the officer's dogs,—the landlady's chairs,—the sisters' house,—the curtain, the curtains,—of the knife, of the knives, —to the fire, to the fires,—the general, the generals,—of the newspaper, of the newspapers,—to the horse, to the horses,—the niece's bonnets,—to the animal, to the animals,—to the street, to the streets, —of the bird, to the birds.

He is,—are we?—am I?—you are,—are they (*f.*)?—thou art,—is she?—they are,—is he?—have you?—I am,—has he?—are you?—we have,—we are,—I have,—she is.

2. La sœur a-t-elle vu[1] le chien de la tante? Les soldats du général sont dans la rue. J'ai deux[2] neveux. C'est[3] le cheval de l'officier. Les journaux sont-ils dans la chambre? Nous sommes les nièces de l'hôtesse. Avez-vous parlé[4] au frère? C'est[3] le prix des chapeaux. Les livres sont sur la table. Le général a-t-il écrit[5] aux officiers? J'ai parlé[4] à la sœur du soldat. Où sont les rideaux? A-t-elle deux[2] chiens? Avez-vous écrit[5] à l'hôtesse de l'oncle? L'officier a-t-il vu[1] les chevaux? Avez-vous vu[1] le livre sur la table?

Has the aunt the uncle's knives? Are you the soldier's brother? Have you seen[1] the generals? We have spoken[4] to the landlady's nephew. Has the officer seen[1] the newspapers? Are the general's horses in the street? I have written[5] to the officer's niece. He has two[2] nephews. I have given[6] the birds to the soldier. The aunt's bonnet is on the chair. We have given[6] the curtains to the officer's sisters. Where are the aunt's cats? We have seen[1] the soldiers. I have written[5] to the uncle. Is she in the room? Has the general's nephew given[6] the knife to the officer?

(*) *at* must be translated like *to.*

[1] *vu,* seen   [2] *deux,* two   [3] *c'est,* that is   [4] *parlé,* spoken   [5] *écrit,* written   [6] *donné,* given.

Questions on Grammar.

1. How are *of the* and *to the* translated before a masculine singular noun commencing with a consonant?
2. How are *of the* and *to the* translated before a feminine singular noun commencing with a consonant?
3. How are *of the* and *to the* translated before a singular noun, whether masculine or feminine, commencing with a vowel or *h* mute?
4. How are *of the* and *to the* translated before a noun in the plural?
5. Can the prepositions *de* or *à* precede the articles *le* or *les*? if not, what must be used instead?
6. What nouns form their plural by adding *x*?
7. What nouns form their plural by changing their termination into *aux*?
8. How do you translate into French, *the brother's book, the dog's nose, the uncle's voice, Charles' hat*?

Conversation.

Where is the uncle's book?	Où est le livre de l'oncle?
The uncle's book is on the chair.	Le livre de l'oncle est sur la chaise.
Who is in the father's room?	Qui est dans la chambre du père?
The aunt is in the father's room.	La tante est dans la chambre du père.
Have you seen the niece's bird?	Avez-vous vu l'oiseau de la nièce?
Yes, sir, the niece's bird is on the table.	Oui, monsieur, l'oiseau de la nièce est sur la table.
Has the landlady's nephew the knife?	Le neveu de l'hôtesse a-t-il le couteau?
Yes, madam, he has the knife.	Oui, madame, il a le couteau.
Have you read (*lu*) the paper, madam?	Avez-vous lu le journal, madame?
Yes, sir, I have read the papers which (*qui*) are on the chair.	Oui, monsieur, j'ai lu les journaux qui sont sur la chaise.
Is your brother (an) officer?	Votre frère est-il officier?
Yes, madam, he is [a] general.	Oui, madame, il est général.
Where have you seen (*vu*) the sister's bonnet?	Où avez-vous vu le chapeau de la sœur?
We have seen her (*son*) bonnet in the brother's room.	Nous avons vu son chapeau dans la chambre du frère.
Is the soldier's dog in the street?	Le chien du soldat est-il dans la rue?
No, madam, he is in the house.	Non, madame, il est dans la maison.
Hast thou seen the mouse in the room?	As-tu vu la souris dans la chambre?
Yes, I have seen the cat and the mouse.	Oui, j'ai vu le chat et la souris.
To whom (*qui*) have you given (*donné*) the curtains?	A qui avez-vous donné les rideaux?
I have given the curtains to the woman.	J'ai donné les rideaux à la femme.

Reading Exercise No. 2.

Tout ce qui brille n'est pas or. Ouvrez la fenêtre.
All that which glitters ,, is not gold   Open the window

Fermez la porte. Où demeurez-vous? Nous demeurons
Shut the door   Where live you   We live

dans cette jolie maison. Quand avez-vous acheté cet
in this pretty house   When have you bought this

habit? Où est votre sœur? Elle est allée se promener
coat   Where is your sister   She is gone herself to walk

avec sa tante. Les jours augmentent(39) sensiblement. Le
with her aunt   The days increase sensibly   The

temps(16) était très beau avant-hier(17). Il ne fait pas aussi
weather was very fine the day before yesterday   It ,, makes not so

froid en Angleterre que dans le Nord de la France. J'ai
cold in England as in the North of the France   I have

oublié d'acheter des gants. Comment s'appellent(39) les sept
forgotten to buy some gloves   How themselves call the seven

jours de la semaine? Ils s'appellent: lundi, mardi,
days of the week   They themselves call Monday Tuesday

mercredi, jeudi, vendredi, samedi et dimanche. Quels
Wednesday Thursday Friday Saturday and Sunday   What

sont les noms des mois de l'année? Janvier, février,
are the names of the months of the year   January February

mars(19), avril,(36) mai, juin, juillet, août(1), septembre(15),
March April May June July August September

octobre, novembre et décembre. Lisez-vous des livres
October November and December   Read you any books

français? Oui, quelquefois. Lisez-vous à haute voix?
French   Yes sometimes   Read you at loud voice

Oui, toujours; car mon professeur m'a dit que c'était la
Yes always for my professor me has said that this was the

seule manière d'acquérir une prononciation correcte.
only manner of to acquire a pronunciation correct

Pouvez-vous me comprendre quand je parle français?
Can you me understand when I speak French

Oui, quand vous ne parlez pas trop vite. Pourriez-vous
Yes when you ,, speak not too quick   Could you

suivre une conversation? Non, monsieur; mon oreille n'est
follow a conversation   No Sir my ear ,, is

pas assez habituée à la prononciation de votre langue.
not enough accustomed to the pronunciation of your language

THIRD LESSON.   *Troisième Leçon*

THE ARTICLE *(continued)* AND THE NOUN *(concluded)*.

The Indefinite Article *a* or *an* is translated:

un before masculine singular nouns; as,—
  un frère, a brother; *un animal*, an animal.

une before feminine singular nouns; as,—
  une hôtesse, a landlady; *une porte*, a door.

NOTE.—*de* before a vowel or *h* mute becomes *d'*; thus,
  d'un, d'une, of a *or* of an

FORMATION OF THE PLURAL OF NOUNS *(concluded)*.
Exceptions to the formation of the Plural of Nouns.

EXCEPTIONS to Rule 1.—a). Seven nouns ending in *ou* add *x* in the plural; viz: *le bijou*, the jewel; *le caillou*, the pebble; *le chou*, the cabbage; *le genou*, the knee; *le hibou*, the owl; *le joujou*, the toy; *le pou*, the louse.—Plural: *les bijoux, les cailloux; &c.*

b). Seven nouns ending in *ail* form their plural by changing that termination into *aux;* viz: *le bail*, the lease; *le corail*, the coral; *l'émail (m.)*, the enamel; *le soupirail*, the air hole; *le travail*, the work; *le vantail*, the leaf of a folding door; *le vitrail*, the stained glass-window.—Plural: *les baux, les coraux*, etc.

EXCEPTIONS to Rule 4.—Five nouns ending in *al* add *s* in the plural; viz: *le bal*, the ball; *le régal*, the feast; *le carnaval*, the carnival; *le chacal*, the jackal; *le nopal*, the cactus.—Plural: *les bals, les régals*, etc.

The following four nouns form their plural irregularly; viz:—
  l'aïeul (m.), the ancestor; Plural: *les aïeux*
  le ciel, the heaven;   ,,   *les cieux*
  l'œil (m.), the eye;   ,,   *les yeux*
  le bétail, the cattle;   ,,   *les bestiaux*

However *ciels* is used when it means *skies*, and in a few compound nouns; *œils* is used in *œils de bœuf*, oval window, and *œils de chat*, cat's eyes (jewels); *aïeuls* is used in the meaning of *grandfathers*.

The Auxiliary Verbs *avoir*, to have, and *être*, to be.
                    Imperfect.

j'avais, *I had*	j'étais, *I was*
tu avais, *thou hadst*	tu étais, *thou wast*
il, elle avait, *he, she had*	il, elle était, *he, she was*
nous avions, *we had*	nous étions, *we were*
vous aviez, *you had*	vous étiez, *you were*
ils, elles avaient,(*) *they had*	ils, elles étaient,(*) *they were*

OBSERVATION: Whenever negations, as: *pas*, not, *rien*, nothing, *jamais*, never, etc. are used with a verb, the particle *ne* is also required. *Ne* can only be used with verbs, and must always precede the verb, as
  je n'ai pas, I have not.   *ne suis-je pas*, am I not?
  n'avais-je pas, had I not? *je n'étais pas*, I was not.

(*) *ent* of all verbs in the 3rd person plural is mute. (vide Exception 39.)

The ball, *la balle*
    plur: *les balles*
 ,, ball (festival), *le bal;* plur: *les bals*
 ,, boy, *le garçon*
 ,, child, *l'enfant m.*
 ,, daughter or girl, *la fille*
	the eye, *l'œil m;*
	    plur: *les yeux*
	 ,, father, *le père*
	 ,, garden, *le jardin*
	 ,, knee, *le genou;*
	    plur. *les genoux*
	 ,, letter, *la lettre*
	 ,, man, *l'homme m.*
		the mother, *la mère* [m.
		 ,, parents, *les parents*
		 ,, pen, *la plume*
		 ,, pencil, *le crayon*
		 ,, son, *le fils*
		 ,, watch, *la montre*
		 ,, woman, *la femme*
		 for, *pour*
		 or, *ou*

Exercise No. 3.

1. A father,—a mother,—a pencil,—a pen,—of a son,—of a daughter,—to a man,—to a woman,—the knee, the knees,—at the ball, at the balls,—of the eye, of the eyes,—the parents' letter,—a child's ball,—the chairs of a room,—the mice or the birds,—the son's aunt,—to the garden,—an animal's knees,—to the curtains,—the noses and the eyes,—the general's nephews,—a herring and the cat,—to the hand,—an officer's horses,—at (to) an hotel,—to the voices,—the door of a church,—a boy's watch,—the uncle's hats,—of the fires,—to a girl,—from a watch,—to a soldier,—at (to) a table,—from (of) the men.

You had,—hadst thou?—had he?—they (*f.*) had,—had we?—I had,—had they?—she had,—was she?—they were,—thou wast,—were you?—was I?—we were,—were they (*f.*)?—he was,—he is not,—have I not?—are we not?—you have not,—were they not?—he has not,—you had not,—you are not,—I had not,—has she not?—they have not,—are they (*f.*) not?

2. Avez-vous une plume et un crayon? La fille de la femme n'a pas la lettre. Qui avait les journaux? Où étaient les fils du général? N'avez-vous pas donné[1] les livres au père? Les enfants n'étaient pas dans un jardin. L'officier est le neveu d'un général. Nous n'avions pas les balles. Le livre est-il sur la table ou sur la chaise? La montre était pour l'oncle. Le fils de l'homme n'avait-il pas un couteau? J'avais écrit[2] une lettre à la mère.

For whom was the letter? Had the uncle a watch? Who has given[1] the balls to the children? Where was the father? He was not in the landlady's house. Has the boy a pencil? I have not written[2] to the man. The eyes of a horse are large (*grands*). Has the mother given[1] the hats to a woman? Was the aunt in the garden or in the house? The parents have not the curtains. Were the newspapers not on a table? The nieces and (the*) nephews were in a garden. Were you at a ball?

(*) In French before every noun the article must be employed, even if in English the article be not repeated.

1 *donné*, given   2 *écrit*, written.

Questions on Grammar.

1. Is the indefinite article *un, une* the translation for *a* or *an* or for both?
2. When is *un* and when is *une* used?
3. How is *of a* or *of an* translated?
4. What is the general (first) rule in French for the formation of the plural of nouns?
5. What is the second rule ⎫
6. What is the third rule ⎬ for the formation of the plural of nouns?
7. What is the fourth rule ⎭
8. How many nouns ending in *ou* and *ail* are exceptions to rule 1, and how do they form their plural?
9. Are there any nouns ending in *al* (rule 4) which do not change into *aux* in the plural?
10. Are there any other exceptions?
11. Are verbs used negatively accompanied by one negation only as in English?
12. What participle can never be used without a verb—that it must always precede?
13. Is *ent* in the 3rd person plural of a verb ever pronounced?

Conversation.

Have you a pen, sir?	Avez-vous une plume, monsieur?
No, madam, I have no *(pas de)* pen, but *(mais)* I have a pencil.	Non, madame, je n'ai pas de plume, mais j'ai un crayon.
Has the uncle a son and two *(deux)* daughters?	L'oncle a-t-il un fils et deux filles?
No, sir, he has two sons and one *(une)* daughter.	Non, monsieur, il a deux fils et une fille.
Have you given *(donné)* the letter to the mother?	Avez-vous donné la lettre à la mère?
No, I have not given the letter to the mother, but to the father.	Non, je n'ai pas donné la lettre à la mère, mais au père.
Has the woman a watch?	La femme a-t-elle une montre?
Yes, she has a watch and a knife.	Oui, elle a une montre et un couteau.
Have they seen *(vu)* the child's ball?	Ont-ils vu la balle de l'enfant?
Yes, madam, they have found *(trouvé)* two balls.	Oui, madame, ils ont trouvé deux balles.
Has the boy large *(de grands)* eyes?	Le garçon a-t-il de grands yeux?
Yes sir, the boy and the girl have large eyes.	Oui, monsieur, le garçon et la fille ont de grands yeux.
What *(que)* have you seen in the street?	Qu'avez-vous vu dans la rue?
We have seen a horse which *(qui)* had both *(les deux)* knees broken *(cass's)*.	Nous avons vu un cheval qui avait les deux genoux cassés.

Reading Exercise No. 3.

Monsieur Robert est-il chez lui? Non, monsieur, il est sorti. Pourriez-vous me dire quand il rentrera? Non, monsieur; mais je ne crois pas qu'il reste longtemps absent. A quelle heure le train part-il? Il part à neuf heures quarante-cinq. N'y a-t-il pas un autre train à dix heures et demie? Je ne pourrais vous donner ce renseignement. Combien d'argent avez-vous dans votre porte-monnaie? J'ai deux cents francs(3) en or; douze francs cinquante centimes en argent et quinze centimes en monnaie de cuivre. Quelle est la valeur du shelling en argent français? Il vaut environ un franc vingt(11)-cinq centimes. Que désirez-vous acheter aujourd'hui? J'ai besoin d'un gilet et d'un pardessus. Ne vous faut-il pas un chapeau? Non, monsieur; mais je voudrais acheter une paire de bottines et une paire de souliers. Que faut-il servir à monsieur? Donnez-moi, s'il vous plaît, un potage au tapioca, une côtelette de mouton, des pommes de terre frites, et un demi-poulet rôti. Avez-vous fait un bon voyage? Non, le temps(16) n'a pas été favorable. Hier(17) soir j'ai perdu mon parapluie.

FOURTH LESSON. *Quatrième Leçon*

The ARTICLE (*concluded*).

The Partitive Article *du, de la, de l', des* must be used in French before every noun *taken in a partitive* (*) *sense; some* or *any* is the translation of the partitive article, which is often omitted in English.

The *partitive article* is in reality the *definite article* with the preposition *de* (of) and is used in the same manner, viz.:

du before a masculine noun singular ⎫ commencing with a
de la ,, ,, feminine ,, ,, ⎬ consonant
de l' ,, any noun singular commencing with a vowel or *h* mute
des ,, ,, ,, plural ; as,—
du vin (*m.*), some *or* any wine   *de la viande* (*f.*), some *or* any meat
de l'argent (*m.*), ,, ,, money *des plumes* (*f.*), ,, ,, pens

Give me some bread, meat, water, and apples. *Donnez-moi du pain, de la viande, de l'eau, et des pommes.*

De or *d'* takes the place of the partitive article *du, de la, de l', des* before a noun in the singular or plural :—

1. After a negation ; as,
pas de viande, no *or* not any meat   *pas d'oiseaux,* no *or* not any birds

2. After adverbs of quantity (like *enough, much,* etc.); as—
assez d'huile, enough oil   *combien de soldats !* how many soldiers

3. After nouns expressing a quantity, weight, measure, etc. (like *a glass, a cup, a pound, a dozen, two yards,* etc.), corresponding here exactly with the English *of*; as,—
un verre de vin, a glass of wine   *une livre de viande,* a pound of meat
une couple d'oiseaux, a couple of birds

4. This is also generally the case if the noun in French is preceded by an adjective ; as,
de bon vin,   (some *or* any) good wine
de jolis oiseaux, (some *or* any) pretty birds

The Auxiliary Verbs *avoir,* to have, *être,* to be.
Future.

j'aurai, *I shall have* | je serai, *I shall be*
tu auras, *thou wilt have* | tu seras, *thou wilt be*
il, elle aura, *he, she will have* | il, elle sera, *he, she will be*
nous aurons, *we shall have* | nous serons, *we shall be*
vous aurez, *you will have* | vous serez, *you will be*
ils, elles auront, *they will have* | ils, elles seront, *they will be*

(*) The word *partitive* implies the idea of an indefinite *part* of anything : Ex. *Give me some bread;* here *some bread* means a part or a portion of bread. *Have you any pens?* here *any pens* means an indefinite number of pens. Buy some tea, coffee, sugar and apples, i.e. *some coffee, some sugar, some apples,* means : Buy a quantity (not distinctly mentioned) of tea, of coffee, of sugar, and an indefinite number of apples.

the apple, *la pomme*	how much (how many), *combien*	the pear, *la poire*
,, beer, *la bière*		,, pound, *la livre*
,, bottle, *la bouteille*	the ink, *l'encre f.*	,, salt, *le sel*
,, bread, *le pain*	,, meat, *la viande*	,, sugar, *le sucre*
,, coffee, *le café*	,, money, *l'argent m.*	,, tea, *le thé*
,, cup, *la tasse*	,, oil, *l'huile f.*	,, water, *l'eau f.*
,, enough, *assez*	,, paper, *le papier*	,, wine, *le vin*
,, glass, *le verre*		

Exercise No. 4.

1. Some (any) bread,—some (any) paper,—some (any) beer,—some (any) meat,—some (any) money,—some (any) ink,—some (any) books,—some (any) apples,—some coffee, meat, oil, and pears,—paper, ink, and pens,—cups, bottles, and glasses,—beer, coffee, and meat,—not any bread, no* beer,—not any money,—no sons,—(some *or* any) good (*bonne*) ink,—(some *or* any) bad (*mauvais*) tea,—enough wine,—how much sugar?—many (*beaucoup*) pears,—a glass of water,—a cup of coffee,—a dozen (*douzaine f.*) of chairs,—enough paper,—some water,—a bottle of beer,—some books,—a pound of salt,—some (any) sugar and bread,—some newspapers,—no tables,—some (any) oil,—no beer,—some children.

We shall have,—shall I have?—he will have,—will they (*f.*) have?—you will have,—wilt thou have?—will she be?—they will be,—thou wilt be, — will you be? — I shall be, — shall we be? — I shall not have,—I have not,—shall we not be?—we were not,—you have,—you will not have,—will you be?—we are not,—they will have,—were they (*f.*)?

2. Achetez[1] une livre de sucre et une bouteille de vin. Aurons-nous du café? Ils n'auront pas de thé. Avez-vous de l'encre et des plumes? La mère a assez de poires. Donnez-moi[2] un verre de bière. J'aurai de bonne (*good*) huile. Voilà[3] de l'eau et du vin. Combien d'argent a l'officier? Qui a du sel? Combien de chaises avez-vous dans la chambre? J'ai de la viande et du pain. Nous avons vu[4] des oiseaux dans le jardin. Avez-vous de la bière, du vin, ou du café?

We shall have some coffee. Officers and soldiers are in the house. Have they any money? Has he any apples and pears, bread and salt? Give me[2] a cup of coffee and a glass of water. I have not enough sugar. He has not any bread. How many cups of tea have you? There are[3] paper and ink. Has the general any bad (*mauvais*) horses? The father will be in the garden. Buy[1] a bottle of oil and a pound of meat. Have you not any ink? Has she some pencils? Have you seen[4] any animals? I have not any beer. There is[3] a glass of wine.

(*) *No* as well as *not* must be translated *pas*.

1 *achetez,* buy 2 *donnez-moi,* give me 3 *voilà,* there is, there are 4 *vu* seen

French Grammar.

Questions on Grammar.

1. What is the partitive article in French?
2. Is the partitive article similar to the definite article?
3. What words in English are the translation of *du, de la*, etc.
4. Are these words always expressed in English?
5. When must the partitive article be used?
6. What is the meaning of partitive?
7. How is the partitive article rendered after a negation or an adverb of quantity, or before an adjective?
8. When is *de* used instead of the partitive article?

Conversation.

What (*que*) have you in your (the) hand?	Qu'avez-vous dans la main?
I have a pear and some bread in my (the) hand.	J'ai une poire et du pain dans la main.
How much tea did you buy (have you bought (*acheté*)?	Combien de thé avez-vous acheté?
We did not buy any tea, but (*mais*) we have bought a bottle of wine, two (*deux*) pounds of meat, some coffee, some ink and some paper.	Nous n'avons pas acheté de thé, mais nous avons acheté une bouteille de vin, deux livres de viande, du café, de l'encre et du papier.
Do you prefer (*préférez-vous*) a cup of coffee to a glass of wine?	Préférez-vous une tasse de café à un verre de vin?
Thank you, madam; we prefer (*nous préférons*) coffee.	Merci, madame; nous préférons du café.
Have you seen (*vu*) the uncle's knife?	Avez-vous vu le couteau de l'oncle?
Yes, madam, I have seen the uncle's knife on the table	Oui, madame, j'ai vu le couteau de l'oncle sur la table.
Who has given (*donné*) some oil to the little (*petit*) boy?	Qui a donné de l'huile au petit garçon?
I have not given any oil to the boy.	Je n'ai pas donné d'huile au petit garçon.
What have you done (*fait*) with (*avec*) the money?	Qu'avez-vous fait avec l'argent?
We have bought some apples, some sugar, and some salt.	Nous avons acheté des pommes, du sucre et du sel.
Has the officer's son some pens?	Le fils de l'officier a-t-il des plumes?
No, sir, he has no pens, but some pencils.	Non, monsieur, il n'a pas de plumes, mais des crayons.
To whom have you given a watch?	A qui avez-vous donné une montre?
I have given a watch to the woman's niece.	J'ai donné une montre à la nièce de la femme,
For whom have you bought a garden?	Pour qui avez-vous acheté un jardin?
I have not bought any garden, but we have bought a house.	Nous n'avons pas acheté de jardin mais nous avons acheté une maison.

Reading Exercise No. 4.

Translate this and the following anecdotes. Words which the student has already learnt are omitted and indicated by a . and those which are the same or nearly the same in English as in French are indicated by a —

Esope et le piéton.
    Æsop . . foot-passenger

Esope, le célèbre fabuliste, était trés pauvre. Il faisait
Æsop . celebrated fabulist . very poor . made

souvent à pied des excursions d'une ville à l'autre. Il
often on foot . — . town . another .

rencontra un jour un piéton : celui-ci l'arrêta et lui dit :
met . day . foot passenger this him stopped . to him said

"Voudriez-vous me dire quelle distance me sépare de la
Would . — tell what — — separates . .

ville qui est sur la colline." Esope prit un air stupide et
town which . . . hill Æsop took . — stupid .

répondit : "Vous n'avez qu'à marcher, et vous y arriverez."
answered . „ . but to walk . . there will arrive

L'étranger sourit et dit : "Je sais parfaitement cela ; mais
. stranger smiled . said . know perfectly that but

je désirerais savoir combien de temps il me faudra pour
. should wish to know . . time . — will be necessary for

faire le chemin." Esope parut s'offenser et répéta les
make . way Æsop appeared himself to offend . repeated .

mêmes paroles. "Cet homme n'est pas tout à fait lucide :
same words This man „ . . quite lucid

il ne me dira rien," pensa le piéton ; et il continua son
. „ — will tell nothing thought . foot-passenger . . continued his

chemin. Quelques minutes plus tard il entendit qu'on
way Some — later . heard that one

l'appelait : il se retourna et vit Esope que le suivait.
him called . himself turned round . saw Æsop . him followed

"Que me voulez-vous," lui demanda-t-il ? "Je veux vous
What from me wish . to him demanded . . wish .

dire, dit Esope, que vous serez à la ville dans une heure et
. to say said Æsop that . will be . . town . . hour .

demie." "Et pourquoi ne m'avez-vous pas répondu immé-
a half . why „ me . . . answered imme-

diatement." "C'est parce qu'il était nécessaire que je visse
diately. This . because it . necessary that she see

comment vous marchiez."
how . walked

Fifth Lesson.   *Cinquième Leçon.*

Words which are the same or nearly the same in English and French.

Words which are the same, are nearly all nouns or adjectives, ending as follows:

in al	Ex.:	*central, filial*	in age	Ex.:	*âge, village*
in ble	,,	*table, visible*	in uge	,,	*déluge, refuge*
in ce	,,	*distance, vice*	in ent	,,	*prudent, diligent*
in ade	,,	*sérénade, parade*	in ion	,,	*nation, station, commission*
in ude	,,	*habitude, solitude*			

REMARK.—Letters which are accented in French drop their accent in English.

Words which undergo a slight modification.

	change that termination into		Ex.:	
English words ending in { ary	aire	,,	solitary	—*solitaire*
ory	oire	,,	glory	—*gloire*
cy	ce	,,	clemency	—*clémence*
ty	té	,,	charity	—*charité*
ous	eux	,,	pious	—*pieux*
our	eur	,,	favour	—*faveur*
or	eur	,,	doctor	—*docteur*
ic	ique	,,	comic	—*comique*
ive	if	,,	active	—*actif*
ian	ien	,,	historian	—*historien*

Many English verbs ending in *ise*, *ize* or *use*, end in French in *iser*, *user*.—Examples: realise, *réaliser;* exercise, *exercer;* abuse, *abuser;* amuse, *amuser.*

	change this ending into		
Verbs ending in { ate	er	moderate	—*modérer*
fy	fier	modify	—*modifier*

NOTE.—There are few exceptions to the above rules; they will greatly assist the student in rapidly acquiring a large number of words.

Verbs *avoir*, to have, and *être*, to be.
Present Conditional,

j'aurais, *I should have*	je serais, *I should be*
tu aurais, *thou wouldst have*	tu serais, *thou wouldst be*
il, elle aurait, *he, she would have*	il, elle serait, *he, she would be*
nous aurions, *we should have*	nous serions, *we should be*
vous auriez, *you would have*	vous seriez, *you would be*
ils, elles auraient, *they would have*	ils, elles seraient, *they would be*

apppentice, *apprenti* m.	great, *grand*	small, *petit*
ass, *âne* m.	here, *ici*	there, *là*
boot, *botte* f.	large, *grand*	time, *temps* (16) m.
cousin, *cousin* m.	master, *maître* m.	to-morrow, *demain*
cousin(f.), *cousine* f.	morning, *matin* m.	trade, *métier* m.
day, *jour* m.	pair, *paire* f.	useful, *utile*
foot, *pied* m.	shoe, soulier m. [m.	very, *très*
friend, *ami* m.	shoemaker, *cordonnier*	work, *travail* m.

Exercise No. 5.

1. General(")(*)—respectable—conscience—escalade—aptitude—heritage(')—febrifuge(')—accident—admiration—military—history—decency(')—beauty—curious—ardour—horror—aquatic—adjective—comedian(')—to idealize(')—to refuse—to accelerate(")—to stupefy (')—moral—anniversary—honorable—captivity—musical—obligatory—similitude—adversary—city—pretentious(')—to analyse—evidence—(')—firmament—naval - original—capable—inactive—illusion—to moderate(')—lion—charitable—calamity—visage—motion—direction—vanity - instrument—to indemnize—colonnade—rage—imprudence—notary—civic—notable—adversity.

You would have—I should be—would he have ?—they would be—thou wouldst be—I should have—she would not be—we should not have—we should be—should we have ?—would you be ?—we should have—thou wouldst have—she would be—he would have—would they *(f.)* have?—you would be—he would have—we should not be—wouldst thou have?—should I be—we should not be—she would have—they *(m.)* would have.

2. Les bottes et les souliers de votre¹ ami sont à la station. Nous aurions attendu² mon³ cousin. Ceci⁴ est obligatoire. Cette (*this*) capitulation serait honorable. Votre action n'est pas charitable. Vous ne seriez pas sur⁵ le rivage. Seraient-ils dans la cité. Je ne serais pas capable de⁶ refuser.

The instrument is very useful. The boots of the general are in the room. He has a large foot. This⁷ would be a great (*grande*) imprudence (*f.*). It would have a great (*grande*) importance (*f.*) My⁸ friend would be impatient. The shoemaker would not have finished⁹ the boots. We should have a good master. You would be capable to¹⁰ simplify the question. His¹¹ apprentice was very laborious. Your¹² cousin has a very good trade. You will have a pair of boots and his¹³ cousin (*f.*) a pair of shoes. Would he have the time? He would not be there. We should be here to-morrow morning. His charity is immense. The ass is an animal which¹⁴ is very useful.

---

1 *votre*, yours 2 *attendu*, waited for 3 *mon*, my 4 *ceci*, this 5 *sur*, on 6 *de*, to 7 this, *ce* 8 my, *mon* 9 finished, *fini* 10 to, *de* 11 his, son 12 your, *votre* 13 his, *sa* 14 which, *qui*

(*) The apostrophes placed between brackets indicate that as many acute accents are required in the French word.

Questions on Grammar.

1. What are the endings which are generally the same in French as in English?
2. What becomes of the accents which exist in the French words when such words also exist in the English language?
3. What are the endings which are nearly the same in French as in English?
4. How can French words be formed from English words ending in *ary* and *ory*?
5. How do English words in *ty* and *cy* end in French?
6. How can French words be formed from English words ending in *ous*, *our*, or.
7. How do English words ending in *ic*, *ive* and *ian* change those terminations?
8. How do most of the English verbs ending in *ise*, *ize* and *use* end in French?
9. How do verbs ending in *ate* and *fy* end in French?

Conversation.

Has the shoemaker an apprentice?	Le cordonnier a-t-il un apprenti?
Yes, he has two apprentices in his (*son*) workshop (*atelier*).	Oui, il a deux apprentis dans son atelier.
Where are the boots?	Où sont les bottes?
The boots are in my (*mon*) uncle's room.	Les bottes sont dans la chambre de mon oncle.
Are the shoes too (*trop*) small?	Les souliers sont-ils trop petits?
No, they are rather (*plutôt*) too large.	Non, ils sont plutôt trop grands.
Has your (*votre*) cousin a large foot?	Votre cousin a-t-il un grand pied?
No, his (*son*) foot is very small.	Non, son pied est très petit.
Will the boots be ready (*prêtes*) to-morrow morning?	Les bottes seront-elles prêtes demain matin?
Yes, they will be here.	Oui, elles seront ici.
What (*quel*) is your friend's trade (the trade of your friend)?	Quel est le métier de votre ami?
He is (a) shoemaker.	Il est cordonnier.
Have you two pairs of boots?	Avez-vous deux paires de bottes?
No, I have only (*seulement*) one pair of boots; but (*mais*) I have also (*aussi*) a pair of shoes.	Non, j'ai seulement (je n'ai qu') une paire de bottes; mais j'ai aussi une paire de souliers.
Where is my friend's ass?	Où est l'âne de mon ami?
It is in the garden.	Il est dans le jardin.
Is it (*ce*) a useful animal?	Est-ce un animal utile?
Yes: it (*il*) is very useful.	Oui, il est très utile.

Reading Exercise No. 5.

Un de nos͡amis avait besoin d'une paire de bottes.
. . our . . need . . . . .
Il alla chez le cordonnier et lui dit: Faites-moi, s'il vous
. went to , . . to him said make me if . you
plaît, une paire de bottes, mais je désire qu'elles soient de
please . . . but I wish . . should be .
première qualité. Il faut͡aussi que je vous dise quelque
first — It is necessary also . . . may say some
chose. Je me suis cassé une jambe, dans ma jeunesse; c'est
thing . myself broke . leg in my youth this .
pourquoi j'ai un pied plus gros que l'autre. Vous devez
why . . . . larger than . other . must
donc faire une botte plus large que l'autre. Le cordonnier
then make . . wider than . other . .
promit de faire attention et prit mesure. Trois jours͡après
promised . to do — . took measure three . afterwards
l'apprenti du cordonnier apportait les bottes à mon͡ami; .
. . . . brought . . . my friend
celui-ci les͡essaya immédiatement: il mit la plus grande
this them tried immediately . put . larger
botte au plus petit pied, et ce dernier y entra très facile-
. . smaller . . this last there entered very easi-
ment. Il voulut͡ensuite mettre la plus petite botte au
ly . wished afterwards to put . smaller . .
plus grand pied: mais il ne put naturellement pas͡y
larger . but . ,, could naturally . in it
réussir. Il se fâcha alors et dit͡à l'apprenti: Votre
succeed . got angry then . said . . .
maître ne comprend pas son métier. Je lui avais recom-
. ,, understands . his . . him . recom-
mandé de faire une botte plus large que l'autre et je trouve
mended . to make . . larger than . other . . find
tout le contraire: il a fait l'une beaucoup plus͡étroite que
all . contrary . . made . . much more narrow than
l'autre. Prenez ces bottes et remportez-les, afin qu'il
. other take these . . take away them in order that .
se conforme à mes͡instructions.
himself may conform . my —

SIXTH LESSON.   *Sixième Leçon.*

The Adjective.

There are two kinds of adjectives: those which express some quality belonging to the noun or pronoun to which they refer and are therefore called *qualifying;* and those which determine or define more clearly than the article, and are called *determinative.*

Adjectives are variable words and take the gender and number of the noun which they qualify or determine.

Qualifying Adjectives.
FORMATION OF THE FEMININE.

RULE I.—Adjectives form their feminine by adding *e* to the masculine; as,—*grand,* large, *grande; petit,* small, *petite; joli,* pretty, *jolie; aisé,* easy, *aisée*

RULE II.—Adjectives ending in *e* mute remain the same in the feminine; as,
modeste, modest, *modeste; fidèle,* faithful, *fidèle*

RULE III.—Adjectives ending in *on, an, et, el, eil, ien,* double the final consonant and add an *e;* as,
bon, good, *bonne; paysan,* peasant, *paysanne; muet,* dumb *muette; éternel,* eternal, *éternelle; pareil,* alike, *pareille; chrétien,* christian, *chrétienne*

EXCEPTIONS.—*complet,* complete; *concret,* concrete; *discret,* discreet; *inquiet,* uneasy; *replet,* stout; *secret,* secret, form their feminine by putting a grave accent on the *e* before the *t,* and adding an *e* to the masculine; thus: *complète, discrète, inquiète,* &c.

RULE IV.—Adjectives ending in *x* change *x* into *se;* as,
heureux, happy, *heureuse; jaloux,* jealous, *jalouse*

EXCEPTIONS.—*doux,* sweet, *douce; roux,* reddish, *rousse; faux,* false, *fausse; vieux,* old, *vieille.*

RULE V.—Adjectives ending in *f* change *f* into *ve;* as,
neuf, new, *neuve; actif,* active, *active*

RULE VI.—Adjectives ending in *er* change *er* into *ère;* as,
fier, proud, *fière; premier,* first, *première; singulier,* singular, *singulière*

The Auxiliary Verbs *avoir,* to have and *être,* to be.
Past Indefinite.

(Compound tenses in French are formed with the tenses of an auxiliary verb and the past participle).

J'ai eu, *I have had*	J'ai été, *I have been*
tu as eu, *thou hast had*	tu as été, *thou hast been*
il, elle a eu, *he, she has had*	il, elle a été, *he, she has been*
nous avons eu, *we have had*	nous avons été, *we have been*
vous avez eu, *you have had*	vous avez été, *you have been*
ils, elles ont eu, *they have had*	ils, elles ont été, *they have been*

advice, *avis m*
alone, *seul*
anxious, *anxieux*
bad, *mauvais*
courageous, *courageux*
embarrassment, *embar-*
good, *bon* [*ras m.*
  andwriting, *écriture f.*
hard, *dur*
honest, *honnête*
impossible, *impossible*
lame, *boiteux*
last, *dernier*
misfortune, *infortune f.*
neighbour, *voisin m.*
news, *nouvelle f.*
no, *non*
old, *vieux*
person, *personne f.*
positive, *positif*
prudent, *prudent*
small, *petit*
too, *trop*
town, *ville f.*

Exercise No. 6.
Write the feminine of the following adjectives.

1. Patient—savant—égal—obtus—renommé—ardu—hardi—agreste—mignon—coquet—solennel—vermeil—payen—secret—audacieux—doux—récréatif—dernier—rond—malade—sujet—obstiné—fameux—faux—opulent—inactif—vieux—content—dur—lourd—actuel—facile—net—vertueux—roux—réservé—comique—laborieux—serein—complet—droit—triste—naturel—boiteux—habile—lent—religieux—plein—juste—ancien—libéral—vicieux—discret—incliné—intelligent.

We have been—I have not had—they (*f.*) have been—have we had?—I have not been—he has not had—we have not had—thou hast had—he has had—thou hast been—have you not had?—you have not had—have they (*m.*) had?—has she been?—have they (*f.*) had?—you have been—have I not been?—have we had?—have they (*m.*) not been?—they (*m.*) have been—we have not been.

2. La maison est grande. La ville est petite. Ma¹ mère était seule. J'ai été prudente. Nous avons eu le courage. Sa² sœur est boiteuse. Cette³ chambre ne serait pas trop grande. Elle a été généreuse(*). Cette³ ville est très vieille. La nouvelle est positive. Son⁴ écriture est très mauvaise. Cette personne était très honnête. Mon⁵ écriture n'était pas bonne. Il est impossible (de) refuser un avis à notre⁶ voisin dans son⁴ embarras et dans son infortune. La dernière nouvelle est bonne. Cette viande est dure. Cette personne est très discrète.

She has been happy. My⁷ room is not very large. He had had patience. This⁸ woman is old. Our⁹ sister is good. His¹⁰ misfortune is great. This⁸ person is anxious to see¹¹ the town. My mother was alone in her¹² large room. This handwriting is very bad. You have been prudent (*f.*) in your¹³ advice. She was very courageous in her¹⁴ embarrassments. The news is too positive. The old woman is lame. Is this⁸ person honest and discreet?

(*) Some adjectives which are not found in the vocabulary must be looked for on the opposite page.
1 *ma*, my 2 *sa*, his 3 *cette*, this 4 *son*, his 5 *mon*, my 6 *notre*, our 7 my. *ma* 8 this, *cette* 9 our, *notre* 10 his, *son* 11 to see, *de voir* 12 her, *sa* 13 your, *vos* 14 her, *ses*

Questions on Grammar.

1. How many kinds of adjectives are there in French?
2. What is the difference between qualifying and determinative adjectives?
3. How do adjectives agree with the nouns they qualify or determine?
4. How do adjectives form their feminine in French?
5. How do adjectives ending in *e* mute form their feminine?
6. What are the endings of adjectives which double their final consonant in the feminine?
7. Give the adjectives in *el* which form their feminine by changing that ending into *èle*?
8. How do adjectives ending in *x* form the feminine?
9. Give the exceptions to the above rule.
10. How do adjectives ending in *f* form the feminine?
11. How do adjectives ending in *er* form the feminine?

Conversation.

Who (*qui*) has written (*écrit*) this (*cette*) letter?	Qui a écrit cette lettre?
My (*mon*) friend has written the letter.	Mon ami a écrit la lettre.
To whom has this letter been (*été*) written (*écrite*)?	A qui cette lettre a-t-elle été écrite?
It (*elle*) has been written to my father.	Elle a été écrite à mon père.
Is the handwriting of your (*votre*) friend very bad?	L'écriture de votre ami est-elle très mauvaise?
No, it is very good.	Non, elle est très bonne.
Is it possible to write (*d'écrire*) a letter with (*avec*) this bad pen?	Est-il possible d'écrire une lettre avec cette mauvaise plume?
No, it (*c'*) is impossible.	Non, c'est impossible.
Is it (*il*) possible that the old shoemaker should come (*vienne*) tomorrow?	Est-il possible que le vieux cordonnier vienne demain?
It (*ce*) would be possible if (*s'*) he were (*était*) not lame.	Ce serait possible s'il n'était pas boiteux.
Have you seen (*vu*) this news in the last newspaper?	Avez-vous vu cette nouvelle dans le dernier journal?
Yes, I have seen the news in the newspaper which (*que*) the postman (*facteur*) brought (*a apporté*) this (*ce*) morning.	Oui, j'ai vu la nouvelle dans le journal que le facteur a apporté ce matin.
Is the news positive?	La nouvelle est-elle positive?
Yes, it (*elle*) is quite (*tout à fait*) true (*vraie*).	Oui, elle est tout à fait vraie.

Reading Exercise No. 6.

Un͡homme avait reçu une lettre et voulait͡y répondre
pour son malheur il ne pouvait pas͡écrire et il se trouva
dans l'embarras. Il alla voir un de ses voisins et lui
demanda conseil. "Allez chez notre vieux sacristain" lui
dit le voisin; "il écrit souvent des lettres pour d'autres
gens." L'homme suivit son͡avis, alla chez le sacristain
et lui expliqua son͡embarras. "Je suis fâché de ne pas
pouvoir écrire votre lettre" répondit le sacristain; "je
suis boiteux." L'homme fut͡étonné. "Vous͡êtes boiteux,"
dit-il, "et cela vous͡empêche d'écrire ma lettre! écrivez-
vous donc avec le pied?" "Non," répliqua le sacristain
"j'écris͡avec la main; mais mon͡écriture est si mauvaise
que je puis seul la lire. Les gens͡étaient͡obligés de m'envoyer chercher pour que je lusse les lettres que j'avais
écrites. Maintenant, comme je suis paralysé, il m'est
impossible d'aller trouver ceux qui ont reçu mes lettres;
et comme la personne à qui vous voulez͡écrire habite une
autre ville, elle ne pourrait pas venir dans ma maison.
Il est donc impossible que j'écrive votre lettre, comme
vous me le demandez."

SEVENTH LESSON. *Septième Leçon.*

Qualifying Adjectives (*continued*).

FORMATION OF THE FEMININE (*continued*).

RULE VII.—Adjectives ending in *eur* and derived from present participles by changing *ant* into *eur* form their feminine by changing *r* into *se;* as,

trompeur, deceptive, *trompeuse; menteur*, liar, *menteuse.*

EXCEPTIONS.—*Vengeur*, avenger; *enchanteur*, enchanter; *pécheur*, sinner, and some adjectives used only as law terms as, *demandeur*, plaintiff &c., although derived from present participles, have for their féminines *vengeresse, enchanteresse, pécheresse* and *demanderesse*.

RULE VIII.—Adjectives ending in *érieur* form their feminine by the simple addition of *e* to the masculine; as,

supérieur, superior, *supérieure; inférieur*, inferior, *inférieure*

REMARK.—*Majeur*, major; *mineur*, minor and *meilleur*, better follow the same rule.

RULE IX.—Adjectives ending in *teur* not derived from present participles form their feminines by changing *teur* into *trice;* as,

admirateur, admirer, *admiratrice; créateur*, creator, *créatrice*

RULE X.—Adjectives in *au* and *ou* form their feminines by changing *au* into *elle*, and *ou* into *olle;* as,

beau, beautiful, *belle; nouveau*, new, *nouvelle; mou*, soft, *molle*

REMARK.—*beau, nouveau, mou, fou* (mad) and *vieux* become *bel, ouvel, mol, fol* and *vieil* before a masculine noun beginning with a vowel or mute *h*.

RULE XI.—The following adjectives double the final consonant and add an *e* to the masculine:

nul	void	nulle	gros	large	grosse	épais	thick	épaisse
sot	silly	sotte	gras	fat	grasse	las	tired	lasse
gentil	nice	gentille	bas	low	basse	exprès	express	expresse

RULE XII.—The following adjectives are irregular:

aigu*	acute	aiguë	long	long	longue	favori	favorite	favorite
frais	fresh	fraîche	public	public	publique	devin	guesser	devineresse
sec	dry	sèche	caduc	decrepit	caduque	malin	malicious	maligne
blanc	white	blanche	turc	Turkish	turque	bénin	benign	bénigne
franc	frank	franche	grec	Greek	grecque	coi	still	coite
tiers	third	tierce	hebreu	Hebrew	hebraïque	traître	treacherous	traîtresse

Present Indicative of the verb *donner*, to give.
(*First Conjugation, including all verbs ending in* er.)

je donn-e,(†) *I give*	donné-je, *do I give?*	je ne donne pas, *I do not give*
tu donn-es, *thou givest*	donnes-tu, *dost thou give*	tu ne donnes pas, *thou dost not —*
il donn-e, *he gives*	donne-t-il, *does he give*	il ne donne pas, *he does not —*
nous donn-ons, *we give*	donnons-nous, *do we give?*	nous ne donnons pas, *we do not—*
vous donn-ez, *you give*	donnez-vous, *do you give?*	vous ne donnez pas, *you do not—*
ils donn-ent, *they give*	donnent-ils, *do they give?*	ils ne donnent pas, *they do not—*

(*) All adjectives ending in *gu* take the diæresis on the *e* (*ë*) in the feminine.

(†) The *endings* have been separated from the *root* by a hyphen and must be placed after the root of any verb of the same conjugation; **as,** —*je parl-e*, I speak; *tu march-es*, thou walkest; *il chant-e*, he sings, &c.

answer, *réponse f.*
clever, *habile*
cow, *vache f.*
doctor, *docteur m.*
dress, *robe f.*
exercise, *exercice m.*
gentleman, *monsieur*
health, *santé f.*
ill, *malade*

lady, *dame f.*
lesson, *leçon f.*
nothing, *rien*
physician, *médecin m.*
pretty, *joli*
quick, *vite*
red, *rouge*
song, *chanson f.*

to-day, *aujourd'hui*
to like, to love, *aimer*
to sing, *chanter*
to speak, *parler*
to walk, *marcher*
visit, *visite f.*
well, *bien*
with, *avec*

Exercise No. 7.

Write the feminine of the following adjectives.

1. Rieur—intérieur—générateur—jumeau—fou—réclameur—vengeur—majeur—consolateur—beau—sot—blanc—aigu—malin—nul—frais—caduc—contigu—enchanteur—gentil—joueur—exprès—sec—bénin—gros—favori—mineur—mou—las—gras—blanc—pécheur—épais—franc—public—devin—meilleur—bas—ambigu—nouveau—long.

We give—do I give?—you do not give—do they (*f.*) give?—he gives—thou givest—they (*f.*) do not give—it (*f.*) gives—does he give? —I speak—we like—I give—do we give?—they (*m.*) do not give—do you give?—I do not give—you give—she walks—they (*f.*) sing—she does not give—do we speak?—they (*m.*) give—doest thou give?—do they (*m.*) give?—we do not give—do they (*m.*) sing?—she gives—she likes.

2. La dame a eu une visite. Le médecin parle bien. Vous marchez vite. Mon¹ père donne une robe*b*(*) blanche*a* à ma² petite cousine. Ma voisine est la sœur*b* jumelle*a* de ce³ monsieur. Donnez-vous une meilleure pomme à votre⁴ frère? Je ne donne pas la grosse poire au petit garçon. Avez-vous une vache*b* grasse*a*? Nous chantons aujourd'hui. Donnent-ils leurs⁵ exercices au professeur? Qu'⁶avez-vous dans votre main?—Rien. Leur⁷ vache est malade. Elle chante bien.

We sing to-day with your⁸ sister. My⁹ cousin walks very quickly. My¹⁰ dress is white and red. They (*m.*) give some large apples to the little girl. She was a great friend of my¹⁰ aunt. This¹¹ is my favorite*b*(*) song*a*. Her¹² answer was ambiguous. Do you give this¹³ long lesson to the little boy? This¹³ girl is very clever. You speak well. The lady is ill; she has received¹⁴ the visit of the physician. My¹⁵ mother gives these¹⁶ apples and these pears to the little boy and to the pretty little girl.

(*) *b..a* indicate that the word marked *a* must be placed before the word marked *b*.

1 *mon*, my 2 *ma*, my 3 *ce*, this 4 *votre*, your 5 *leurs*, their 6 *qu'*, what 7 *leur*, their 8 *your, votre* 9 my, *mon* 10 my, *ma* 11 this, *c'* 12 her, *sa* 13 this, *cette* 14 received, *reçu* 15 my, *ma* 16 these, *ces*

Questions on Grammar.

1. How do adjectives ending in *eur* derived from present participles form the feminine?
2. Give the adjectives which change *eur* into *eresse* in the feminine.
3. Which are the adjectives ending in *eur* which form the feminine by adding *e* to the masculine?
4. How do adjectives ending in *teur*, not derived from present participles, form the feminine?
5. How do adjectives in *au* and *ou* form the feminine?
6. Give the forms used instead of *beau, nouveau, mou, fou* and *vieux* before masculine nouns beginning with a vowel or a mute *h*.
7. Give the feminine of *gentil, gros, gras, épais, sot, nul*.
8. Give the feminine of *frais, sec, blanc, long, public, favori, malin*.
9. What is the sign which must be placed on the final *e* of the feminine form of adjectives ending in *gu* in the masculine?

Conversation.

Where (*où*) is the lady?	Où est la dame?
The lady is in the room with the physician.	La dame est dans la chambre avec le médecin.
Is she ill?	Est-elle malade?
No (*non*); but (*mais*) she wishes (*désire*) to have his (*son*) advice on (*sur*) the health of her (*sa*) daughter.	Non, mais elle désire avoir son avis sur la santé de sa fille.
Is the doctor clever?	Le docteur est-il habile?
Yes; a gentleman told me (*m'a dit*) that he was very clever.	Oui; un monsieur m'a dit qu'il était très habile.
Do you like the dress of this (*cette*) little girl?	Aimez-vous la robe de cette petite fille?
Yes, I like it (*l'*) (very) much (*beaucoup*).	Oui; je l'aime beaucoup.
Do you walk quickly?	Marchez-vous vite?
No, I do not walk very quickly.	Non, je ne marche pas très vite.
Have you seen (*vu*) my (*mon*) neighbour's cow?	Avez-vous vu la vache de mon voisin?
Yes, it is very pretty; it is brown and white.	Oui, elle est très jolie; elle est brune et blanche.
Have you received (*reçu*) an answer from your brother?	Avez-vous reçu une réponse de votre frère?
Yes, sir; he is in very good health.	Oui, monsieur; il est en très bonne santé.
Is he always (*toujours*) with your (*votre*) sister in the country (*à la campagne*)?	Est-il toujours avec votre sœur à la campagne?
No, he is alone now.	Non, il est seul maintenant.

Reading Exercise No. 7.

Une dame avait ͡un *soin* exagéré de sa *santé*. Elle
. . . a care exaggerated . her . .
était *dans* la *plus grande inquiétude*, au sujet de la *plus*
. . . greatest uneasiness on the subject . . most
légère indisposition et *envoyait* ͡immédiate*ment* chercher
slight — . sent . immediately to fetch
le *docteur*. Ce médeci*n* était ͡un ͡homme très habile et
. — this . . . , . clever .
avait *conséquemment* ͡une *grande clientèle*. Il lui était
. consequently . . practice . to him .
donc très *désagréable* d'être *dérangé inutilement* de ses ͡
then . disagreeable . to be disturbed uselessly from his
autres ͡*occupations*. Il résolut de corriger cette dame de
other . . resolved to correct . . .
sa *manie*. *Un* jour qu'elle avait remarqué une tache rouge
her mania . . that . . remarked . spot .
sur sa *main*, elle le fit ͡aussitôt ͡appeler. Il v*int*, regarda
on her . . him made at once call . came looked at
la *main* et dit : "vous ͡avez très b*ien* fait de me faire venir
. . . said . . well done of — to make come
aujourd'hui." La dame fut ͡épouv*antée en* l'*entendant*
. . . . . frightened on him hearing
parler ͡ainsi et lui d*emanda* si elle était d*angereusement*
speak thus . him asked if . . dangerously
malade. "Pas le m*oins* du *monde*," répondit le docteur.
. . . least . world answered . —
"Mais si vous ͡aviez ͡atten*du* jusqu'à dem*ain*, la tache
but if . . waited till to-morrow . spot
aurait certaine*ment* disparu sans mon traite*ment* et j'aurais
. certainly disappeared without any treatment .
perdu le prix de cette visite." La dame comprit probable-
lost . . . this visit . . understood probably
ment la leçon, car le médeci*n*, après ͡avoir raconté cette
. . for . . after . related this
anecdote, ajoutait que la dame ne l'avait jamais fait ͡
— added that . . „ him . never made
appeler, depuis ce jour-là, sinon lorsqu'elle était réelle*ment*
call since that . there but when . . really
malade.

Eighth Lesson. *Huitième Leçon.*

Qualifying Adjectives *(continued).*
FORMATION OF THE PLURAL.

RULE.—Adjectives form their plural according to the rules given for nouns. (Lessons 1, 2 & 3.)

EXCEPTION 1.—Adjectives ending in *eu* take *s* in the plural instead of taking an *x*; as,—*bleu*, blue, *bleus; feu*, defunct, *feus*

2.—The following adjectives ending in *al* take *s* in the plural instead of changing *al* into *aux;* they are very seldom used in the plural.

| *fatal* | fatal | *glacial* | glacial | *natal* | natal |
| *final* | final | *jovial* | jovial | *naval* | naval |

and a few others very little used.

Degrees of Comparison.

There are three degrees of comparison of adjectives : the *positive*, the *comparative* and *superlative*.

The *positive* is the adjective itself, without any comparison between the noun which it qualifies and any other noun ; as,

cet homme est pauvre, this man is poor

The comparative is the degree which indicates that a comparison is made between the object qualified by the adjective and one or several other objects of the same kind. Comparatives are formed in French by placing the adverbs *plus*, more, *moins*, less, *aussi*, as, before the adjectives.

cet homme est plus généreux que moi, this man is more generous than I
cet homme est moins généreux que moi, this man is less generous than I
cet homme est aussi généreux que moi, this man is as generous as I

It may be seen from these examples that *than*, as well as *as*, at the beginning of the second term of the comparison is translated *que*.

The superlative is the degree which indicates that the object qualified by the adjective possesses the quality in a very high degree (*superlative absolute*) or in the highest degree (*superlative relative*). The *superlative absolute* is formed by placing *très*, *fort* or *bien*, very before the adjective ; as,

cet homme est très pauvre, this man is very poor

The *superlative relative* is formed by placing the article *le*, *la*, *les* before the comparative ; as,

cet homme est le plus généreux, this man is the most generous
les hommes les plus sages, the wisest men

Imperfect of the verb *donner*, to give.

Je donn-ais, *I gave* or *I was giving*	donnais-je, *did I give* or *was I giving*
tu donn-ais, *thou gavest*	donnais-tu, *didst thou give*
il donn-ait, *he gave*	donnait-il, *did he give*
nous donn-ions. *we gave*	donnions-nous, *did we give*
vous donn-iez, *you gave*	donniez-vous, *did we give*
ils donn-aient, *they gave*	donnaient-ils, *did they give*

beautiful, *beau*	London, *Londres m.*	rich, *riche*
blue, *bleu*	month, *mois m.*	soon, *bientôt*
coat, *habit m.*	new, *nouveau*	sound, *son m.*
debt, *dette f.*	painter, *peintre m.*	sum, *somme f.*
end, *bout m. fin f.*	painting, *tableau m.*	tall, *grand*
family, *famille f.*	perfect, *parfait*	to give, *donner*
flower, *fleur f.*	poor, *pauvre*	wide, *large*
glove, *gant m.*	ribbon, *ruban m.*	young, *jeune*

Exercise No. 8.

1. The tall[b] men[a] —the tall[b] women[a] —the beautiful flowers —some blue[b] coats[a] — some blue[b] dresses[a] —the beautiful gardens—the nasal[b] sounds[a] —a larger street—the largest house—a wide[b] river[a] —the widest[b] rivers[a] —a more intelligent[b] gentleman[a]—some more intelligent[b] ladies[a] —a very rich[b] friend[a] —some very old hats—the bad debts— the poor[b] families[a] —some beautiful flowers—some richer[b] men[a].

He gave—we did not give—did I give?—she did not give—he sang—did we give?—thou gavest—he hid not give—you did not sing— they (*m.*) walked—they (*m.*) did not sing—we gave—didst thou give?— did you speak?—you did not give—did he give?—I gave—we walked —did you give?—they (*f.*) did not give—I spoke—you gave— did she speak?—they (*m.*) gave—thou didst not give—did they (*f.*) give?— I did not give.

2. Le peintre a envoyé[1] de très beaux tableaux à mon[2] ami. Ma[3] sœur aime les rubans bleus. Les nouveaux régiments ont des habits rouges. Mon[2] père a des chevaux moins beaux que les vôtres.[4] Les maisons de la nouvelle rue sont très belles. Les rues du nouveau Paris sont plus larges que les rues de Londres. Les fleurs de votre[5] jardin sont d'une parfaite beauté. Mes[6] frères donnaient (des) avis à leurs[7] amis. Les couteaux que[8] vous donniez à mes[6] sœurs étaient aussi bons que les miens.[9] Donniez-vous des[10] fleurs à mon[2] ami.

He will pay[11] his[12] debts at the end of the month. These[13] flowers will soon[b] be[a] perfect. These[13] paintings are less beautiful than those.[14] My[15] brother is as rich as I.[16] My[15] father was the tallest of the family. The sounds of my[15] instrument are more beautiful than those.[14] London is larger than Paris. These[13] gentlemen[17] are very rich. The songs which[18] he sang were very pretty. We did not give any blue[b] ribbons[a] to the youngest girl. She will pay this[19] sum[b] soon[a]. They *(m)* gave their[20] old coats to the poor. These[13] gloves are less pretty than those.[14] This[21] painter is very young.

---

1 *envoyé*, sent 2 *mon*, my 3 *ma*, my 4 *les vôtres*, yours 5 *votre*, your, 6 *mes*, my 7 *leurs*, their 8 *que*, which 9 *les miens*, mine 10 *des*, any 11 will pay, *paiera* 12 his, *ses* 13 these, *ces* 14 those, *ceux-là* 15 my, *mon* 16 I, *moi* 17 gentlemen, *messieurs* 18 which, *qu'* 19 this, *cette* 20 their, *leurs*, 21 this, *ce.*

Questions on Grammar.

1. How do adjectives form the plural?
2. How do adjectives ending in *eu* form the plural?
3. Give some adjectives ending in *al* which take *s* when used in the plural.
4. How many degrees of comparison are there in adjectives?
5. Give an example of an adjective used in the positive?
6. What does the comparative of an adjective indicate?
7. How are comparatives formed in French?
8. What does the superlative indicate?
9. How is the superlative absolute of an adjective formed in French?
10. How is the superlative relative formed in French?

Conversation.

Where does the painter live (*demeure*)?	Où demeure le peintre?
The painter lives in the new street.	Le peintre demeure dans la nouvelle rue.
Has the painter finished (*fini*) your (*votre*) portrait?	Le peintre a-t-il fini votre portrait?
Yes, it is (*c'est*) a very good painting.	Oui, c'est un très bon tableau.
In which (*quelle*) room is your portrait?	Dans quelle chambre est votre portrait?
It is (*il est*) in my father's room.	Il est dans la chambre de mon père.
When (*quand*) will you be in (*à*) London?	Quand serez-vous à Londres?
I shall be[b] there[a] (*y*) at the end of the month.	J'y serai à la fin du mois.
Will you be in Paris[b] soon[a]?	Serez-vous bientôt à Paris?
I shall be there in twelve (*douze*) days and your brother in a month.	J'y serai dans douze jours et votre frère dans un mois.
Are his (*ses*) ribbons blue or red?	Ses rubans sont-ils bleus ou rouges?
They are blue, white (*blancs*) and red.	Ils sont bleus, blancs et rouges.
He will pay (*paiera*) a large sum of money to my father.	Il paiera une grosse somme d'argent à mon père.
How much will he pay?	Combien paiera-t-il?
Two thousand (*deux mille*) francs.	Deux mille francs.
Is he richer than you?	Est-il plus riche que vous?
No, I am much (*beaucoup*) richer than he (*lui*).	Non, je suis beaucoup plus riche que lui.

Reading Exercise No. 8.

Un homme, très riche mais aussi avare que riche, désirant avoir son portrait, s'adressa à un artiste de talent et lui promit de le payer généreusement si le portrait était d'une ressemblance satisfaisante. Le peintre se mit à l'ouvrage et, au bout de quelques mois, il avait achevé un tableau qui ne laissait rien à désirer, ni pour le fini du travail, ni pour la ressemblance qui était parfaite. Mais l'original essaya d'obtenir une diminution sur le prix convenu, et voyant que l'artiste était résolu à ne pas céder, il lui déclara qu'il pouvait garder son tableau : car il se disait que, ne pouvant le vendre à personne, le peintre serait bien obligé de le lui donner meilleur marché. Que fit le peintre? Il fit encadrer le portrait, y mit une inscription: "je suis ici parce que je ne paie pas mes dettes," et le plaça au-dessus de la porte de sa maison. Or, l'original était connu de tout le monde et bientôt il était devenu la risée de la ville entière. Alors le Crœsus ne put résister au ridicule et se hâta de payer la somme qu'il avait refusée auparavant.

NINTH LESSON.   *Neuvième Leçon.*

Qualifying Adjectives *(concluded)*.
DEGREES OF COMPARISON OF ADJECTIVES *(concluded)*.

There are three adjectives in French which form their comparatives and superlatives irregularly, viz:

bon	good	*meilleur* better	*le meilleur*	the best
mauvais	bad	*pire* worse	*le pire*	the worst
petit	little, small	*moindre* less, smaller	*le moindre*	the smallest

The corresponding adverbs are also irregular in the formation of their comparatives and superlatives:

bien	well	*mieux* better	*le mieux*	the best
mal	badly	*pis* worse	*le pis*	the worst
peu	little	*moins* less	*le moins*	the least

REMARK 1.—The regular comparatives and superlatives of *mauvais*, *petit* and *mal* are also used.

Ex.: *ce pain-ci est plus mauvais que l'autre*, this bread is worse than the other
ce livre est le plus petit, this book is the smallest
il écrit plus mal que moi, he writes worse than I

2. It must be noticed that *meilleur* and *mieux* are both translated *better*; *pire* and *pis*, *petit* and *peu*, *moindre* and *moins* also translate the same English words *worse*, *little* and *less*. In order to know when he has to use either of these words, the student must refer to the definitions of the parts of speech. *Meilleur, pire, petit* and *moindre* are adjectives and consequently must be be used when *better, worse, little* and *less* qualify nouns.

Ex.: *ce pain est meilleur que le vôtre*, this bread is better than yours
ce livre-ci est pire que celui-là, this book is worse than that
cet endroit est plus petit que celui-là, this place is smaller than that
mon chapeau est petit, my hat is small

Mieux, pis, peu and *moins* are adverbs and will be used when *better, worse, little* and *less* determine verbs, adjectives or adverbs.

Ex.: *il lit mieux que moi*, he reads better than I
il chante plus mal que son frère, he sings worse than his brother
il parle peu, he speaks little
nous voyageons moins souvent que vous, we travel less often than you

PLACE OF ADJECTIVES.

The place of adjectives in French is generally after the nouns. However some adjectives, principally those which are of one or two syllables, like *bon, grand, beau, joli, petit, mauvais* are placed before the noun. As a rule, the longer word is placed last.

Future of the Verb *donner*, to give *(continued)*.

je donn-erai, *I shall give*	donnerai-je, *shall I give*
tu donn-eras, *thou wilt give*	donneras-tu, *wilt thou give*
il donn-era, *he will give*	donnera-t-il, *will he give*
nous donn-erons, *we shall give*	donnerons-nous, *shall we give*
vous donn-erez, *you will give*	donnerez-vous, *will you give*
ils donn-eront, *they will give*	donneront-ils, *will they give*

bed, *lit m.*
business, *affaire f.*
care, *souci m.*
clerk, *commis m.*
climate, *climat m.*
contented, *content*
country, *pays m.*
dish, *plat m.*

grape, *raisin m.*
gun, *fusil m.*
joy, *joie f.*
joyful, *joyeux*
kind, *espèce f.*
laziness, *paresse f.*
milk, *lait m.*
o'clock, *heure f.*

parcel, *paquet m.*
reason, *raison f.*
salary, *salaire m.*
thing, *chose f.*
to eat, *manger*
to find, *trouver*
vice, *vice m.*
workman, *ouvrier m.*

Exercise No. 9.

1. A better dish—the best milk—a worse climate—the worst weather—a smaller book—the least care—he speaks better—you sing the best—she dances badly—she sings worse—he sings the best—I walk little—we speak less—they (*m.*) walk the least—the best workmen—a better gun—the best dish—a smaller bed—I eat very little.

We shall give—will you give?—he will not give—I shall walk—shall we sing?—he will love—thou wilt give—shall I give?—we shall not give—will he speak?—will he give?—you will not give—I shall give—will you sing?—he will walk—I shall not give—will you walk?—you will give—will they (*f.*) give?—wilt thou give?—they (*m.*) will not give—she will not sing—he will give—they (*m.*) will give—shall we give?—thou wilt not give—we shall not speak.

2. Nous donnerons la meilleure plume à votre[1] fils. Il donnera la plus mauvaise pomme à son[2] frère. Il sera content de[3] la moindre chose. Il avait un[4] des meilleurs chevaux. Il est de la pire espèce. Il mange peu. Vous donnerez moins à votre[1] voisin. Il chante le mieux de tous[5] ses[6] amis. Cet[7] oiseau mange moins que le nôtre[8]. La paresse est le pire de tous[5] les vices. Cette[9] maison est plus petite que la vôtre[10]. Je donnerai le meilleur de mes[11] fusils à mon[12] cousin. Nous marcherons moins demain qu'aujourd'hui. Cet[7] enfant est très petit.

She will sing better to-morrow. He was better than his[13] brother. She spoke little of that[14] business. She will dance less in that[14] town. Will you speak a little with me[15]? She will not speak to your[16] cousin. I shall give less to my[17] new clerk. The apples are better in your[16] country. He will give his[18] best grapes to our[19] uncle. His[18] reasons are worse than ever[20]. His[13] bed is better than mine[21]. This[22] work-man had the least salary. We shall eat little: the least thing will be sufficient[23]. This[24] parcel is very small. He gives less than I[25]. Give me[26] some better wine.

---

1 *votre*, your 2 *son*, his 3 *de*, with 4 *un*, one 5 *tous*, all 6 *ses*, his 7 *cet*, this 8 *le nôtre*, ours 9 *cette*, this 10 *le, la vôtre*, yours 11 *mes*, my 12 *mon*, my 13 his. *son.* 14 that, *cette* 15 me, *moi* 16 your, *votre* 17 my, *mon* 18 his, *ses* 19 our, *notre* 20 ever, *jamais* 21 mine, *le mien* 22 this, *cet* 23 will be sufficient, *suffira* 24 this *ce* 25 I, *moi* 26 give me, *donnez-moi*.

Questions on Grammar.

1. What are the three French adjectives which form their comparatives and superlatives irregularly?
2. Give the comparatives of those three adjectives?
3. What are the three adverbs which are irregular in the formation of their comparatives and superlatives?
4. Give the superlative of those three adverbs?
5. What are the adjectives and adverbs of which the regular forms of comparatives and superlatives can also be used?
6. What are the English words which are both adjectives and adverbs and are translated by two different words in French?
7. When must *meilleur, pire, petit* and *moindre* be used?
8. When must *mieux, pis, peu* and *moins* be used?
9. What is generally the place of adjectives in French?
10. What are the adjectives which are placed before the nouns?

Conversation.

Where did you find this parcel?	Où avez-vous trouvé ce paquet?
found this parcel in the street.	J'ai trouvé ce paquet dans la rue.
Where was it?	Où était-il?
It was before (*devant*) the door of my (*mon*) father's house.	Il était devant la porte de la maison de mon père.
Was the money upon (*sur*) the bed?	L'argent était-il sur le lit?
No; it was upon the table.	Non; il était sur la table.
Is your (*votre*) father's clerk contented with (*de*) his (*son*) salary?	Le commis de votre père est-il content de son salaire?
Yes; he is very contented.	Oui; il est très content.
What (*qu'*) have you eaten at dinner (*dîner*)?	Qu'avez-vous mangé à dîner?
I have eaten some meat, some bread, apples and grapes.	J'ai mangé de la viande, du pain, des pommes et des raisins.
Why (*pourquoi*) is the workman so (*si*) joyful?	Pourquoi l'ouvrier est-il si joyeux?
Because he has earned (*gagné*) a good salary.	Parcequ'il a gagné un bon salaire.
At what (*quelle*) o'clock will you eat this evening?	A quelle heure mangerez-vous ce soir?
At six (*six*) o'clock, if (*si*) my father has (*est*) arrived (*arrivé*).	A six heures, si mon père est arrivé.
Will your brother be here (*ici*)?	Votre frère sera-t-il ici?
I hope (*espère*) so (*que oui*).	J'espère que oui.

Reading Exercise No. 9.

Un͡ouvrier avait deux fils : l'*un* d'eux͡était un͡enfant
. . . . . two . the one . them . .
bon et diligent qui se levait tous les mat*in*s à six͡heures ;
. . — who himself raised all . . at six .
l'autre, qui était paresseux, restait dans son lit jusqu'à
. other who . lazy remained . his . until
dix͡heures. Un mat*in* l'enfant laborieux trouva devant
ten . . . . . . — found before
la porte de la maiso*n* *un* paquet contenant dix͡écus ; et
. . . . . . containing ten crowns .
naturelleme*nt* il *en* fut très joyeux et apporta l'argent͡à
naturally . of it . . . brought . .
son père, qui partagea sa joie. Celui-ci alla directeme*nt*͡
his . who shared his . this one went/ directly
à la chambre de ses͡enfants et y trouva le paresseux qui
. . . . his . . there found . lazy who
était͡encore couché. Il l'éveilla, lui montra l'argent͡et
. still laid down . him awoke him showed . money .
lui dit : "Regarde ce que t*on* frère a trouvé dans la rue.
him said look that which thy . . found . . .
Mais pourquoi est-il si heureux ? c'est parce qu'il se lève
but why . . so happy this is because . himself raises
chaque mat*in* à six͡heures. Tu ne trouveras jamais rien
every . . six . . ,, wilt find never nothing
de semblable, puisque, à dix͡heures, tu es͡encore dans
of similar since . ten . . . still .
t*on* lit." Le jeune garçon qui n'était pas͡encore parfaite-
thy . . . . who ,, . . yet perfectly
ment réveillé, se frotta les yeux͡et répondit : "Vous
awaken to himself rubbed . . . answered .
avez tout à fait raiso*n*, m*on* père, et je ne vous contredirai
. altogether right my . . ,, you shall contradict
pas. Mais, ne croyez-vous pas que celui qui a perdu le
. but ,, believe . . . he who . lost .
paquet qui contenait son͡argent aurait bien mieux fait de
. which contained his . . much . done to
rester comme moi dans son lit. Il serait plus riche de
remain like me . his . . . . .
dix͡écus."
ten crowns

Tenth Lesson.   *Dixième Leçon.*
Determinative Adjectives.
Numeral Adjectives.

Numeral adjectives are of two kinds : the Cardinal Numeral adjectives and the Ordinal.

Cardinal Numeral Adjectives.

Cardinal Numeral adjectives merely indicate the quantity; as *vingt hommes*, twenty men; *trente-six livres*, thirty-six books.

They are called Cardinal because they are the principal, those from which others are derived.

1	*Un*, one	21	*Vingt et un*, twenty-one
2	*Deux*, two	22	*Vingt deux*, twenty-two
3	*Trois*, three	23	*Vingt trois*, twenty-three, &c.
4	*Quatre*, four	30	*Trente*, thirty
5	*Cinq*, five	31	*Trente et un, &c.*, thirty-one, &c.
6	*Six*, six	40	*Quarante*, forty
7	*Sept*, seven	50	*Cinquante*, fifty
8	*Huit*, eight	60	*Soixante*, sixty
9	*Neuf*, nine	70	*Soixante-dix*, seventy
10	*Dix*, ten	71	*Soixante et onze*, seventy-one
11	*Onze*, eleven	72	*Soixante-douze*, seventy-two &c.
12	*Douze*, twelve	80	*Quatre-vingt*, eighty
13	*Treize*, thirteen	81	*Quatre-vingt-un*, eighty-one, &c.
14	*Quatorze*, fourteen	90	*Quatre-vingt-dix*, ninety
15	*Quinze*, fifteen	91	*Quatre-vingt-onze*, ninety-one
16	*Seize*, sixteen	92	*Quatre-vingt-douze*, ninety-two &c.
17	*Dix-sept*, seventeen	100	*Cent*, one hundred
18	*Dix-huit*, eighteen	101	*Cent-un*, one hundred and one, &c
19	*Dix-neuf*, nineteen	1000	*Mille*, one thousand
20	*Vingt*, twenty	1,000,000	*Un million*, one million

Remarks—1. Cardinal numbers are invariable except *quatre-vingt*, eighty, and *cent*, hundred, multiplied by another number, when not followed by another number.—Ex.: *quatre-vingts hommes*, eighty men; *trois cents soldats*, three hundred soldiers.

Exceptions.—*Cent* et *vingt* are invariable at the end of dates.
  Ex.: *l'an mil huit cent*, the year 1800.

2. *Mille*, only takes an *s* in the plural when it means *miles*.
  Ex,: *il y a trois milles d'ici*, it is three miles from here

3. *Million* and *milliard* are considered as nouns, and always take an *s* in the plural.—Ex.: *deux millions d'hommes*, two millions of men; *cinq milliards de francs*, five milliards of francs.

4. *Mil* is used instead of *mille* in dates.
  Ex.: *l'an mil-huit cent-quatre-vingt-deux*, the year 1882.

Conjugation of *donner*, to give

Je donn-erais(*), *I should give, &c.* | Je ne donnerais pas, *I should not give*

(*) See for the other persons the Conditional of *avoir* and *être* as the endings for that tense are identical in all verbs.

beast, *bête f.*	fleet, *flotte f.*	ox, *bœuf m.*
dead, *mort*	for, *pour*	sailor, *matelot m.*
death, *mort f.*	franc, *franc m.*	sheep, *mouton m.*
English, *anglais*	how, *comment*	ship, *navire m.*
faithful, *fidèle*	grief, *douleur f.*	stable, *écurie f.*
farm, *ferme f.*	loss, *perte f.*	to ask, *demander*
farmer, *fermier m.*	mile, *mille m.*	tree, *arbre m.*
fatigue, *fatigue f.*	orchard, *verger m.*	year, *an m.*

Exercise No. 10.

1. Thirty-two horses—forty-five cows—fifty-six apples—sixty-nine pears—seventy-three years—eighty-five soldiers—ninety-four sheep—one hundred and two oxen—two hundred clerks—three hundred and five miles—four hundred and twenty three ships—five hundred and thirty-one francs—six hundred and seventy-five pounds—seven hundred and eighty sailors—eight hundred and ninety houses—nine hundred and forty-one trees—one thousand eight hundred and eighty-one.

We should give—I should not give—would you give?—I should sing—would he give?—I should give—we should not give—would they (*m.*) give?—thou wouldst not give—he would give—they (*f.*) would not give—should I give?—you would not give—you would give—he would speak—wouldst thou give?—she would walk—I would ask—thou wouldst give—they (*m.*) would give—thou wouldst not give—should we give?—we should like.

2. Nous donnerions dix mille-cinq cents francs pour cette[1] maison. Le matelot a voyagé[2] pendant[3] deux cent-trente et un jours. Notre[4] fermier a trois cent-cinquante-six moutons, cent-vingt bœufs, trente vaches et trois taureaux. Mon[5] ami a hérité de[6] deux cent mille francs à la mort de son père. La flotte anglaise était composée[7] de trente-deux navires. Il y a[8] cinquante arbres dans mon[5] petit verger. Sa douleur était grande à[9] l'occasion de la perte de son[10] fidèle ami.

He would give two thousand francs to his[11] nephew. My[12] farmer has two hundred and sixty beasts on[9] his[13] farm. We should ask: he would give fifty francs to our[14] brother. My[15] fatigue was greater than his[16]. I had made[17] thirty miles the same[18] day. How would you give this[19] letter to his[20] sister? I should like to[21] speak to your[22] professor. There are[24] three hundred and fifty houses in the street. The regiment is composed[25] of two thousand five hundred men. I gave two hundred francs for that[26] painting.

---

1 *cette*, this 2 *voyagé*, travelled 3 *pendant*, during 4 *notre*, our 5 *mon*, my 6 *hérité de*, inherited 7 *composée*, composed 8 *il y a*, there are 9 *à* on 10 *son*, his 11 his, *son* 12 my, *mon* 13 his, *ses* 14 our, *notre* 15 my, *ma* 16 his, *la sienne* 17 made, *fait* 18 same, *même* 19 this, *cette* 20 his, *sa* 21 to, *à* 22 your, *votre* 23 his, *ses* 24 there are, *il-y-a* 25 composed, *composé* 26 that, *ce*

Questions on Grammar.

1. How many kinds of numeral adjectives are there in French?
2. What do cardinal numeral adjectives indicate?
3. Why are cardinal numeral adjectives so called?
4. Give the first ten numbers in French?
5. Give the numbers from *eleven* to *twenty*?
6. Translate *thirty, forty, fifty, sixty, seventy, eighty, ninety one hundred, one thousand.*
7. Translate *twenty-one, seventy-one, eighty-one, ninety-one.*
8. Translate *twenty-two, seventy-three, eighty-four, ninety-five.*
9. Which are the two cardinal numbers which take *s* in the plural, and when does that alteration take place?
10. Do *vingt* and *cent* ever take *s* in dates?
11. When does *mille* take an *s* in the plural?
12. How are *million* and *milliard* spelt in the plural?
13. When is *mil* used instead of *mille*?

Conversation.

How many (*combien de*) beasts has your (*votre*) farmer on his farm.	Combien de bêtes votre fermier a-t-il à sa ferme?
He has more than (*de*) four hundred sheep, about (*environ*) twenty-three oxen and forty cows.	Il a plus de quatre cents moutons, environ vingt-trois bœufs et quarante vaches.
Is the bull dead?	Le taureau est-il mort?
Yes, it died (*est mort*) this (*ce*) morning at six o'clock.	Oui, il est mort ce matin, à six heures.
How much (*combien*) had your father paid (*payé*) for this (*cet*) animal?	Combien votre père avait-il payé pour cet animal?
He had paid five hundred and sixty-three francs.	Il avait payé cinq cent-soixante-trois francs.
Is it not (*n'est-ce pas*) a great loss for your father?	N'est-ce pas une grande perte pour votre père?
Yes; but it was getting old.	Si; mais il devenait vieux.
What (*quel*) was its (*son*) age?	Quel était son âge?
It was (*il avait*) nine years and eight months (old).	Il avait neuf ans et huit mois.
Where is your (*votre*) faithful friend?	Où est votre ami fidèle?
He is in my (*mon*) father's orchard under (*sous*) the large tree.	Il est dans le verger de mon père, sous le grand arbre.
Good bye.	Adieu.

Reading Exercise No. 10.

Un malheur n'arrive jamais seul. *Un* jeune homme
. misfortune „ happens never . . .
de pro*vin*ce demeurait⌒à Paris pour étudier à l'université
. — lived in — to study . . —
qu*an*d⌒il reçut⌒*un* jour la visite d'*un* serviteur de son
when . received . . . . . servant . his
père. "Comme*n*t se portent-ils à la maiso*n*?" demanda
. . themselves carry . . . .
l'étudi*an*t. "Quelle nouvelle m'apportez-vous?" "Aucune,
. student what . to me bring . none
répo*n*dit le serviteur, "si ce n'est celle de la mort du chat."
replied . servant if this . . that . . . .
—"Comme*n*t, le chat est mort; et de quoi est morte la
. . . . what . dead .
pauvre bête?"—"D'*in*digestion; pour avoir mangé trop
poor . — . . eaten too much
de vi*an*de."—"Et qui d*on*c lui avait donné cette vi*an* e?"
. . . who then to it . given this .
—"Personne, si ce n'est vos pauvres chevaux."—"Nos
nobody if this . . your . . . our
chevaux aussi s*on*t-ils d*on*c morts? Expliquez-vou ."—
. also are . then . explain yours if
"Certaineme*n*t; les pauvres⌒animaux s*on*t morts de fa igue
certainly . . . . . . —
pour avoir trop porté d'eau."—"Et à quoi cette eau était-
. . too much carried . . . to what this .
elle destinée?"—"A éteindre l'*in*cendie de votre maiso*n*."—
. destined to extinguish . fire . your .
"L'*in*cendie de notre maiso*n*!"—"Oui, vraiment; par suite
. fire . our . . indeed by consequence
de la néglige*n*ce de la serva*n*te, qui avait⌒oublié d'étei*n*dre
. . — . . . maidservant who . forgotten to put out
les torches."—"De quelles torches voulez-vous parler?"—
. — . what — wish .
"De celles qui avaient servi aux funérailles de votre mère."
. those which . served . funeral . your .
—"Que dites-vous? ma mère est morte! et vous ne me le
. what say . my . . dead . . „ —
disiez pas⌒immédiateme*n*t!"
said . immediately

Eleventh Lesson.   Onzième Leçon.

Numeral Adjectives *(concluded)*.
Ordinal Numeral Adjectives.

Ordinal numeral adjectives are so called because they indicate the order or the rank of persons or things. They are formed in French by adding *ième* to the cardinal numbers; as, *troisième*, third formed from *trois*, three; *dixième*, tenth from *dix*, ten.

Except: *premier*, first and *second*, second.

Unième can only be used after *vingt, trente, quarante, cinquante, soixante, quatre-vingt, cent* and *mille*. The *f* of *neuf*, nine, is changed into *v* in *neuvième*, ninth. The final *e* of cardinal numbers is suppressed in ordinal adjectives; as,—*quatrième*, fourth from *quatre*, four; *trentième*, thirtieth from *trente*, thirty; a *u* is added after the *q* of *cinq*, five: *cinquième*, fifth.

The following is a list of Ordinal Numeral Adjectives.

Premier, -ère (f.) first	*Seizième*, sixteenth
Deuxième or *second, -e* (,̂)	*Dix-septième &c.*, seventeenth
Troisième, third [second	*Vingtième*, twentieth
Quatrième, fourth	*Vingt-et-unième &c.*, twenty-first
Cinquième, fifth	*Trentième*, thirtieth
Sixième sixth	*Quarantième*, fortieth
Septième, seventh	*Cinquantième*, fiftieth
Huitième. eighth	*Centième*, hundredth
Neuvième, ninth	*Cent-unième*, hundred and first
Dixième, tenth	*Deux-cent trente troisième*, two hundred and thirty-third
Onzième, eleventh	
Douzième, twelfth	*Millième*, thousandth
Treizième, thirteenth	*Mille deux cent-quatrième*, one thousand two hundred and fourth
Quatorzième, fourteenth	
Quinzième, fifteenth	*Millionième*, millionth

Remarks 1.—The ordinal numbers which are used in English to indicate the day of the month, or the order of succession among kings of the same name in a country, are replaced in French by the cardinal numbers, except first which is translated *premier*.

Ex.: *Charles trois*, Charles the third; *Louis quatorze*, Louis the fourteenth; *Le trois Mars*, the third of March; *le trente et un Mai*, the thirty-first of May; *le premier Août*, the first of August; *Charles premier*, Charles the first.

2. Charles the fifth (Emperor of Germany) is translated *Charles Quint* and Sixtus the fifth (the pope) *Sixte Quint*.

Compound tenses of *donner*, to give.

They are formed with the auxiliary *avoir* and the past participle *donn-é*.

J'ai donné &c., *I have given*	Je n'ai pas donné, *I have not given*
J'avais donné &c., *I had given*	Je n'avais pas donné, *I had not given*
J'aurai donné &c., *I shall have given*	Je n'aurai pas donné, *I shall not have given*
&c. &c. &c.	

birthday, *jour de nais-* [*sance m.*]
by, *par*
carriage. *voiture f.*
chapter, *chapitre m.*
Charles, *Charles m.*
happy, *heureux*
Henry, *Henri m.*
illness, *maladie f.*
king, *roi m.*
line, *ligne f.* [*m.*]
misfortune, *malheur*

modest, *modeste*
pain, *douleur f.*
part, *partie f.*
peasant, *paysan m.*
profound, *profond*
sincere, *sincère*
volume, *volume m.*
when, *quand, lorsque*
world, *monde m.*
year, *année f.*
January, *Janvier m.*

February, *Février m.*
March, *Mars m.*
April, *Avril m.*
May, *Mai m.*
June, *Juin m.*
July, *Juillet m.*
August, *Août m.* [*m.*
September, *Septembre*
October, *Octobre m.* [*m.*
November, *Novembre*
December, *Décembre m.*

Exercise No. 11.

1. The second volume—the sixth house—the ninth chapter—the twelfth tree—the fifteenth letter—the nineteenth line—the twentieth year—the thirty-second carriage—the forty-fifth book—the fifty-first birthday—the sixteenth of May — the seventy-first regiment—the eightieth battalion—the ninety-third day—the hundredth anniversary—the thousandth part—the second of January—the third of March—the first of April—Charles the second—Henry the first.

He has given—we have spoken—they *(f.)* had walked—have you spoken?—they *(m.)* will not have sung—I shall have given—we should have spoken—had she walked?—they *(m.)* would have given—we shall have spoken—has he given?—he would not have given—shall we have spoken?—you had sung—would she have found—we had not found.—we had given—have you walked?—I had not given.

2. Ma¹ deuxième sœur était avec mon² frère à Paris. J'ai donné le premier volume à votre³ cousin. Il était dans sa⁴ quarante-septième année. J'avais trouvé votre³ oncle dans la vingt-septième avenue. Le seizième chapitre de ce⁵ livre est très bien écrit⁶. Vous trouverez cela⁷ à la vingt-huitième ligne. La cinquième maison de cette⁸ rue est très belle. Henri quatre a été un très grand roi de France. Je verrai⁹ votre³ mère le¹⁰ trois Avril.

We had walked the first day. I shall see¹¹ his¹² aunt (on) the second of January. I like the tenth chapter of the book; but I do not like the(*) eleventh. I was then¹³ in my¹⁴ fortieth year. I have served¹⁵ in the ninety-ninth regiment. It is¹⁶ her¹⁷ thirty-first birthday. Have you read of¹⁸ the death of Charles the first. I shall come¹⁹ (on) the third of March. Four is the fifth part of twenty. He came²⁰ yesterday²¹ for the third time²².

1 *ma,* my 2 *mon,* my 3 *votre,* your 4 *sa,* his 5 *ce,* this 6 *écrit,* written 7 *cela,* that 8 *cette,* this 9 *verrai,* shall see 10 *le,* on the 11 shall see, *verrai* 12 his, *sa* 13 then, *alors* 14 my, *ma* 15 served, *servi* 16 it is, *c'est* 17 her, *son* 18 read of, *lu* 19 I shall come, *je viendrai* 20 he came, *il est venu* 21 yesterday, *hier* 22 time, *fois (f.)*

(*) The *e* of *le* is not elided before *onze* and *onzième.*

Questions on Grammar.

1. Why are ordinal numeral adjectives so called?
2. How are ordinal numbers formed from cardinal numbers in French?
3. Translate *first* and *second*, *twenty-first* and *thirty-second*.
4. Translate *fourth*, *fifth* and *ninth*.
5. Translate *third, sixth, seventh, eighth, tenth, eleventh, twelfth, thirteenth, seventeenth, nineteenth*.
6. Translate *twentieth, thirtieth, sixtieth, seventieth, seventy-first, seventy-third, seventy-seventh, eightieth, eighty-second, ninetieth, ninety-second, ninety-fourth, hundredth, thousandth*.
7. How are ordinal numbers used in English for dates translated into French?
8. What are the numeral adjectives which must be used in French after names of kings to indicate their order of succession?
9. Translate *Charles the first; the first of March*.
10. Translate *Charles the fifth (Emperor of Germany)*.

Conversation.

Have you not seen (*vu*) your (*votre*) brother Charles in his (*sa*) carriage?	N'avez-vous pas vu votre frère Charles dans sa voiture?
No, I have not seen my (*mon*) brother Charles; but I have seen my brother Henry.	Non, je n'ai pas vu mon frère Charles, mais j'ai vu mon frère Henri.
How old are (*quel âge ont*) your (*vos*) two brothers?	Quel âge ont vos deux frères?
They are twins (*jumeaux*) and will be (*auront*) sixteen (*seize ans*) (on) the third of March.	Ils sont jumeaux et auront seize ans le trois Mars.
And you; how old are you (*quel âge avez-vous*)?	Et vous; quel âge avez-vous?
I shall be (*j'aurai*) sixty-four years (on) the twenty-eighth of April next.	J'aurai soixante-quatre ans, le vingt-huit Avril prochain.
The peasant's grief seems (*semble*) very profound. What is the matter with him (*qu'a-t-il*)?	La douleur du paysan semble très profonde. Qu'a-t-il?
He lost (*perdu*) his daughter (on) the second of January.	Il a perdu sa fille le deux Janvier.
Was he not very happy formerly (*auparavant*)?	N'était-il pas très heureux auparavant?
Yes, he was (*c'était*) the happiest man in the (*du*) world.	Si, c'était l'homme le plus heureux du monde.

Reading Exercise No. 11.

Un paysan se croyait certainement à l'abri des caprices de la fortune, lorsqu'un jour sa vache fut enlevée soudain par une maladie épidémique. Le pauvre homme se désolait de ce malheur, quand il fut affligé d'un malheur bien plus terrible encore: sa femme mourut. Il se disait qu'il ne se consolerait jamais d'une perte semblable. Il reçut alors la visite de tous les principaux habitants du village qui venaient lui offrir leurs condoléances: mais presque tous, après avoir épuisé leurs meilleurs arguments, finissaient en lui rappelant qu'on ne saurait rester seul dans ce monde, lorsqu'on est encore jeune et vigoureux. L'un avait plusieurs filles parmi lesquelles il pourrait choisir, l'autre avait une sœur qui serait heureuse de devenir la mère de ses enfants; celui-là, une parente qui dirigerait à merveille le ménage de notre veuf. Il les laissa parler; mais il faisait remarquer plus tard à l'un de ses amis qu'il valait mieux dans ce pays-là perdre sa femme qu'une vache: car chacun lui avait offert de remplacer la première tandis que personne n'avait parlé de la dernière."

TWELFTH LESSON. *Douzième Leçon.*

Demonstrative Adjectives.

Demonstrative adjectives are so called because they point to a person or thing.

Demonstrative adjectives, which always precede nouns, must not be confounded with demonstrative pronouns which like any other pronouns stand inside of nouns. In French different words are used when adjectives or pronouns, to translate *this, that, these, those.*

The Demonstrative adjectives are as follows:

Masc. Sing.	Fem. Sing.	Pl. of both Gend.
ce, cet, this or that	cette, this or that	ces, these or those

REMARK I.—*Ce* is used before masculine nouns beginning with consonants and *cet* before masculine nouns beginning with vowels or *h* mute; as,

ce chien, this or that dog; *ce héros*, this or that hero
cet animal, this or that animal; *cet homme*, this or that man

II.—When it is necessary to make in French the same distinction which is made in English by using *this* or *that*, the adverbs *ci* or *là* are placed after the nouns which are perceded by *ce, cet, cette* or *ces*; as,

ce cheval-ci, this horse; *ce cheval-là*, that horse
cet homme-ci, this man; *cet homme-là*, that man
cette femme-ci, this woman; *cette femme-là*, that woman
ces maisons-ci, these houses; *ces maisons-là*, those houses

Ci refers to the person or thing nearer to the speaker, *là* to the farther.

The hyphen must always be placed between the nouns and the adverbs *ci* and *là*.

Conjugation of the verb *finir*, to finish.

Verbs ending in *ir* belong to the second conjugation of regular verbs.

Present Indicative.

je fin-is, *I finish*	finis-je, *do I finish*
tu fin-is, *thou finishest*	finis-tu, *doest thou finish*
il fin-it, *he finishes*	finit-il, *does he finish*
nous fin-issons, *we finish*	finissons-nous, *do we finish*
vous fin-issez, *you finish*	finissez-vous, *do you finish*
ils fin-issent, *they finish*	finissent-ils, *do they finish*

anger, *colère f.*
axe, *hache f.*
bridge, *pont m.*
clock, *horloge f.*
custom, *habitude f.*
ear, *oreille f.*
hamlet, *'hameau m.* (*)
hatred, *'haine f.*
hedge, *'haie f.*

herb, *herbe f.*
history, *histoire f.*
hospital, *hôpital m.*
hut, *'hutte f.*
image, *image f.*
inkstand, *encrier m.*
island, *île f.*
lobster, *'homard m.*
meadow, *prairie f.*

messenger, *messager m*
name, *nom m.*
owl, *'hibou m.*
plate, *assiette f.*
shed, *'hangar m.*
tower, *tour f.*
to build, *bâtir*
to grow, *grandir*
winter, *hiver m.*

Exercise No. 12.

1. This *or* that cat—this *or* that hamlet—this *or* that tree—this *or* that hospital—this *or* that table—this *or* that axe—this *or* that island—this *or* that history—these *or* those friends—these *or* those owls—these *or* those inkstands—these *or* those winters—these *or* those streets—these *or* those hedges—these *or* those images—these *or* those customs—this bridge—that shed—this bird—that hotel—this tower—that hatred—this water—that herb—these horses—those lobsters—these officers—those coats—these girls—those huts—these plates—those clocks.

We finish—does he finish?—I do not finish—I build—he does not finish—thou finishest—they *(f.)* do not finish—do I finish?—does she finish?—they *(m.)* finish—she does not finish—we build—thou dost not finish—do we finish?—I finish—dost thou finish?—we do not finish—you build—does he grow?—you finish—we grow—do you finish?—you do not finish—they *(m.)* build—he grows—he finishes.

2. Nous finissons cette leçon. Ils finissent ce pont. Bâtissez-vous ces maisons? Elles grandissent beaucoup[1]. Ces chevaux-ci sont plus beaux que ces chevaux-là. Cette île-ci est plus grande que cette île-là. Nous avons acheté[2] cette table-ci et cette chaise-là pour notre[3] sœur. Cet habit est trop grand. Cette tour-là est plus vieille que cette tour-ci. Mettez[4] les homards sur ces assiettes-là.

This house is larger than that house. These boys and those girls will go[5] to the town. Give me[6] these plates. Those clocks are very good. He finishes this lesson. He is in this hospital with his[7] father. These hedges grow well. Put[8] the bread on the table. I like these customs. These flowers are beautiful. He builds a house in this street. This lobster is good; that lobster is bad. This hospital is large. This inkstand is small. These customs are very old.

---

1 *beaucoup*, much 2 *acheté*, bought 3 *notre*, our 4 *mettez*, put 5 will go. *iront* 6 give me, *donnez-moi* 7 his, *son* 8 put, *mettez*

(*) The apostrophe indicates that the *h* is aspirated. (See lesson 1).

French Grammar

Questions on Grammar.

1. Why are demonstrative adjectives so called?
2. What is the difference between a demonstrative adjective and a demonstrative pronoun?
3. Is there any difference in English between demonstrative adjectives and demonstrative pronouns?
4. What are the demonstrative adjectives in French?
5. When is *cet* used before a masculine noun instead of *ce*?
6. What are the adverbs which are placed after French nouns preceded by *ce, cet, cette, ces,* in order to make a distinction between *this* and *that* or *these* and *those*?
7. What does *ci* refer to?
8. What does *là* refer to?
9. What is the sign which must always be placed between *ci* or *là* and the noun?

Conversation.

What *(quels)* animals did you see *(avez-vous vus)* in the meadow?	Quels animaux avez-vous vus dans la prairie?
I saw (have seen) two horses and ten cows in this meadow.	J'ai vu deux chevaux et dix vaches dans cette prairie.
Was the peasant with his *(son)* horse in that meadow?	Le paysan était-il avec son cheval dans cette prairie?
Yes; he was[b] there[a] *(y)* with his horse and his *(ses)* cows.	Oui; il y était avec son cheval et ses vaches.
Have you sent *(envoyé)* a messenger to the master of this meadow?	Avez-vous envoyé un messager au maître de cette prairie?
Yes, I have sent the peasant's neighbour.	Oui, j'ai envoyé le voisin du paysan.
What did the master say *(dit)* to this man?	Qu'a dit le maître à cet homme?
The master was very angry and said *(dit)* that the peasant would be punished *(puni)* for putting his cows in this meadow.	Le maître était dans une grande colère et a dit que le paysan serait puni pour avoir mis ses vaches dans cette prairie.
What did the peasant answer *(répondit)* to this menace?	Que répondit le paysan à cette menace?
The peasant's answer was very insolent.	La réponse du paysan fut très insolente.
But what was his answer?	Mais quelle fut sa réponse?
He said that he would cut off *(couperait)* the master's ears.	Il dit qu'il couperait les oreilles du maître.

Reading Exercise No. 12.

Un gentilhomme, qui possédait une grande propriété, remarquait depuis longtemps que des animaux étrangers étaient conduits dans ses pâturages et y faisaient un dégât considérable. Il établit une surveillance et bientôt on vint lui dire le nom d'un paysan qu'on avait surpris au moment où il sortait avec son cheval de la prairie. Le gentilhomme chargea l'un de ses serviteurs d'aller chez lui et de le prévenir que la première fois que son cheval serait trouvé paissant dans le pré il lui ferait couper la queue. Mais le paysan répondit au messager: "Je me tiens pour averti: mais tu diras à ton maître que s'il fait couper la queue à mon cheval, je lui couperai les oreilles." Le messager rapporta la réponse au gentilhomme qui entra dans une violente colère; il envoya chercher le paysan et lui dit: "Comment oses-tu me faire transmettre une réponse aussi insolente et me menacer?" — "Moi, vous menacer, Monsieur;" répliqua le paysan. "Vous me permettrez de vous faire observer que vous vous êtes trompé. Il est vrai que j'ai dit que si Monsieur coupait la queue de mon cheval, je lui couperais les oreilles; mais j'ai voulu parler des oreilles de ce dernier

THIRTEENTH LESSON. *Treizième Leçon*

Possessive Adjectives.

Possessive adjectives are so called because they indicate possession. The following is a list of them.

Sin. Masc.	Fem.	Plu. of all Gen.	Sin. Masc.	Fem.	Plu. of all Gen.
mon	ma	mes, my	notre	notre	nos, our
ton	ta	tes, thy	votre	votre	vos, your
son	sa	ses, his, her, its	leur	leur	leurs, their

REMARK 1.—*Mon, ton, son* are used instead of *ma, ta, sa* before feminine nouns beginning with a vowel or an *h* mute.

Ex.: *mon âme*, my soul; *ton histoire*, thy history; *son image*, his image.

II.—In French possessive adjectives of the third person take the gender of the noun which they determine, and not as in English, the gender of the possessor.

Ex.: *son frère*, her brother; *sa sœur*, his sister.

III.—Possessive adjectives as well as any other determinative adjectives must be repeated before every noun.

Indefinite Adjectives.

Indefinite adjectives are so called because they determine nouns in an indefinite manner.

They are as follows:

certain, certain, some	*chaque*, every, each
nul, no	*même*, same
tout, every, all, whole	*quelque*, some, any
aucun, not any, not one	*plusieurs*, several
un tel, such a	*un...quelconque*, any...whatever
quel, which, what	*différents*, different
maint, many a	*divers*, diverse, various

REMARK I.—*Nul, aucun* and *chaque* are never used in the plural: therefore, the noun that follows them must be also in the singular. Ex.: *Je n'ai aucun ami*, I have no friends.

If it were necessary to translate the noun in the plural, *no* would be translated *pas de*. Ex.: *Je n'ai pas de maisons*, I have no houses.

II.—*Plusieurs, différents*, and *divers* are never used in the singular; *plusieurs* does not change in the feminine.

III.—*Un quelconque* any ... whatever, becomes in the plural *des ... quelconques*.

IV.—The plural of *tout* is *tous* for the masculine, and *toutes* for the feminine. *Tout* means *every* when no article or determinative adjective is placed before the noun. It means *the whole* when the noun, being preceded by an article or determinative adjective, is in the singular. Ex.: *Tout homme*, every man; *toute la ville*, the whole town; *tous mes amis*, all my friends.

after, *après*
arm, *bras m.*
army, *armée f.*
battle, *bataille f.*
cannon-ball, *boulet m.*
carpenter, *charpentier*
city, *cité f.* [*m.*
difficulty, *difficulté f.*

fault, *faute f.*
floor, *étage m.*
fork, *fourchette f.*
head, *tête f.*
interesting, *intéres-*
leg, *jambe f.* [*sant*
member, *membre m.*
mouth, *bouche f.*

nation, *nation f.*
needle, *aiguille f.*
rule, *règle f.*
soul, *âme f.*
subject, *sujet m.*
queen, *reine f,*
wood, *bois m.*
wound, *blessure f.*

Exercise No. 13.

1. My book—my sister—my soul—my arms—thy brother—thy aunt—thy friend *(f.)*—thy feet—his pencil—her dog—its head—his pen—her house—its mouth—her needle—his eyes—her hands—its legs—our father—our army—our members—our boots—your coat—your dress—your bed—your rooms—their uncle—their aunt—their children—their faults—certain men—certain rules—certain friends — certain women—no boy—no girl—no towns—no villages—every tree — every city—the whole nation—all the words—all my sisters—such book — such letter—such knives—such forks—which dish—which plate—which kings—which queens—many a man—many a daughter—many soldiers—many flowers—each volume—each page—the same floor—the same house—the same gloves—the same streets—some friend—some cousin *(f.)*—some men—some ladies—several hamlets—several cities—any book whatever—any plant whatever—any hats whatever—any persons whatever—different subjects — different reasons — diverse climates—diverse rivers.

(*)We finished—did I finish?—you did not finish—we built—did we finish?—he finished—I did not finish—did he build?—we did not finish—I built—I finished—did they finish?—they *(m.)* built—did you finish?—thou didst not finish—you finished—we did not build—did he build?—didst thou finish?—she did not finish—thou finishedst—they *(m.)* finished—you built—they *(f.)* did not finish—did he finish?

2. Nous aimons votre famille. Leur histoire est intéressante. Il a maint ami dans notre ville. Il finissait sa leçon. J'ai été dans différents villages. Il habite[1] dans la même rue que[2] moi[3]. Ses yeux sont bleus. Sa bouche est petite. Ses mains sont blanches. Nous n'avons pas de chambres dans notre hôtel. Nos gants sont plus beaux que ceux[4] de notre cousin.

The houses of our village are large. The whole book is interesting. What lesson have you learnt[5]? All the dishes were very good. Show me your hat. I have some friends in this town. I find certain rules very difficult.

(*) Exercise on the imperfect of *finir*, to end (see Supplement, page 11).
1 *habite*, lives 2 *que*, as 3 *moi*, I 4 *ceux*, those 5 learnt, *apprise*

Questions on Grammar.

1. Why are possessive adjectives so called?
2. Give the masculine singular of possessive adjectives?
3. Give the feminine singular of possessive adjectives?
4. Give the plural of possessive adjectives?
5. How are *my, thy, his, her, its* translated before a feminine noun beginning with a vowel or *h* mute?
6. Do possessive adjectives of the third person agree in gender with the possessed object or with the possessor?
7. What are the words which must be repeated before every noun?
8. Why are indefinite adjectives so called?
9. Which are the indefinite adjectives that are never used in the plural?
10. What indefinite adjective is never used in the singular?
11. What is the plural masculine of *tout*?
12. When does *tout* mean *whole*; when *every*?

Conversation.

Who *(qui)* are the soldiers who *(qui)* are on the second floor?	Qui sont les soldats qui sont au second étage?
They are *(ce sont)* my cousins.	Ce sont mes cousins.
What is the colour of their coats?	Quelle est la couleur de leurs habits?
They are blue.	Ils sont bleus.
Do they belong *(appartiennent-ils)* to the English[b] army[a]?	Appartiennent-ils à l'armée anglaise?
No; they are French *(Français)*.	Non; ils sont Français.
Who *(qui)* has made *(fait)* this table?	Qui a fait cette table?
The carpenter.	Le charpentier.
Is the wood good?	Le bois est-il bon?
Yes; it is very good.	Oui; il est très bon.
Do you find any difficulty whatever in this grammar *(grammaire)*?	Trouvez-vous une difficulté quelconque dans cette grammaire?
No, I find this grammar very easy *(facile)*; the rules are explained *(expliquées)* with clearness *(clarté)* and simplicity.	Non; je trouve cette grammaire très facile; les règles sont expliquées avec clarté et simplicité.
How many *(Combien de)* mistakes had you in your lesson?	Combien de fautes aviez-vous dans votre devoir?
Twelve.	Douze.
Have you learnt *(appris)* any foreign language?	Avez-vous appris quelque langue étrangère?
Yes; I have learned all European languages.	Oui; j'ai appris toutes les langues européennes.

Reading Exercise No. 13.

Un capitaine avait perdu une jambe dans⌢une bataille
      captain   lost

C'était⌢un très bon⌢officier, et il était très⌢aimé des soldats
He

et très⌢estimé de *son* général. Cepen*dant* ce général le
    esteemed   —   However   —   him

considérant comme *incapable* de servir à l'avenir, lui écrivit
considering   as   —   . to serve .. future him wrote

pour le prévenir qu'il allait lui faire obtenir une *pension*.
   . him to inform   .. was going him to make obtain .   —

Mais le capitaine *en* fut très⌢affligé : et *un* mois⌢après,
  .. captain of it was . afflicted .

lorsque sa blessure fut guérie, il se fit faire une jambe de
.   .   .   .   cured . to himself made to make .

bois et alla chez le général pour lui dem*an*der de modifier
.. went to . — . him to ask .

sa décis*ion* : "Je peux⌢aussi bi*en* marcher," lui dit-il, "avec
. — . can as well . to him said he

cette jambe artificielle que je le faisais⌢avec ma jambe
. . artificial as . it did . .

naturelle. D'*ailleurs*, si je vais⌢au *com*bat, c'est pour me
natural Moreover if . go to the — it . .

battre et *non* pour me sauver." Le général consentit⌢après
fight . not . myself to save . — consented .

beauc*ou*p d'hésita*tion* et le capitaine rejoignit *son* régiment.
. — .. captain rejoined . —

Peu de temps⌢après, ce régim*en*t fut⌢engagé dans⌢une
Little . . . — engaged . .

bata*ille* et notre officier se conduisait⌢avec *un* courage
. . . himself conducted . . —

héroïque, lorsqu'*un* boulet lui coupa sa jambe de bois ; il
heroical . . ball to him cut . . . .

fut renversé et les soldats qui se trouvaient près de lui,
was thrown down . . . who themselves . near . him

appelèrent⌢*un* chirurgien. "Taisez-vous *donc*," leur dit⌢
called . surgeon Be silent then to them said

alors le capitaine, "ce n'est pas⌢*un* chirurgien qu'il me
then . captain it „ . . surgeon that . to me

faudrait ; *en*voyez-moi *un* charpentier."
would be necessary send me

FOURTEENTH LESSON.   *Quatorzième Leçon.*

The Pronoun.

There are in French six classes of Pronouns, viz: *Personal, Demonstrative, Possessive, Relative, Interrogative* and *Indefinite*.

Personal Pronouns.

They are so called because they are used to designate persons. There are three persons: the 1st person who speaks, the 2nd to whom one speaks, and the 3rd of whom one speaks.

Personal pronouns are *conjunctive*, that is to say used in connection with the verb, or *disjunctive* used separately from the verb.

Conjunctive pronouns are always placed before the verb; *disjunctive*, which may be used without a verb, are, when used with a verb, placed after it.

Personal pronouns are as follows:

Conjunctive Pronouns.

		1st Person.	2nd Person.	3rd Person. Mas.	3rd Person. Fem
Sing.	Nom.	*je*, I	*tu*, thou	*il*, he	*elle*, she
	Acc.	*me*, me	*te*, thee	*le*, him	*la*, her
	Dat.	*me*, to me	*te*, to thee	*lui*, to him	*lui*, to her
Plur.	Nom.	*nous*, we	*vous*, you	*ils*, they	*elles*, they
	Acc.	*nous*, us	*vous*, you	*les*, them	*les*, them
	Dat.	*nous*, of us	*vous*, to you	*leur*, to them	*leur*, to them

Disjunctive Pronouns.

	1st Person.	2nd Person.	Mas. 3rd Person.	Fem.
Sing.	*moi*, I, me	*toi*, thou, thee	*lui*, he, him	*elle*, she, her
Plur.	*nous*, we, us	*vous*, you	*eux*, they, them	*elles*, they, them

There are besides four more personal pronouns of the third person, viz: *se, soi, en, y.*

Se, himself, herself, themselves, one's self, is conjunctive and always precedes the verb.

    Ex.: *il se flatte*, he flatters himself; *ils se trompent*, they deceive themselves (they make a mistake).

Soi, one's self, is disjunctive and used after the verb.

    Ex.: *ne penser qu'à soi*, to think only of one's self.

En generally translates *of him, of her, of it, of them* and is principally used in speaking of things.

    Ex.: *nous en parlons*, we speak of it.

Y generally translates *to it, to them* and can only be used in speaking of things.

    Ex.: *il y réfère souvent*, he often refers to it.

RULE.—Personal pronouns, when objects of verbs, always precede them in French.

    Ex.: *il me connaît*, he knows me; *nous les verrons*, we shall see them.

EXCEPTION.—Personal pronouns follow the verb in the Imperative and disjunctive pronouns are used, except for pronouns of the 3rd person.—*Donnez-moi*, give me; *dépêche-toi*, hasten; *parlez-lui*, speak to her; *dites-leur*, say to them.

afternoon, *après-midi f.*	mind, *esprit m.*	terrace, *terrasse f.*
always, *toujours*	new, *nouveau*	to deceive, *décevoir*
baker, *boulanger m.*	often, *souvent*	to-morrow, *demain*
butcher, *boucher m.*	park, *parc m.*	to leap, *sauter*
cheap, *bon marché*	pleasure, *plaisir m.*	to meet, *rencontrer*
difficult, *difficile*	ready, *prêt*	to supply, *fournir*
grocer, *épicier m.*	shop, *magasin m.*	upon, *sur* [*croisée f.*
joiner, *menuisier m.*	strength, *force f.*	window, *fenêtre f.*,

Exercise No. 14.

1. I like him.—Thou knowest[1] them.—He liked me.—We shall speak to you.—You would speak to us.—They (*m.*) will give the book to them.—He knows[2] me.—She spoke to me.—They (*f.*) knew[3] us.—They spoke to us.—I like thee.—I speak to thee.—He knew[4] you—He will speak to you.—I met him.—We spoke to him.—We meet them.—You speak to them.—I like her.—I shall write[5] to her.—He was with me.—He will be with us.—He spoke of thee.—Shall I dance with you?—It[6] is he.—We spoke with them (*m.*).—It[6] was she.—I came[7] with them (*f.*).

(†)We receive—do I receive?—he does not receive—we deceive—I do not receive—I receive—she does not receive—you do not deceive—does he receive?—dost thou receive?—he receives—we do not receive—they (*f.*) do not deceive—you do not receive—he deceives—you receive—do you receive?—I deceive—they (*m.*) deceive—do we receive?—thou receivest—they (*m.*) do not receive—thou dost not receive—do they (*f.*) receive?—they (*m.*) receive—you deceive.

2. Ils nous reçoivent toujours avec un nouveau plaisir. Nous sommes prêts à les recevoir. Je l'ai vu[8] à la fenêtre. C'[9]est lui qui[10] me reçoit. Je le rencontrerai dans le parc cette après-midi. Nous les avons achetés[11] dans le magasin de votre frère. Je les ai vus dans le jardin. Nous les avons donnés[12] à votre sœur. Je lui parlerai demain. Ils reçoivent leurs amis avec affabilité. Les recevez-vous souvent? Ils déçoivent notre père. Nous le finirons demain matin.

I have given them to the carpenter. The butcher sells[13] them cheap. Our baker supplies them. I have given it (*m.*) to the grocer. The joiner has made[14] these windows for them (*m.*). We meet them very often. His friend receives him always in his beautiful garden. We like you. They will give that new book to us. We give these apples to you. I like them.

---

1 knowest, *connais* 2 knows, *connaît* 3 knew, *connaissaient* 4 knew, *connaissait*
5 shall write, *écrirai* 6 it, *c'* 7 came, *vins*
8 *vu*, seen 9 *c'*, it 10 *qui*, who 11 *achetés*, bought 12 *donnés*, given
13 sells, *vend* 14 made, *fait*

(†) See the Present Indicative of *recevoir* 3rd conjugation (Supplement, page 12).

Questions on Grammar.

1. How many classes of pronouns are there in French?
2. Why are personal pronouns so called?
3. What are the three persons?
4. How many kinds of personal pronouns are there; what are they?
5. What is the place of conjunctive and disjunctive personal pronouns?
6. Give the personal pronouns of the 1st person?
7. Give those of the 2nd person?
8. Give those of the 3rd person?
9. What is the meaning of the pronouns *se* and *soi* and what are their respective places?
10. What is the meaning of *en* and *y*?
11. What is the place of personal pronouns when objects of the verb?
12. When are they placed after the verb?

Conversation.

When will the baker come (*viendra*)?	Quand viendra le boulanger?
The baker will come this afternoon.	Le boulanger viendra cette après-midi.
Is the bread which he sells good?	Le pain qu'il vend est-il bon?
Yes, it is good and cheap.	Oui, il est bon et bon marché.
Is the new grocer's shop open (*ouvert*)?	Le nouveau magasin d'épicier est-il ouvert?
No the carpenters and joiners have not yet (*pas encore*) finished their work.	Non, les charpentiers et les menuisiers n'ont pas encore fini leur travail.
When do you think that everything will be ready?	Quand pensez-vous que tout soit prêt?
It will be difficult to get everything ready (to prepare everything) before to-morrow.	Il sera difficile de tout préparer avant demain.
Have you been in the park this afternoon?	Avez-vous été dans le parc cette après-midi?
No, the wind blew (*soufflait*) very strongly.	Non, le vent soufflait très fort.
Have you heard (*entendu dire*) anything about the (*au sujet de la*) storm?	Avez-vous entendu dire quelque chose au sujet de la tempête?
Yes; they say (*on dit*) that many panes of glass have been broken (*cassés*).	Oui; on dit que beaucoup de carreaux ont été cassés.

Reading Exercise No. 14.

On raconte l'anecdote suivante au sujet de Thomas
More, Lord Chancelier d'Angleterre. Au commencement de sa carrière, il habitait une maison sur la terrasse de laquelle il se promenait souvent : un jour qu'il se livrait à cette récréation, un fou que l'on gardait dans la maison voisine échappa à la surveillance de ses gardiens et sauta de la fenêtre sur la terrasse. Apercevant le chancelier il courut vers lui et le prenant par le bras : "Vous sauterez dans la rue," lui dit-il d'une voix furieuse, ' ou je vous y précipiterai." Le chancelier le regarda et vit que c'était un homme d'une force bien supérieure à la sienne et qu'il y aurait folie à chercher à se défendre. Mais il ne perdit pas sa présence d'esprit. "Je suis prêt," dit-il "à faire ce que vous me demandez, mais permettez-moi de vous faire observer que cela ne présente aucune difficulté. Il serait beaucoup plus difficile de sauter de la rue sur cette terrasse, et c'est ce que je vous propose de faire." Le fou réfléchit un instant d'un air soupçonneux, puis éclata de rire et consentit à la proposition. Le chancelier s'empressa d'en profiter et échappa de cette manière à ce pressant danger.

FIFTEENTH LESSON. *Quinzième Leçon.*

Personal Pronouns *(concluded)*.

REMARKS. 1.—Personal pronouns when preceded by prepositions follow the verb. Disjunctive pronouns are used then.
Je parle de vous. I speak of *you*. *Il vint avec* moi. He came with *me*.

2. When the verb has two personal pronouns of different persons as complements, one in the accusative case (direct object) and the other in the dative (indirect object), they are both placed before the verb, in the order of priority of persons, that is to say, the pronouns of the 1st and 2nd persons before those of the 3rd.
Il me le *dit.* He says *it to me*. *Je* te le *donne.* I give *it to thee*.

3. If the two pronouns were of the 3rd person, the direct object would be placed before the indirect object.
Je le lui *envoie.* I send *it to him. Nous* les leur *donnons.* We give *them to them.*

4. If the verb be in the imperative the direct object always precedes the indirect object.
Donnez-le moi. Give *it to me*. *Prêtez*-le leur. Lend *it to them*.

5. When the verb being in the imperative is accompanied by a negation the pronouns precede the verb and are placed respectively, as explained before (R. 2 and 3).
  Ne me le *donnez pas.* Do not give *it to me*.
  Ne le leur *prêtez pas.* Do not lend *it to them*.

6. *Se*, which generally translates *himself, herself, itself, themselves, one's self*, also translates *each other, one another*, when placed in English after reciprocal verbs(*) in the 3rd person plural.
  Ils s'aiment tendrement. They love *each other* tenderly.
  Ils s'écriront. They will write *to each other*.

7. *En* which generally translates *of him, of her, of it, of them*, also translates the same personal pronouns, preceded by other prepositions when these prepositions ought to be translated in French by the preposition *de*.
  J'en suis content. I am satisfied *with it*.
  Son succès en *dépend.* His success depends *upon it*.

8. *En* also translates *some* or *any* when placed after a verb.
  J'en ai. I have *some*. *Je n'en ai pas.* I have *not any*.

9. *En* is sometimes an adverb of place and translates *from thence*.
  J'en arrive. I arrive *from thence*.

10. *En* is a preposition when preceding a noun or a present participle.
  En *France.* In France. En *lisant.* By reading.

11. *Y* which generally translates *to it, to them*, also translates the same pronouns preceded by other prepositions, when these prepositions ought to be translated by the preposition *à*.
  J'y pense. I think *of it*. *Il y demeure.* He lives *in it*.

12. *Y* is often an adverb of place and translates *there*.
  Il y est. He is *there*.

13. *En* and *y* occur sometimes together, *y*, adverb always preceding *en*, pronoun, which is always placed immediately before the verb.
  Il y en a. He has *some there*.

(*) Verbs which imply an idea of reciprocity as, *se saluer*, to salute one another, *se haïr*, to hate each other, &c.

among, *parmi*
to advise, *conseiller*
bank, *bord m.*
betrothed, *fiancée f.*
to burn, *brûler*
to call, *appeler*
to commence, *commencer*
despair, *désespoir m.*
dinner, *dîner m.*

eve, *veille f.*
to fall, *tomber*
fish, *poisson m.*
finger, *doigt m.*
flesh, *chair f.*
girl, *fille f.*
guest, *convive m.*
incredible, *incroyable*
to lend, *prêter*

lip, *lèvre f.*
place, *endroit m.*
relation, *parent m.*
research, *recherche f.*
ring, *bague f.*
to send, *envoyer.*
sign, *signe m.*
strange, *étrange*
token, *gage m.*

Exercise No. 15.

1. We speak of you.—I will come[1] with them *(m.)*.—You will be there without me.—He gives it to me.—He lends it to us.—I shall give it to thee.—We shall lend them to you.—I give it to him.—We shall give it to her.—I shall lend it to them *(m.)*.—I should lend them to them *(f.)*.—Give them to us.—Lend them to him.—Do not give them to us.—Do not send them to him.—He burns himself.—She will burn herself.—They *(m.)* would burn themselves.—They *(f.)* burned themselves.—They *(m.)* write[2] to each other.—They *(f.)* hated[3] one another.—He speaks of him.—We shall speak of her.—He would speak of it.—We spoke of them.—He struck[4] his dog with it.—You will have some.—He had not any.—He has arrived[5] from thence.—They are in town.—You will learn[6] it by speaking.—He alluded[7] to it.—My hat hangs[8] from it.—We were there.—We have some there.

(*)**2.** Je le lui dirai[9] demain. Nous vous le donnerions avec plaisir. Donnez-le lui avec son nouveau livre. Ne le leur prêtez pas si vous ne voulez[10] pas le perdre[11]. Ils se prêtent de l'argent. J'en reçois souvent des lettres. J'en ferai[12] un paquet pour votre frère. Où est votre ami? Il est en France avec sa mère. Il apprend[13] beaucoup en lisant[14] ces livres. Il y va[15] aujourd'hui avec ses cousins. Y en avez-vous?

We shall send[16] him some. Give it to him and he will give it to me to-morrow afternoon. We shall lend them to you. I have some flowers; have you any? Where does he go[17]? Do you receive any letters from them? Have you any friends there? No[18], I have not any there. Do not say[19] it to them. I have not any relations in France, but I have some here. Do they write[20] often to each other? They write to one another every month. Will you give it to them?

1 will come, *viendrai* 2 write, *écrivent* 3 hated, *haïssaient* 4 struck, *frappa*
5 has arrived, *est arrivé* 6 will learn, *apprendrez* 7 alluded, *faisait allusion*
8 hangs, *est pendu* 9 dirai, shall say 10 *voulez*, wish 11 *perdre*, to lose
12 *ferai*, shall make 13 *apprend*, learns 14 *lisant*, reading 15 *va*, goes
16 shall send, *enverrons* 17 does he go, *va-t-il* 18 no, *non* 19 say, *dites*
20 do they write, *écrivent-ils*

(*) As the exercises of this lesson necessitate the use of several verbs, we have thought preferable not to give here any special exercise on a new tense of the verb *recevoir*.

Questions on Grammar.

1. What is the place of personal pronouns when preceded by prepositions?
2. What are the respective places of the two personal pronouns, one being direct object and the other indirect object of the verb, when they are of different persons?
3. What are their places when they are both of the 3rd person?
4. What are their places when the verb is in the Imperative?
5. How are they placed when the verb being in the Imperative is accompanied by a negation?
6. What is the meaning of *se* before reciprocal verbs?
7. Does *en* always translate personal pronouns of the third person preceded by the preposition *of*?
8. What are the other meanings of *en*?
9. Does *y* aways translate personal pronouns of the 3rd person preceded by the preposition *to*?
10. What is the other meaning of *y*?
11. What are the respective places of *y* and *en* when occurring together before the verb?

Conversation.

You have a fine dog; who gave it to you?	Vous avez un beau chien; qui vous l'a donné?
My cousin Charles gave it to me; but I shall return it to him.	Mon cousin Charles me l'a donné; mais je le lui rendrai.
Have you also some birds?	Avez-vous aussi des oiseaux?
Yes, I have some.	Oui, j'en ai.
How many have you (of them)?	Combien en avez-vous?
I have six (of them).	J'en ai six.
Have you been in the garden? they are there.	Avez-vous été dans le jardin? ils y sont.
No, I have not been there.	Non, je n'y ai pas été.
You have two canaries: will you *(voulez-vous)* give me one (of them)?	Vous avez deux canaris: voulez-vous m'en donner un?
With pleasure; but you will not give it to anybody.	Avec plaisir; mais vous ne le donnerez à personne.
No; if my best friend should ask *(demandait)* me (for) it, I would not give it to him.	Non; si mon meilleur ami me le demandait, je ne le lui donnerais pas.
You told *(avez dit)* me that you had some friends in Paris: have you still any of them there?	Vous m'avez dit que vous aviez des amis à Paris: y en avez-vous encore.
Yes, I have still two of them there.	Oui, j'y en ai encore deux.

Reading Exercise No. 15.

C'était à la fin du dîner, au moment où la conver-
              when
sation s'anime et où les anecdotes les plus étranges, et les
       enlivens   when
plus incroyables éclosent sur les lèvres et souvent dans
                      bloom
l'imagination des convives. Mon oncle, fit signe qu'il
                                              made
voulait parler. "Il y a quelques années," commença-t-il,
 wished   ago
un de mes amis était à la veille de se marier; parmi les
                           eve   to marry
présents qu'il avait faits à sa fiancée se trouvait une
          which   made
bague d'un certain prix, et cette jeune personne la portait
                  value   wore
au doigt en gage de leur engagement: lorsque, se promenant
                                when   walking
un jour sur les bords de la rivière, elle se pencha pour
                                              bent
cueillir un nénuphar et la bague, qui était un peu trop
to pick   water-lily   which
grande, glissa de son doigt et tomba dans l'eau. La jeune
        slipped
fille était au désespoir: on fit, mais en vain, des recherches
                            they made
à l'endroit où le bijou avait disparu. Ses parents et ses
             jewel   disappeared
amis lui conseillaient de rompre son engagement, effrayés
                        to break   frightened
de ce qu'ils appelaient un mauvais présage. Elle persista
      which   persisted
néanmoins. Le mariage eut lieu. Mais au repas de noces,
nevertheless   marriage took place   repast   wedding
un énorme poisson ayant été servi, quelle fut la satisfaction
   enormous   served   what was
générale lorsqu'en le découpant, on y trouva ...." "La
                     carving   they in it found
bague," s'écrièrent tous les auditeurs à l'unisson!" "La
         exclaimed   unison
chair la plus délicate et de très petites arêtes."
                                            bones

Sixteenth Lesson. *Seizième Leçon.*

Demonstrative Pronouns.

Demonstrative pronouns are used to point to persons or things which have just been named before or will be named immediately after the verb.

Demonstrative pronouns are as follows :

Ce, ceci, celui-ci, celui	this
Ce, cela, celui-là, celui	that
Ceux-ci, ceux	these
Ceux-là, ceux	those

Remarks. 1.—*Ce*, pronoun is the same word as *ce*, demonstrative adjective (See Lesson 12). But, as a pronoun, *ce* is invariable, instead of assuming different forms in the feminine and plural. It translates indifferently *this, that, these,* or *those.*

C'est ma sœur, this is my sister.
Ce sont mes frères, these are my brothers.

Ce can only be used before the verb *être*, or the relative pronouns *qui, que, dont.*

Ce sera la première fois, this will be the first time.
Dites-moi ce que vous pensez, tell me (that which) *what* you think.

Ce, translates the personal pronouns, *he, she, it, they* before the auxiliary *to be,* when this verb is followed by a noun, (*)pronoun verb in the infinitive, or adverb.

C'est bien, it is right. *Ce sont mes frères, they* are my brothers
C'est mon ami, he is my friend. *C'est moi, it* is I.

Ce is also used to translate *it* and *they* when the verb *être* is followed by an adjective, when this adjective refers to an idea mentioned precedingly, but not to a noun.

Apprenez à nager, c'est très utile, learn how to swim, *it* is very useful.

II.—*Ceci,* this, and *cela* that, are formed from the same demonstrative pronoun *ce,* to which the adverbs *ci*, here, and *là,* there, have been added, in the same way as they are to nouns, preceded by demonstrative adjectives (See page 64).

Ceci me plaît plus que cela, *this* pleases me more than *that.*
Je vous donnerai ceci ; *mais vous me donnerez* cela, I will give you *this*, but you will give me *that.*

Ceci and *cela* can only be used in speaking of things or referring to whole sentences. *This* and *that* used in a general sense as complements of verbs are always translated *ceci* and *cela.*

Je ferai plutôt ceci *que* cela, I will rather do *this* than *that.*

(*) However personal pronouns are used when the noun which follows the verb *être* is preceded by the indefinite article, which is not translated ; as,
He is a doctor. *Il est médecin.*

to announce, *annoncer*	happiness, *bonheur m.*	postman, *facteur m.*
better, *meilleur*	industrious, *laborieux*	sight, *vue f.*
convenient, *commode*	more, *plus*	still, *encore*
to cost, *coûter*	never, *jamais*	than, *que*
dear, *cher*	night, *nuit f.*	to think, *penser*
easy, *facile*	to occupy, *occuper*	time, *fois f.*
French, *français* [*f.*]	only, *seulement*	tongue, *langue f.*
governess, *gouvernante*	to perceive, *apercevoir*	to work, *travailler*

Exercise No. 16.

1. This is my brother.—This is my sister.—These are my nephews.—Those are my nieces.—This will be difficult.—That would be very dear.—This was very convenient.—This is what (that which[1]) I think.—He is my friend.—She is my neighbour.—It is a good dog.—They are my cousins (*m.*).—It is well.—It is you.—This is better than that.—Do[2] this.—Do that.—I like this and you like that.—He gives me that.—This pleases[3] you.

(*)They (*f.*) received—you received—did I receive?—he did not receive—I perceived—did you receive?—I received—we did not receive—we perceived—they did not perceive—she perceived—did he receive?—he received—didst thou receive?—you did not receive—she received—I did not receive—you perceived—we received—she did not receive—did we receive?—did they (*m.*) receive?—they (*f.*) did not receive—thou receivedst—did I perceive?—thou didst not receive—They (*m.*) perceived—did they (*f.*) receive?—he did not perceive—they (*m.*) received.

2. C'est mon père. C'est ma mère. Ce sont des soldats. C'est lui. C'est une femme heureuse. Ce sont des enfants laborieux. Ce n'est pas ce que[4] vous m'avez dit[5]. Ceci me plaît plus que cela. Ceci est facile; cela est difficile. Donnez-moi cela. Ceci coûte plus cher[6] que cela. Il donne ceci à mon frère et cela à ma sœur. Je recevais cela chaque jour. Vous receviez ceci. C'est moi. Est-ce vous? Ce n'est pas mon ami. Etait-ce son frère? Recevez cela.

He is an officer in the French army. She was a governess in my cousin's family. This is a good book. This is what (that which) you gave me the other day. I received this and you received that. That costs twenty-two pounds. I have given that to the postman. I give you this and that. Do what (that which) you have promised.[7] This will be the first time. She was a very good woman. It is a pretty sight. Those are my boots. I have said[8] that to the soldier. What[9] do you take[10]: this or that? This is a very convenient[b] house[a]. She is a pretty girl.

1 which, *que* 2 do, *faites* 3 pleases, *plaît*
4 *que*, which 5 *dit*, said 6 *plus cher*, dearer
7 promised, promis 8 said, *dit* 9 what, *que* 10 do you take, *prenez-vous*
(*) See the Imperfect of the verb *recevoir*, to receive (Supplement, p.p. 12, 18 & 19).

Questions on Grammar.

1. What are demonstrative pronouns?
2. Give the four pronouns which translate *this*?
3. Give the four pronouns which translate *that*?
4. How do you translate *these*?
5. How do you translate *those*?
6. What is the difference between *ce* adjective and *ce* pronoun?
7. Before what words can *ce* be used?
8. When does *ce* translate *he, she, it, they*?
9. When does *ce* translate *it* and *they*, the verb *être* being followed by an adjective?
10. What is the derivation of *ceci*?
11. When can *ceci* be used to translate *this*, after a verb?

Conversation.

How do you find this?	Comment trouvez-vous ceci?
I find this better than that.	Je trouve ceci meilleur que cela.
How much does this cost?	Combien coûte ceci?
This costs three pounds.	Ceci coûte trois livres sterling.
What is the price of that?	Quel est le prix de cela?
That is worth (*vaut*) thirty pounds.	Cela vaut trente livres sterling.
Give me this.	Donnez-moi ceci.
No, I shall give you that.	Non, je vous donnerai cela.
Is it cheap?	Est-ce bon marché?
No, it is dearer than the other.	Non, c'est plus cher que l'autre.
Who (*qui*) received (has received) this?	Qui a reçu ceci?
It is the gentleman who occupies the rooms on the first floor.	C'est le monsieur qui occupe les chambres du premier étage.
Who is the most industrious, your brother or you?	Qui est le plus laborieux: votre frère ou vous?
(It is) my brother.	C'est mon frère.
Tell me (*dites-moi*) if the governess finds her rooms convenient.	Dites-moi si l'institutrice trouve ses chambres commodes.
I do not know (*je ne sais pas*) (that).	Je ne sais pas cela.
Here is (*voici*) the postman.	Voici le facteur.
For whom are the letters?	Pour qui sont les lettres?
This is for my father; those are for my cousin.	Celle-ci est pour mon père; celles-là sont pour mon cousin.

Reading Exercise No. 16.

Lord Macartney avait occupé une position honorifique
honorary
dans l'armée et il se vantait non seulement de n'avoir
boasted
jamais rien demandé, mais encore d'avoir refusé les faveurs
anything
qui lui avaient été offertes. Il ne connaissait pas, disait-
which   offered   knew   said
il, de plus grand bonheur que celui d'être indépendant et
any   independent
de faire ce qui lui plaisait. Le roi, ayant été instruit de
to do which pleased   informed
cela, voulut voir si cette opinion était sincère. Un jour
wished to see
donc il le prit à part et lui demanda mystérieusement s'il
then   took aside   mysteriously
savait l'espagnol. "Non, Sire," répondit Macartney, mais
knew   Spanish   answered
je l'apprendrai immédiatement, si cela fait plaisir à votre
shall learn   immediately   does
majesté." "Oui, vraiment," répliqua le roi, "je vous le
replied
conseille, et vous aurez à vous en féliciter." Macartney
advise   yourself for it to congratulate
conclut de cette simple conversation que le roi avait l'in-
concluded   simple
tention de lui confier quelque importante mission diplo-
entrust   important
matique. Il se mit à travailler jour et nuit, et trois mois
himself put
après il annonçait au roi qu'il savait parfaitement la langue
perfectly
espagnole. "Tant mieux," répondit le roi, "cela vous
So much the better
permettra de lire Don Quichotte dans l'original."
will allow   Quixote

SEVENTEENTH LESSON. *Dix-septième Leçon.*

The Demonstrative Pronoun *(concluded).*

III.—*Celui-ci,* this, is derived from *ce,* this, *lui,* he and *ci,* here. It is used in speaking of persons or things every time it is necessary to indicate that the person or thing pointed to is of the masculine gender and singular number, and is nearer to the speaker than another person or thing; *celui-là* (that-he-there) being used to point to the farther.

Vous voyez ces deux chevaux: *celui-ci* est plus cher que *celui-là.* You see these two horses: *this one* is dearer than *that.*

Celui-ci and *celui-là* are often translated *the latter* and *the former.*

Mon père et mon frère sont partis; *celui-là* va à Paris et *celui-ci* va à Rome. My father and brother have departed; *the former* goes to Paris and *the latter* goes to Rome.

Ceux-ci, these, and *ceux-là,* those, derived from *ce-eux-ci* or *là* refer to a masculine plural noun.

Avez-vous vu les officiers et les soldats; *ceux-là* ont de plus beaux uniformes que *ceux-ci?* Have you seen the officers and soldiers; *those* have finer uniforms than *these.*

Celles-ci, these, or *celles-là,* those, *ce, elles, ci* or *là* point to a feminine plural noun.

De ces fleurs, *celles-ci* sont plus belles que *celles-là.* Of these flowers *these* are more beautiful than *those.*

IV.—*Celui, celle, ceux, celles,* derived respectively from *ce-lui, ce-elle, ce-eux, ce-elles* are used in the same manner as *celui-ci, celle-ci, &c.,* but before relative pronouns and prepositions only, the adverbs *ci* and *là* being no longer necessary to point more accurately.

J'aime cette maison, mais je préfère *celle* de mon père. I like this house, but I prefer *that* of my father (my father's).

Ces livres sont intéressants; mais je préfère *ceux* que vous m'avez donnés hier. These books are interesting, but I prefer *those* which you gave me yesterday.

Celui, celle, ceux, celles translate indifferently *this* or *that,* and *these* or *those.*

They often translate *the one* or *the ones* and the personal pronouns *he, she, him, it, they, them* before relative pronouns.

Ce n'est pas *celui* que je pensais. It is not *the one* I thought.
Je connais *celui* qui a dit cela. I know *him* who said that.

author, *auteur m.*	to deceive, *décevoir*	polite, *poli*
bill, *note f.*	to flatter, *flatter*	rare, *rare*
to buy *acheter*	grammar, *grammaire f.*	soup, *soupe f.*
cake, *gâteau m.*	grandfather, *grand-père*	spacious, *spacieux*
clear, *clair*	to inhabit, *habiter* [*m.*	stream, *ruisseau m.*
coin, *pièce f.*	learned, *instruit*	to study, *étudier*
cold, *froid*	object, *objet m.*	tailor, *tailleur m.*
to compose, *composer*	piece, *pièce f.*	warm, *chaud*
		yesterday, *hier*

Exercise No. 17.

1. I like this horse; but I do not like that.—This one is good: that one is bad.—Give me this book and I shall give you that.—I understand[1] this rule, but I do not understand that. — These houses are more spacious than those.—My pen is worse than this.—Your garden is prettier than that. — These birds are rarer than those. — This book is not my father's (that of my father). — These gloves are my grandfather's (those of my grandfather). — This wine is that which[2] I bought (have bought) this morning. I like him who is a good son.

(*)We shall receive—I shall not receive—shall I receive?— they (*f.*) will not receive—will he receive?—I shall receive—will you not receive?—he will not receive—they (*m.*) will receive—we shall not receive—he will receive—they (*m.*) will not receive—wilt thou receive?—she will not receive—shall we receive?—you will receive—I will deceive—will you receive?—shall we not deceive?—shall I not receive?—she will receive—thou wilt receive—you will not receive — they (*f.*) will receive—thou wilt not receive.

2. De ces deux jeunes filles, celle-ci est plus instruite que celle-là. Ces grammaires-ci sont meilleures que celles-là. Ces messieurs-ci sont plus polis que ceux-là. Ce ruisseau-ci est plus clair que celui-là. Cette eau-ci est plus froide que celle-là. Cette soupe-ci est plus chaude que celle-là. Ce vin-ci est bon, mais celui de mon père est meilleur. J'ai vu[3] le chien de votre frère, mais je n'ai pas vu celui de son ami. J'aime cette couleur-ci mais je n'aime pas celle de la robe de votre cousine.

He who studies every day will soon become[4] learned. These boots are not the ones I bought the other day. That glass is larger than your friend's (that of your friend). Give me these coins and I will give you those. I have received[5] my tailor's bill, I shall receive my shoemaker's[5] this morning. We have received your cousin's visit, we shall receive that of his friend this afternoon. We like this house, we do not like that. These chairs are better than those. This gentleman writes[6] quicker than that one. This ink is clearer than that.

---

1 understand, *comprends*   2 which, *que*
3 *vu*, seen
4 will become, *deviendra*   5 received, *reçu*   6 writes, *écrit*
(*) See Future of *recevoir*, and the conjugation of verbs interrogatively and negatively (Supplement, p.p. 12, 18 & 19).

Questions on Grammar.

1. From what words is *celui-ci* derived?
2. When is *celui-ci* used to translate *this?*
3. Give the etymology of *celui-là?*
4. What is the feminine of *celui-ci* and *celui-là?*
5. What is the plural masculine of *celui-ci;* from what is it derived?
6. Give the plural feminine of *celui-là* and its etymology?
7. When are *celui, celle, ceux, celles,* used instead of *celui-ci, celle-ci, ceux-ci, celles-ci?*
8. How are *the one who* (or *he who*) translated?
9. How do you translate *he who?*

Conversation.

Which stuff will you take (*prendrez-vous*) this one or that?	Quelle étoffe prendrez-vous; celle-ci ou celle-là?
I shall take (*je prendrai*) this one; but I think that one is better, only it is too dear for me.	Je prendrai celle-ci, mais je pense que celle-là est meilleure; seulement elle est trop chère pour moi.
Take (*prenez*) that one: it will last (*durera*) longer (*plus longtemps*).	Prenez celle-là: elle durera plus longtemps.
Is it not the one which (*que*) you have sold (*vendue*) to my friend Mrs. ... (*Madame*)?	N'est-ce pas celle que vous avez vendue à mon amie, Madame...?
No it is that which (*que*) I showed (*ai montrée*) you in the other room.	Non c'est celle que je vous ai montrée dans l'autre chambre.
What (*quel*) is the price of that?	Quel est le prix de celle-là?
That costs two francs and fifty centimes a (*le*) metre (*mètre*).	Celle-là coûte deux francs cinquante centimes le mètre?
Are these gloves those which (*que*) my sister saw (has seen) (*vus*) yesterday?	Ces gants sont-ils ceux que ma sœur a vus hier?
No, Miss (*Mademoiselle*), they are not the same.	Non, Mademoiselle; ce ne sont pas les mêmes.
Is this parcel mine (*le mien*)?	Ce paquet-ci est-il le mien?
No, it is Mrs.'s...(that of Mrs....).	Non, c'est celui de Madame ...
Will you send (*enverrez*) that to my hotel?	Enverrez-vous celui-là à mon hôtel?
Yes, Madam, with the greatest pleasure.	Oui, Madame, avec le plus grand plaisir.

Reading Exercise No. 17.

Un poète avait un jour composé une pièce de vers
sur les gâteaux que faisait un pâtissier renommé de la ville
qu'il habitait. Le pâtissier, quoiqu'il ne cultivât pas
beaucoup les Muses, fut cependant flatté dans son orgueil,
à la réception d'un exemplaire de cette poésie : il voulut
en témoigner sa satisfaction à l'auteur et crut qu'il ne
pouvait mieux faire que de lui envoyer un des objets qui
avaient éveillé son inspiration. Le poète reçut d'abord
cet envoi avec plaisir et se mit à déguster le chef-d'œuvre
appétissant ; mais quelle ne fut pas son humiliation en
découvrant que le pâtissier s'était servi de la pièce de vers
elle-même pour le faire cuire au four. Il lui écrivit donc
une lettre indignée, où il l'accusait du crime de lèse-poésie
"De quoi vous plaignez-vous ?" lui répondit le pâtissier ;
"Je n'ai fait qu'imiter vos procédés. Vous aviez fait une
poésie sur mes gâteaux et, moi, j'ai fait un gâteau sur
votre poésie."

Eighteenth Lesson. — *Dix-huitième Leçon.*

Possessive Pronouns.

Possessive Pronouns are those which express possession. They are as follows:

Singular.		Plural.		
Masc.	*Fem.*	*Masc.*	*Fem.*	
le mien	la mienne	les miens	les miennes	mine
le tien	la tienne	les tiens	les tiennes	thine
le sien	la sienne	les siens	les siennes	his, hers, its
le nôtre	la nôtre	les nôtres	les nôtres	ours
le vôtre	la vôtre	les vôtres	les vôtres	yours
le leur	la leur	les leurs	les leurs	theirs

REMARKS. I.—It must be noticed that the *o* of *nôtre* and *vôtre*, when pronouns, has the circumflex accent, which does not exist in *notre* and *votre*, possessive adjectives.

II.—The words *nôtre*, *vôtre* and *leur* do not change in the feminine.

III.—The rule given in Lesson 13 for possessive adjectives of the the third person must also be applied to possessive pronouns; thus,

ce livre et *le sien*, translates as well this book and *his*, as this book and *hers*.

To avoid the lack of precision which may result from it, when it is necessary to indicate to whom an object belongs, possession is expressed by the verb *être*, to be, followed by the preposition *à* and the disjunctive personal pronouns.

Etre is in such cases the translation of the English verb *to belong*.

Ce livre est *à lui*, this book is *his* or belongs *to him*.
Ce livre est *à elle*, this book is *hers* or belongs *to her*.
Cette maison est *à moi*, this house is *mine* or belongs *to me*.
Ces chevaux sont *à nous*, these horses are *ours* or belong *to us*.

IV.—*Le mien, le tien, le sien, &c.*, are generally used instead of *à moi, à toi, à lui* or *à elle*, when it is necessary to make a distinction between different objects of the same kind.

Ce chapeau-ci est *le mien*, celui-là est *le vôtre*. This hat is *mine*, that one is *yours*.

Cette maison-là est *la leur*, celle-ci est *la nôtre*. That house is *theirs*, this one is *ours*.

to address, *adresser*
already, *déjà*
boat *bateau m.*
to dare, *oser*
deep, *profond*
demand, *demande f.*
to desire, *désirer*
dictionary, *dictionnaire m.*

face, *figure f.*
fine, *beau*
to frighten, *effrayer*
jewel, *bijou m.*
key, *clef f.*
to lend, *prêter*
Miss, *Mademoiselle f.*
now, *maintenant*

to oblige, *obliger*
project, *projet m.*
refusal, *refus m.*
to refuse, *refuser*
sigh, *soupir m.*
spoon, *cuiller f.*
umbrella, *parapluie m.*
young lady, *demoiselle f.*

Exercise No. 18.

1. This dog is mine,—that flower is thine,—these shoes are his,—these boots are hers,—these keys are ours,—those rooms are yours,—these children are theirs,—that fork is mine,—this knife is thine,—this spoon is his,—these jewels are ours,—those plates are yours,—these dishes are theirs,—this hat belongs to me,—that coat belongs to thee,—this stick belongs to him,—that dress belongs to her,—the large house belongs to us,—the small garden belongs to you,—the fine carriage belongs to them *(m.)*,—that residence belongs to them *(f.)*.

(*)We should receive—should I receive?—thou wouldst not receive—would he receive?—I should receive—would you receive?—they would receive—they *(m.)* would not receive—you would receive—should we receive?—should we not receive?—thou wouldst receive—would they *(m.)* receive?—I should deceive—wouldst thou receive?—he would not receive—we should not deceive—he would receive—would she receive?

2. Cet enfant-ci est le mien. Ce chat est-il à vous? Je recevrais sa lettre aujourd'hui; quand recevrait-il la mienne? J'ai reçu[1] leur visite ce matin, je recevrai la sienne cette après-midi; quand recevrai-je la vôtre. Cette pendule est à moi. Ces gants-ci sont-ils les vôtres? ceux-ci sont les miens. Cette montre est-elle à vous? Vous avez reçu vos robes, quand recevrons-nous les nôtres? Ces livres sont à eux. Ces albums[2] sont à elles.

I have read[3] your lesson[4], I shall read[5] his now. Give me your book and I will give you mine. This boat belongs to me, that one belongs to them *(m.)*. Is this gun yours or is it mine? This umbrella is mine, that one is hers. He lent me his horse and I lent him mine. This dictionary belongs to me. If I received your friend, would you receive mine? Your shoemaker is good; ours is very bad. I gave (have given) him his hat, he gave me mine.

---

1 *reçu*, received 2 *albums*, albums
3 read, *lu* 4 lesson, *devoir* 5 shall read, *lirai*

(*) See the Conditional of *recevoir*, and the conjugation of verbs used negatively and interrogatively (Supplement, p.p. 12, 18 & 19).

Questions on Grammar.

1. What are possessive pronouns?
2. What are the possessive pronouns which translate *mine*?
3. What are those which translate *thine*?
4. Translate *his, hers, its*.
5. Translate *ours*.
6. Translate *yours*.
7. Translate *theirs*.
8. Translate *this pen is his* and *this pen is hers*.
9. What is the way to translate *his* and *hers* by different expressions?
10. When must *le mien, le tien, &c.* be used instead of *à moi, à toi, &c.*

Conversation.

Whose (*à qui*) are these umbrellas?	A qui sont ces parapluies?
The white one is mine, the brown is theirs, and I think that the green is yours.	Le blanc est le mien; le brun est le leur et je pense que le vert est le vôtre.
Give me mine if you please.	Donnez-moi le mien, s'il vous plaît.
Here it is.	Le voici.
Of these horses which (*lequel*) do you prefer, his or mine?	De ces chevaux, le quel préférez-vous le sien ou le mien?
I prefer yours.	Je préfère le vôtre.
To whom (*à qui*) does this book belong?	A qui est ce livre.
It belongs to me.	Il est à moi.
Which (*quelle*) is the pen that belongs to you, this or that?	Quelle est la plume qui est à vous: celle-ci ou celle-là?
This is mine, that is your cousin's.	Celle-ci est la mienne : celle-là est à votre cousin.
Do these dogs belong to them?	Ces chiens sont-ils à eux?
No, they belong to us; they were theirs, but they gave them to us a few weeks ago (*il y a quelques semaines*).	Non, ils sont à nous : ils étaient à eux, mais ils nous les ont donnés, il y a quelques semaines.
When will you go (*irez-vous*) to their country-house (*maison de campagne*)?	Quand irez-vous à leur maison de campagne?
We shall not go to theirs but to ours.	Nous n'irons pas à la leur, mais à la nôtre.
Is this overcoat yours, or is it mine?	Ce pardessus est-il le vôtre, ou est-ce le mien?
It is mine; yours is in the ante-room.	C'est le mien; le vôtre est dans l'antichambre.

Reading Exercise No. 18.

Un jeune garçon d'*environ* douze *ans* accosta *un* jour
     about   accosted

une demoiselle qui passait *dans⌢*une des rues les plus
     who was passing

fréqu*en*tées de Paris avec sa gouvern*an*te, et lui dem*an*da
 frequented

de lui donner⌢*un* franc comme aumône. "Comment," lui
      as alms

dit la jeune fi*ll*e, "osez-vous⌢adresser une telle dem*an*de
said

aux pass*an*ts?" "Je vous⌢*en* prie, Mademoiselle," ré-
 passers by   of it beg

p*on*dit le jeune garçon, "ne me refusez pas ce que je vous
answered   "   which

dem*an*de; votre refus m'obligerait à pr*en*dre une terrible
          to take

résoluti*on*." Et comme il n'obt*en*ait pas ce qu'il dé*s*irait,
      " obtained which

il s'éloigna avec *un* prof*on*d soupir. La jeune fi*ll*e, effrayée
 went away

de la c*on*sternati*on* qui était p*ein*te sur *son* visage, craignit
   — which painted   feared

qu'il ne p*en*sât⌢à accomplir quelque funeste projet, et ne
  " might think accomplish fatal   "

voul*an*t pas⌢avoir à se reprocher d'avoir été la cause
wishing   " to reproach

*in*directe d'*un* malheur, elle fit rappeler le m*en*di*an*t et lui
         made recall beggar

donna les v*in*gt sous qu'il sollicitait. Puis⌢elle voulut
   half pence solicited Then wished

savoir quelle était l'extrême résoluti*on* à laquelle il faisait⌢
to know what

allusi*on* quelques minutes⌢auparav*an*t. "Oh! Mademoi-
      before

selle," rép*on*dit-il, "je me voyais déjà obligé de travai*ll*er."
  answered myself was already

NINETEENTH LESSON.   *Dix-neuvième Leçon.*

Relative and Interrogative Pronouns.

Relative pronouns are those which relate to other words which precede and are called their antecedents. They are as follows:

Invariable
- *Qui* — who, which, that, whom
- *Que* — whom, which, that, what
- *Quoi* — what
- *Dont* — whose, of whom, of which

Variable
- *Quel, quelle, quels, quelles* — whoever, whatever
- *Lequel, laquelle, lesquels, lesquelles* — which, what

Interrogative pronouns are those which are used at the beginning of an interrogative sentence. They have no antecedents. They are as follows:

Invariable
- *Qui* — who, whom, which
- *Que* — what
- *Quoi* — what

Variable
- *Quel, quelle, quels, quelles* — which, what
- *Lequel, laquelle, lesquels, lesquelles* — which, what

REMARKS. I.—*Whom* is translated by *qui* at the beginning of interrogative sentences and after prepositions:—*Qui connaissez vous ?* whom do you know ?

Le monsieur avec *qui* vous êtes venu. The gentleman with *whom* you came.

In ordinary sentences *qui* translates indifferently *who* or *which*.

L'homme *qui* est là. The man *who* is there.
Le livre *qui* est intéressant. The book *which* is interesting.

II.—*Que* translates *whom* or *which* in the middle of sentences, and *what* at the beginning of interrogative sentences.

L'homme *que* je connais. The man *whom* I know.
Le livre *que* je lis. The book *which* I read.
Que dites vous ? *What* do you say ?

III.—*Quoi* can only be used by itself or after prepositions.

Quoi ? what ? De *quoi* parlez-vous ? of *what* do you speak ?

IV.—*Dont* translates *whose, of whom, of which* in the middle of sentences, but can never be used at the beginning.

L'enfant *dont* vous êtes le père. The child *whose* father you are.

V.—*Quel, quelle, &c.*, translate *which* or *what* in referring to nouns which are placed after the verb *to be*.

Quelle est cette fleur ? *what* is this flower ?

Placed before *que* it is used in the sense of whoever, whatever.

Quel qu'il soit je le verrai. Whoever he may be I shall see him.

VI.—*Lequel, laquelle, &c.*, translate *which* or *what* in referring to nouns already mentioned or before nouns from which they are separated by *de*.

Voici deux fleurs, *laquelle* préférez-vous ? Here are two flowers, *which* do you prefer? *Lequel* de ces deux livres ? Which of these two books?

VII.—*Duquel, auquel, desquels, auxquels, &c.*, translate *of which, to which, &c.*, and must be used instead of *de qui, à qui, &c.*, which can never be used in speaking of *animals* or *things*.

Le chien *duquel* je parle, the dog *of which* I speak.

branch, *branche f.*	merchant, *marchand m.*	pupil, *élève m.*
to bring, *apporter*	mountain, *montagne f.*	to seek, *chercher*
to build, *bâtir*	music, *musique f.*	spot, *endroit m.*
castle *château m.*	narrow, *étroit*	taste, *goût m.*
to hear, *entendre*	nearly, *presque*	to wait, *attendre*
to hope, *espérer*	player, *joueur m.*	why, *pourquoi*
hunger, *faim f.*	portrait, *portrait m.*	without, *sans*
loaf, *miche, pain f.*	to publish, *publier*	wolf, *loup m.*

Exercise No. 19.

1. Who is there?—The child who is in the room.—The book which is on the table.—The horse that is in the street.—Whom do you like?—The cousin whom you like.—The bird which you sell.—The dog that I saw[1].—What do you like?—What?—Of what do you speak?—The merchant whose son he is (of whom he is the son).—The master from whom he brings a letter.—The grammar of which we speak.—What is your name?—Of these two flowers, which do you give me?—Which (*m. p.*) do you like?—Which (*f. p.*) do you buy?

(*)We sell—do I sell(†)?—he does not sell—they (*m.*) do not sell—do they (*m.*) sell?—does he sell?—I sell—we hear—they (*f.*) wait—do you hear?—I do not hear—I do not sell—he sells—dost thou sell?—we do not sell—thou sellest—you do not sell—they (*m.*) hear—you sell—I hear—he does not wait—they (*f.*) sell—do we sell?—she does not sell—she sells—do they (*f.*) sell?—I wait—you hear—does she sell?—thou dost not sell—they (*m.*) sell—do you sell?

2. De qui avez-vous reçu cette lettre? Qui est dans la chambre? Lequel achèterez-vous? De quoi? Que dites[2]-vous? A qui parlez-vous? Dans quoi mettrez[3]-vous cela? Lequel de ces habits donnez-vous à ces pauvres enfants? Quel est votre chapeau? Le lit qui est dans ma chambre est très large; celui que vous avez est très étroit. Le château dont vous voyez les tours est celui qui a été bâti l'année[b] dernière[a]. De qui vient cette lettre? Sur lequel étiez-vous? Les amis que vous avez sont très fidèles. Desquels? Auxquelles avez-vous écrit[4]? Que vendez-vous? Qui recevrez-vous aujourd'hui?

In which (*f, s.*) is your book? What is that? Whom have you seen[5] this afternoon? I have seen the gentleman whom you know[6]. What do you sell? Who speaks? I have the portrait which has been published (the) last[b] week[a]. The boys who are in the room are my brother's pupils. The apples which you sell are not good. I hear your sister's voice who speaks in the other room. (For) Whom do you wait? I wait (for) the lady who wrote[7] to me the other day.

---

1 I saw, *je vis* 2 *dites*, say 3 *mettrez*, will put 4 *écrit*, written
5 seen, *vu* 6 know, *connaissez* 7 wrote, *a écrit*

(*) See the Present Indicative of *rendre*, to render (Supplement, page 13).
(†) *Est-ce que je vends.*

Questions on Grammar.

1. What are relative pronouns?
2. What are interrogative pronouns?
3. Which are the invariable relative pronouns?
4. Which are the variable interrogative pronouns?
5. When does *qui* translate *whom*?
6. When does *que* translate *what*?
7. When does *quoi* translate *what*?
8. When can *dont* be used to translate *whose, of whom, of which*?
9. When does *quel* translate *which* or *what*?
10. When is *lequel* used to translate *which* or *what*?
11. When must *lequel, laquelle, duquel, &c.*, be used instead of *qui, que, dont*?

Conversation.

Which of these gentlemen is your brother?	Lequel de ces Messieurs est votre frère?
It is he who is before the table.	C'est celui qui est devant la table?
What is he doing *(fait-il)*?	Que fait-il?
He is reading *(lit)* the book which you lent him the other day.	Il lit le livre que vous lui avez prêté l'autre jour.
What is this gentleman's name?	Quel est le nom de ce monsieur?
I do not know *(ne sais pas)*; ask (to) the gentleman who is standing *(debout)* near *(près de)* the window.	Je ne sais pas; demandez au monsieur qui est debout près de la fenêtre.
Of what are they speaking *(parlent-ils)*?	De quoi parlent-ils?
They speak of the news which is contained *(contenue)* in to-day's papers *(les journaux d'aujourd'hui)*?	Ils parlent de la nouvelle qui est contenue dans les journaux d'aujourd'hui.
What is this news?	Quelle est cette nouvelle?
The large bell which has been cast *(fondue)* for St. Paul's cathedral arrived (is arrived) yesterday morning.	La grosse cloche qui a été fondue pour la cathédrale de Saint-Paul est arrivée hier matin.
What do they say *(dit-on)* about *(à propos de)* politics?	Que dit-on à propos de politique?
It is said *(on dit)* that we shall have war with Egypt and that Turkey will be our ally.	On dit que nous aurons la guerre avec l'Egypte et que la Turquie sera notre alliée.

Reading Exercise No. 19.

Un joueur de cornemuse traver*sant⌢un* jour les montagnes
           bagpipe   crossing
de l'Ulster en Irlande, rencontra *un* loup affamé. L'endroit
   „   Ireland   hungry
était⌢entièrement désert; il n'y avait aucune habitation à
   entirely —   there was   no   dwelling
proximité, où le pauvre ménétrier pût⌢essayer de chercher
  —   minstrel could try
refuge, ni même au*cun*⌢arbre sur les branches duquel il
     nor even   —   of which
pût grimper. Que faire pour se tirer d'*un* da*n*ger aussi
 climb   What to do   himself to get out of. — so
pres*sant*? Le malheureux se rappela qu'il avait da*n*s sa
pressing   remembered
valise une miche de pai*n*-presque tout⌢entière et *un* petit
wallet   quite entire
morceau de viande. Peut-être pourrait-il assouvir la faim
piece   could to satiate
de l'animal *en* lui abandonna*n*t ces provisio*ns*: il les lui
    —   in   abandoning   —
jeta morceau par morceau; mais⌢hélas! sa*ns*⌢*en*⌢obtenir le
threw piece   alas   from it to obtain
résultat qu'il avait⌢espéré. Il fallait do*n*c avoir recours
              hoped   was necessary then recourse
à *un*⌢autre moy*en*, et il n'imagi*n*a rie*n* de mieux que d'avoir
  another expedient „ imagined   better
recours à sa cornemuse. Quel ne fut pas so*n* conte*n*tement,
                           „   satisfaction
qua*n*d, aux premiers so*n*s qu'il *en* tira, le loup se mit⌢à
                         from it drew   put
s'enfuir da*n*s la directio*n* des m*o*ntagnes avec plus de ra-
fly
pidité qu'il n'*en*⌢était venu quelques⌢*in*sta*n*ts⌢auparava*n*t.
  —   „ from them. come   —   before
"Coqui*n*," s'écria le pauvre ménétrier, "pourquoi n'ai-je
  Rascal exclaimed   minstrel   „
pas connu tes goûts plus tôt; tu peux⌢être certain que je
  known   canst   —
t'aurais donné le dessert avant le souper."
    given   before supper.

TWENTIETH LESSON. *Vingtième Leçon.*

Indefinite Pronouns.

Indefinite pronouns are those which refer to persons or things in an indefinite manner.

The following is a list of them:

quelqu'un, quelqu'une (f), some one, somebody, anybody
quelques-uns, quelques-unes, some ones, some, any, a few
chacun, chacune, each one, every one
aucun, aucune, no one, none
nul, no one, none
l'un, l'une, the one
l'autre, the other
l'un l'autre, l'une autre, each other, one another
l'un et l'autre, l'une et l'autre, both
l'un ou l'autre, l'une ou l'autre, either
ni l'un ni l'autre, ni l'une ni l'autre, neither
(*)*l'un à l'autre, l'une à l'autre*, to one another, to each other
un autre, une autre, another
autrui, d'autres, others
tout le monde, everybody
personne, nobody
tout, everything
tous, all
rien, nothing
quelque chose, something
quiconque, whoever
le même, la même, the same
on, one, they, people

REMARKS. 1.—*L'un, l'autre, l'un l'autre, l'une l'autre*, &c. become in the plural *les uns, les autres, les uns les autres, les unes les autres*, &c.

II.—*Chacun, aucun, tout le monde, autrui, personne, quiconque, rien*, are never used in the plural.

III.—*Aucun, ni l'un ni l'autre, personne, rien*, require the verb to be preceded by the particle *ne*.

Personne *ne* me connaît. Nobody knows me.
Je *n'*ai rien. I have nothing.

IV.—*L'un l'autre, l'un à l'autre*, expressing reciprocity always require the verb to be in the plural and preceded by *se*.

Ils *se* haïssent *l'un l'autre*. They hate *one another*.
Ils *s'*écrivirent *l'un à l'autre*. They wrote *to each other*.

(*) It can be seen that the preposition is placed in French between *l'un* and *l'autre* instead of being placed before *each other* or *one another* as in English.
l'un avec l'autre, with one another; *l'un pour l'autre*, for each other.

to astonish, *étonner*	to happen, *arriver*	robber, *voleur m.*
bullet, *balle f.*	hole, *trou m.*	rude, *grossier*
convent, *couvent m.*	life, *vie f.*	satisfied, *content*
to dare, *oser*	manner, *manière f.*	to send, *envoyer*
to detest, *détester*	monk, *moine m.*	theatre, *théâtre m.*
discontented, *mécontent*	pistole, *pistolet m.*	throat, *gorge f.*
during, *pendant*	pocket, *poche f.*	traveller, *voyageur m.*
forest, *forêt f.*	purse, *bourse f.*	useless, *inutile*

Exercise No. 20.

1. Somebody is in the room.—Some are good, others are bad. —Everyone has it.—No one knows[1] me.—This one is mine, the other is yours.—They like each other.—Both are here.—I shall see[2] either. —Neither is here.—They have sent[3] a letter to each other.—Another will have it.—Everybody knows him. — I know[4] nobody. — He has everything.—All wait in the other room.—He has nothing.—Something will happen.—Whoever knows him likes him.—This (*m.*) is not the same.

(*)We sold—did he sell?—he did not sell—I waited—did we hear? —he waited—I sold—you did not sell—he heard—I heard—did we sell? —they (*f.*) sold—he sold—I did sell—they (*m.*) did not sell—did I wait?—I did not sell—they (*m.*) heard—you sold—did you sell?—We did not sell—thou didst sell—did I hear?—they (*m.*) sold—thou didst not sell—did we wait?—did I sell?—did you wait?—thou soldest—did they (*f.*) sell?

2. J'ai vu[5] quelqu'un qui m'a demandé votre nom.— Comment osez-vous parler d'autrui d'[6]une[c] manière[d] si[a] grossière[b] ? Les uns sont contents, les autres sont mécontents. Il a quelque chose dans sa main. Tous sont là. Il a tout perdu[7]. Tout le monde le connaissait[8] dans cette ville. Ni l'un ni l'autre ne vendent cette marchandise. L'un et l'autre danseront ce soir. Chacun est étonné. Ce cheval n'est pas le même. Rien ne m'étonne. Ils ne vendaient rien.

Both have lost[7] their fortunes. Nobody was with them at the theatre. I have them all. Some like him; others detest him. Neither has bought his house. He has given me something for you. They detest one another. Everyone bought it. I shall have either. I heard nobody. They heard nothing. Nobody is in the house. Nothing is impossible to him. I know[4] the one, but I do not know the other

---

1 knows, *connaît* 2 shall see, *verrai* 3 have sent, *se sont envoyé* 4 I know, *connais* 5 vu, seen 6 d', in 7 perdu, lost 8 connaissait, knew
(*) See the Imperfect of *rendre*, to render (Supplement, page 13).

Questions on Grammar.

1. What are indefinite pronouns?
2. Translate *somebody, everybody, nobody.*
3. Translate *something, nothing, everything.*
4. Translate *either, neither, both, each other.*
5. Translate *the other, the same, others.*
6. What is the plural of *l'un et l'autre?*
7. What indefinite pronouns are never used in the plural?
8. What indefinite pronouns require the verb to be preceded by *ne?*
9. What personal pronoun must be placed before the verb preceded or followed by *l'un l'autre* and *l'un à l'autre?*

Conversation.

Is somebody there?	Quelqu'un est-il là?
Nobody is in the room.	Personne n'est dans la chambre.
Have you seen the one or the other?	Avez-vous vu l'un ou l'autre?
I have seen both.	J'ai vu l'un et l'autre.
Did they give you anything?	Vous ont-ils donné quelque chose
No, they gave me nothing.	Non, ils ne m'ont rien donné.
Is that the same book?	Est-ce le même livre?
No, it is not the same.	Non, ce n'est pas le même.
Did you speak (*vous êtes-vous parlé*) to one another?	Vous êtes-vous parlé l'un à l'autre?
No, I spoke to nobody.	Non, je n'ai parlé à personne.
Do you know either?	Connaissez-vous l'un ou l'autre?
No, I know neither.	Non, je ne connais ni l'un ni l'autre.
Do you know anybody in the town?	Connaissez-vous quelqu'un dans la ville?
No, I know nobody.	Non, je ne connais personne.
Will they come (*viendront*) with each other?	Viendront-ils l'un avec l'autre?
Yes, I expect them both.	Oui, je les attends l'un et l'autre.
My compliments to everybody.	Mes compliments à tout le monde.
I thank you.	Je vous remercie.
Will you see (*verrez-vous*) your cousins there?	Y verrez-vous vos cousins?
Yes, I shall see them all.	Oui, je les verrai tous.
Take (*prenez*) this parcel and I will take (*prendrai*) the other.	Prenez ce paquet et je prendrai l'autre.
I have it.	Je l'ai.

Reading Exercise No. 20.

Le frère quêteur d'un couvent des environs de Paris
    collector   neighbourhood. —
revenait après avoir fait sa tournée dans plusieurs villages
came back   made round
voisins, et rapportait les aumônes qu'il avait recueillies
neighbouring. brought back alms   gathered
pendant la journée. En traversant une forêt, il fut ren-
pendant day   crossing
contré par un voleur qui lui demanda la bourse ou la vie.

Le moine vit bien que la résistance serait inutile et remit
    saw   —   delivered up
au voleur une trentaine de livres; mais il lui demanda
   about thirty
comme faveur de décharger un pistolet qu'il avait à la main,
as   unload
dans l'un des pans de sa robe, afin de prouver au prieur
   flaps   — In order to prove —
qu'il avait été attaqué et qu'il avait fait quelque résistance.
   attacked   made
Le bandit fit ce qu'on lui demandait, mais le moine ne
  — did
voyant pas le trou de la balle, s'étonna de cette circonstance.
seeing not   bullet . astonished circumstance
Le bandit se mit à rire et avoua tout franchement qu'il ne
   — put . laugh . avowed quite frankly
mettait jamais de balles dans ses pistolets et qu'il ne les
put
employait que comme moyens d'intimidation. Cette con-
employed but   ways —
fession lui coûta cher; car le moine, qui était d'une force
  — cost for
remarquable, se jeta sur lui, le prit à la gorge et le terrassa;
remarkable . threw took   flung down
puis ayant cherché dans ses poches, il en retira non seule-
then sought   from it pulled out .
ment les trente livres qu'il lui avait remises auparavant
       delivered before
mais l'argent qu'il avait dérobé à d'autres voyageurs. Le
    robbed
moine ne se fit aucun scrupule de s'en emparer et rentra
 „ . made scruple . of it to take possession . returned
triomphant dans son couvent.
triumphant.

TWENTY-FIRST LESSON.   *Vingt-et-unième Leçon.*

Indefinite Pronouns *(concluded).*

The pronoun *on* is of a very frequent use in the French language; it is used in speaking of persons and translates the English expressions, *one, we, they, people.*

On attend.   *They* wait.
On travaille dans la rue.   *People* work in the street.

On is always of the singular number. Accordingly the verb that follows must be in the singular, as may be seen from the preceding example.

On is of the masculine gender, and accordingly all adjectives which refer to it must be of the same gender. However, these adjectives ought to be in the feminine if the sense clearly indicated that the pronoun *on* refered to a female.

On est toujours fière de sa beauté.   *One* is always proud of one's beauty.
On est heureuse quand *on* est aimée de son mari.   *One* is happy when *one* is loved by *one's* husband.

On is often used, with an active verb, to translate a passive verb.

On croit qu'il viendra.   *It is believed* that he will come.
On dit que sa mère est morte.   *It is said* that his mother is dead.
On me dit.   *I* am told.
On leur disait.   *They* were told.

When *on* is immediately preceded by the conjunctions *et*, and, *si*, if, *que*, that, *ou*, or, and the adverb *où*, where, the euphonic letter *l'* must be placed between the conjunction and the pronoun *on*.

On connaît et *l'on* aime cet homme.   *People* know and like this man.
Si *l'on* m'interroge, je répondrai.   If I am interrogated, I shall answer.
Je crois que *l'on* vient.   I think that *somebody* is coming.
On ne vas pas où *l'on* veut.   *One* does not go where *one* wishes.

However this *l'* ought to be omitted if *on* were followed by a word beginning with an *l*.

On le connaît et *on* l'aime.   *People* know and like him.
Si *on* le savait.   If *people* knew it.
Je ne crois pas qu'*on* le trouve.   I do not believe it will be found.
Il est où *on* l'a mis.   It is where it has been put.

to accept, *accepter*	to imitate, *imiter*	physician, *médecin m.*
act, *acte m.*	judgment, *jugement m.*	to publish, *publier*
to arrive, *arriver*	magnificent, *magnifique*	to recount, *raconter*
care, *soin m.*		repast, *repas m.*
dessert, *dessert m.*	to mix, *mêler* [*m.*	Spain, *Espagne f.*
effect, *effet m.*	monastery, *monastère*	Spaniard, *espagnol*
example, *exemple m.*	necessary, *nécessaire*	trumpet, *trompette f.*
fanaticism, *fanatisme*	patriotism, *patriotisme m.*	wall, *mur m.*
hour, *heure f.* [*m.*		war, *guerre f.*

Exercise No. 21.

1. One thinks.—We wait.—They say¹.—People think.—One works.—One hopes.—They recount—People refuse.—One likes.—One hears.—They give.—People find.—One eats.—One dares.—They desire. —People ask.—It is believed.—It is thought.—I am asked.—He is deceived.—He was obliged.—They speak to him and they say that his brother is ill.—If people knew² it.—I think that they will refuse this. —Do you know³ where one finds that.

(*)I shall sell—we shall not sell—shall we sell?—they (*m.*) will not sell—will she hear?—he will sell—I shall wait—will they sell?—I shall hear—you will not sell—we shall hear—thou wilt sell—you will wait—will you sell?—wilt thou sell?—I shall not sell—they (*f.*) will not sell—you will sell—thou wilt not sell—they (*f.*) will sell—he will not sell—will he sell?—we shall sell—shall I sell?—we shall wait—she will not sell—they (*m.*) will sell.

2. On vendra la maison demain matin. On entend sa voix dans la chambre de votre mère. On raconte que votre ami est⁴ arrivé. On l'imite. On dit que (la) guerre a été déclarée entre⁵ les deux pays. On me déçoit. On pense que je suis très riche. On arrive à Paris en quatre heures. Je pense que l'on est heureux d'⁶avoir un amiᵇ fidèleᵃ. On serait content si l'on avait tout ce que l'on désire. Savez-vous⁷ où l'on publie ce livre. Je crois⁸ qu'on le publie ici. Il croit tout ce qu'on lui dit. Si on l'avait vu⁹ on lui aurait dit cela.

They will sell it. They thought that he was an honest man. It is said that he will arrive to-morrow morning. It is believed that he will be dead before the end of the week. I am told that he is very ill. It is said that he will leave¹⁰ this afternoon. People like him and believe that his patriotism will be rewarded¹¹. People say that this magnificent monastery was (has been) built by the kings of Spain. It is necessary that people should arrive at seven o'clock. If people accepted his invitation he would be very satisfied. Where do they sell that?

---

1 say, *dit* 2 knew, *savait* 3 do you know, *savez-vous* 4 *est*, has 5 *déclarée entre*, declared between 6 *d'*, to 7 *savez-vous*, do you know 8 *crois*, believe 9 *vu*, seen 10 will leave, *partira* 11 rewarded, *récompensé*

(*) See the Future of *rendre* (Supplement, page 11).

Questions on Grammar.

1. What is the meaning of the pronoun *on*?
2. What is the number of the pronoun *on*?
3. What is its gender?
4. Is *on* sometimes of the feminine gender?
5. How are passive verbs often translated in French?
6. What are the conjunctions which require the euphonic letter *l'* to be placed between them and the pronoun *on*?
7. When must that euphonic letter be dispensed with?

Conversation.

Where do they sell these hats?	Où vend-on ces chapeaux?
They are sold in the High Street (*grand'rue*) number thirty-two.	On les vend dans la grand'rue numéro trente-deux.
Do they sell them dear?	Les vend-on cher?
No; they are sold (at) twelve francs fifty centimes.	Non; on les vend douze francs cinquante centimes.
What do they say?	Que dit-on?
They say that the Queen will arrive in (*à*) London to-morrow afternoon.	On dit que la reine arrivera à Londres demain après-midi.
Is it known at what time (*heure*) she will arrive?	Sait-on à quelle heure elle arrivera?
People say that she will be here at two o'clock in (of) the afternoon.	On dit qu'elle sera ici à deux heures de l'après-midi.
Is it believed that people will be admitted in the station?	Croit-on que l'on sera admis dans la station?
I am told that people will not be admitted on the platform.	On me dit que l'on ne sera pas admis sur le quai.
Is it known if the prince will be there?	Sait-on si le prince sera là?
It is said that he will be there with the princess.	On dit qu'il y sera avec la princesse.
Do you believe what they say?	Croyez-vous ce que l'on dit?
I never believe too easily what is reported in some newspapers.	Je ne crois jamais trop facilement ce qui est rapporté dans certains journaux.
Is it believed that this difficult question will soon be resolved by the government?	Croit-on que cette question difficile sera bientôt résolue par le gouvernement?
They think so (that yes).	On croit que oui.

Reading Exercise No. 21.

Pendant les guerres de Napoléon premier en Espagne, le fanatisme et le patriotisme des habitants les portèrent[1] souvent aux actes les plus désespérés.[2] On raconte qu'un général de l'armée du roi Jérôme,[3] étant[4] arrivé un jour sous les murs du monastère de Figuières,[5] envoya un officier au prieur pour lui demander de fournir à ses soldats les vivres[6] qui leur étaient nécessaires. Le prieur répondit[7] que les soldats seraient bien reçus dans la ville, et qu'il donnerait lui-même[8] l'hospitalité au général et à son état-major.[9] Bientôt après, en effet,[10] un repas magnifique était servi ;[11] toutefois[12] le général, sachant[13] combien il était nécessaire de se méfier[14] des Espagnols,[15] crut[16] prudent d'engager le prieur et deux de ses moines à s'asseoir[17] à la table du festin.[18] L'invitation fut acceptée sans hésitation, et les religieux[19] burent[20] et mangèrent copieusement[21] pour donner l'exemple aux officiers français, qui les imitèrent sans la moindre appréhension. Mais au dessert, le prieur se leva[22] et, d'[23]une voix qui fit[24] sur les invités[25] l'effet de la trompette du jugement dernier, il leur annonça qu'un poison mortel[26] avait été mêlé au vin et aux aliments et qu'ils n'avaient pas une heure à vivre.[27] En effet, malgré[28] les soins qui leur furent prodigués[29] par les médecins de l'armée, appelés en toute hâte,[30] au bout[31] de quelques instants, ils expiraient,[32] aussi bien que[33] le prieur et les deux moines, dans des souffrances épouvantables.[34]

1 portèrent, *carried.* 2 désespérés, *desperate.* 3 roi Jérôme, *king Jerome* of (Westphalia). 4 étant, *having.* 5 Figuières, *Figueiras.* 6 vivres, *provisions.* 7 répondit, *answered.* 8 lui-même, *himself.* 9 état-major, *staff.* 10 en effet, *indeed.* 11 servi, *served.* 12 toutefois, *however.* 13 sachant, *knowing.* 14 se méfier, *distrust.* 15 Espagnols, *Spaniards.* 16 crut, *believed.* 17 s'asseoir, *to sit down.* 18 la table du festin, *the convivial table.* 19 religieux, *monks.* 20 burent, *drank.* 21 copieusement, *copiously.* 22 se leva, *rose.* 23 d', *in.* 24 fit, *did.* 25 invités, *guests.* 26 poison mortel, *deadly poison.* 27 à vivre, *to live.* 28 malgré, *in spite of.* 29 leur furent prodigués, *lavished upon them.* 30 appelés en toute hâte, *called with all haste.* 31 au bout de, *at the end of.* 32 expiraient, *expired.* 33 aussi bien que, *as well as.* 34 dans des souffrances épouvantables, *in a dreadful agony.*

Twenty-second Lesson.   *Vingt-deuxième Leçon.*

Verbs.

As we have devoted the whole of the Supplement to verbs, we shall only give here a few general hints, which will be easily understood by the student, if he refer to the table given on the last page of the above mentioned part.

1. All verbs, whatever may be the conjugation to which they belong, whether they be regular or irregular, end in the same manner in the Imperfect of the Indicative (*ais, ais, ait, ions, iez, aient*), in the Future (*rai, ras, ra, rons, rez, ront*), and Conditional (*rais, rais, rait, rions, riez, raient*).

2. The first person singular, if not ending with a vowel (*e* or *ai*) always ends with an *s* (very few verbs with an *x*).

3. The second person singular always ends with *s* (few verbs with *x*).

4. The third person singular when not ending with a vowel (*e* or *a*) always ends with *t* (few verbs with *d*, one with *c*).

5. The first person plural ends in *es* or *ons*.

6. The second person plural ends in *es* or *ez* (always *ez* when the first person plural ends in *ons* except *vous dites, vous faites.*)

7. The third person plural ends always in *nt*.

8. The 1st and 2nd person plural of the present of the Subjunctive are generally the same as the 1st and 2nd person plural of the Imperfect of the Indicative (few irregular verbs excepted).

9. The endings of the Past definite are always *s* (1st conjugation excepted) *s, t, mes, tes, rent*.

10. The endings of the Present of the Subjunctive are always *e, es, e, ions, iez, ent* (few irregular verbs excepted).

11. The endings of the Imperfect of the Subjunctive are always *sse, sses, t, ssions, ssiez, ssent*.

12. There is always a circumflex accent on the vowel in the ending of the 1st and 2nd persons plural of the Past definite and 3rd person singular of the Imperfect of the Subjunctive.

13. The Verbs of the 1st conjugation (*er*) are by far the most numerous, and are all regular but *aller*, to go; *envoyer*, to send, and their compounds.

14. There are only seven regular verbs belonging to the 3rd conjugation (*oir*), viz: *percevoir*, to perceive, *apercevoir*, to perceive, *concevoir*, to conceive, *décevoir*, to deceive, *devoir*, to owe, *redevoir*, to owe still, *recevoir*, to receive.

15. The Imperative has no 1st person in the singular. Many grammarians give a 3rd person singular and plural of the same tense, but these persons belong really to the present of the Subjunctive, and are not formed from the present of the Indicative. This is the reason why we only give the 2nd person singular, 1st and 2nd person plural, which are formed according to the rules of formation. See pages 4, 5 of Supplement.

to accost, *accoster*
to add, *ajouter*
at once, *aussitôt*
to beg, *prier*
to brand, *flétrir*
celebrated, *célèbre*
church, *église f.*
to congratulate, *féliciter*
congratulation, *félicitation f.* [*pointer*
to disappoint, *désap-*

to doubt, *douter.*
eloquent, *éloquent*
even, *même*
future, *avenir m.*
mistake, *erreur f.*
to owe, *devoir*
preacher, *prédicateur m.*
priest, *prêtre m.*
profit, *profit m.*
to punish, *punir*

to quit, *quitter*
reasoning, *raisonnement m.*
to remain, *rester*
to render, *rendre*
short, *court*
to stop, *arrêter* [*m.*
thanks, *remerciments*
to threaten, *menacer*
usurer, *usurier m.*
usury, *usure f.*

Exercise No. 22.
(On the tenses of the verbs which have already been used in the preceding exercises.)

1. Je féliciterai,—nous punirions,—je dois,—il rend,—ne félicitez-vous pas?—nous devons,—nous désappointerons,—donnez-vous?—Je rends,—ils puniraient,—vous finirez,—il reçoit,—il ajoutera,—vous rendez,—il imite?—nous ne chantons pas,—ils finissent,—vous recevez,—nous menacerons,—ils rendent,—vous flétrissez,—nous recevrions,—nous rendons,—je vends,—ils resteraient,—nous quittons,—ils devraient,—ils flétriront,—vous recevrez,—nous vendons,—tu vends,—ils aimaient,—nous bâtissons,—ils vendaient,—elles recevaient,—ils doivent,—il vend,—vous parliez,—ne donneraient-ils pas?—ils bâtissent,—nous vendrons,—vous devez,—nous flétrissions,—ils dansent,—finiraient-ils?—vous flétrirez,—je reçois,—je vendrai,—recevrez-vous?—vous chantez,—ils marchent,—nous recevons,—il vendra,—ils bâtiront,—il doit,—tu rendras,—nous donnerons,—ils punissaient,—vous devrez,—nous ne donnons pas,—vous finissez,—nous rendrons.

2. He sings,—you would love,—we finish,—they *(m.)* receive,—we sold,—they *(m.)* finish,—I give,—he receives,—you did not sell,—I should build,—he would punish,—you walked,—I finish,—did they wait?—I receive,—you punish,—we received,—you sold,—they *(m.)* love,—you owe,—I shall sell,—he received,—I branded,—we should finish,—we congratulate,—he sold,—they *(m.)* would threaten,—we branded,—I received,—he disappoints,—we beg,—he punished,—you owed,—I shall not hear,—I sold,—I added,—he would build,—I shall receive,—we punished,—they *(f.)* finished,—you threatened,—we should receive,—will you wait?—he will owe,—they *(m.)* wait,—we shall commence,—you finished,—I shall finish,—we shall receive,—you hear,—he congratulated,—you imitated,—we should finish,—I should receive,—you will punish,—he would brand,—I shall sing,—you will receive,—he does not sell,—he would owe,—we shall punish,—do we render?—we shall dance,—they *(f.)* will owe,—we should receive,—you will finish,—he sells,—they *(m.)* will speak,—we should commence,—they *(m.)* will build,—you would receive,—I sell.

Questions on Grammar.

1. Which are the three tenses which always end in the same manner whatever may be the conjugation, whether regular or irregular?
2. What is generally the last letter of the 1st person singular?
3. What is always the last letter of the 2nd person singular?
4. What is the last letter of the 3rd person, when not a vowel?
5. What are the two endings which may be found in the 1st person plural?
6. What are the two endings of the 2nd person plural?
7. How does the 3rd person plural always end?
8. Which are the two tenses in which the 1st and 2nd plural are always the same (with very few exceptions)?
9. What are the endings of the Past Definite?
10. What are the endings of the Present of the Subjunctive?
11. What are the endings of the Imperfect of the Subjunctive?
12. In what tenses and persons is the circumflex accent to be always found on the vowel of the ending?
13. Which is the conjugation which includes the greatest number of verbs in French?
14. What are the only regular verbs of the 3rd conjugation?
15. How many persons are there in the Imperative?

Conversation.

What is the most important part of speech in all languages?	Quelle est la partie du discours la plus importante dans toutes les langues?
(It is) the verb.	C'est le verbe.
Can French verbs terminate in the Infinitive in any manner whatever?	Les verbes français peuvent-ils se terminer à l'infinitif d'une manière quelconque?
No; they can only end in four ways, viz: *er, ir, oir, re.*	Non; ils ne peuvent se terminer que de quatre manières, c'est à dire en *er, ir, oir* or *re.*
What is indicated by the ending of the infinitive of a verb?	Qu'indique la termination de l'infinitif d'un verbe?
The conjugation to which it belongs.	A quelle conjugaison il appartient.
What is to be done after ascertaining to what conjugation a verb belongs?	Que faut-il faire après s'être assuré de la conjugaison à laquelle appartient un verbe?
It must be ascertained whether it be regular or irregular.	Il faut s'assurer s'il est régulier ou irrégulier.
How can you ascertain that?	Comment pouvez-vous trouver cela?
By looking at the tables of irregular verbs, Part 14.	En regardant les tableaux des verbes irréguliers, dans la 14ème livraison.
Verbs which are not given, nor composed with any of those which are given therein, are regular.	Les verbes qui n'y sont pas donnés ou qui ne sont composés avec aucun de ceux qui y sont donnés, sont réguliers.

Reading Exercise No. 22.

Un prédicateur célèbre, ayant un jour fait[1] un magnifique sermon dans lequel il avait flétri de la manière la plus éloquente le vice détestable de l'usure, se préparait[2] à quitter l'église, lorsqu'il fut accosté par un usurier, qu'il connaissait[3] parfaitement de[4] réputation. Le prêtre, voyant[5] qu'il cherchait[6] à lui parler, se félicitait intérieurement[7] de l'effet de ses paroles, et s'attendait à ce[8] qu'il allait[9] lui annoncer sa conversion. Il commençait même à le féliciter de sa démarche[10] et de ses meilleures intentions pour l'avenir, lorsque[11] l'usurier l'arrêta court. "Je crains[12]," lui dit-il[13], "que vous ne fassiez[14] erreur: j'ai trouvé en vérité[15] que vous aviez admirablement parlé, et je reconnais[16] toute la force de vos arguments; je vous prie d'agréer[17] mes sincères félicitations, j'ajouterai même, mes remercîments: car je ne doute pas que tous ceux de mes confrères[18] qui se trouvaient à l'église n'aient été[19] profondément[20] émus[21] par votre sermon, et effrayés des châtiments[22] dont vous nous menacez, et qu'ils n'abandonnent[23] aussitôt une si infâme[24] profession. De cette façon[25] je resterai seul à faire l'usure[26]; je ferai[27] des profits considérables, je deviendrai[28] excessivement[29] riche et c'est à vous, ou plutôt[30] à votre sermon, que je devrai tout ce bonheur-là." Le pauvre prédicateur était bien[31] désappointé et il se demanda si peut-être chacun des usuriers n'avait pas fait[32] le même raisonnement.

1 *fait*, made, 2 *se préparait*, was preparing himself, 3 *connaissait*, knew, 4 *de*, by, 5 *voyant*, seeing, 6 *cherchait*, was endeavouring, 7 *intérieurement*, internally, 8 *s'attendait à ce*, expected, 9 *allait*, was going, 10 *de sa démarche*, for his step, 11 *lorsque*, when, 12 *je crains*, I fear, 13 *dit-il*, said he, 14 *fassiez*, make, 15 *en vérité*, indeed, 16 *reconnais*, acknowledge, 17 *d'agréer*, to accept, 18 *confrères*, colleagues, 19 *n'aient été*, have been, 20 *profondément*, deeply, 21 *émus*, moved, 22 *des châtiments*, by the chastisements, 23 *qu'ils n'abandonnent*, that they will abandon, 24 *une si infâme*, such an infamous, 25 *de cette façon*, in this manner, 26 *faire l'usure*, to be an usurer, 27 *ferai*, shall make, 28 *deviendrai*, shall become, 29 *excessivement*, exceedingly, 30 *plutôt*, rather, 31 *bien*, very much, 32 *fait*, made.

TWENTY-THIRD LESSON.　　　　　　　*Vingt-troisième Leçon.*

Adverbs.

The adverb is a word used to modify the sense of a verb, and also of an adjective, participle or another adverb.

In French they follow the verb in simple tenses, and in compound tenses are placed between the auxiliary and the participle.

Il parle souvent. He *often* speaks. *J'ai* bien *dormi*. I have slept *well*.

Adverbs may be divided into ten classes, viz.: adverbs of *manner, time, place, order, quantity, comparison, affirmation, negation, doubt* and *interrogation*.

Adverbs of Manner.

Adverbs of manner express how things are done.

They are formed from qualifying adjectives by the addition of *ment*. Three cases arise in this formation.

RULE. 1.—If the adjective end with a vowel, *ment* is added to the masculine.—*Joli*, pretty, *joliment*, prettily; *aisé*, easy, *aisément*, easily; *honnête*, honest, *honnêtement*, honestly.

EXCEPTIONS.—*Follement*, foolishly; *mollement*, softly; *nouvellement*, newly; *bellement*, gently; *gaiement*, gaily, are formed from the feminine adjectives, *folle, molle, nouvelle, belle, gaie*.

2.—If the adjective end with a consonant, *ment* is added to the feminine.—*Heureux*, happy, *heureusement*, happily; *long*, long, *longuement*, long *or* longly; *doux*, sweet, *doucement*, sweetly.

3.—Adjectives ending in *ant* and *ent* form their adverbs by changing *nt* into *mment:*

Prudent, prudent, *prudemment*, prudently; *constant*, constant, *constamment*, constantly; *innocent*, innocent, *innocemment*, innocently.

EXCEPTIONS.—*Lent*, slow, and *présent*, present, *véhément*, vehement, form their adverbs regularly, *lentement*, slowly; *présentement*, presently, *véhémentement*, vehemently. The adverb formed from *gentil*, nice, is *gentiment*.

REMARKS. 1.—The following adverbs take an acute accent on the *e* which precedes *ment*, when no such accent exists in the adjectives themselves.—*Aveuglément*, blindly (from *aveugle*); *commodément*, conveniently (from *commode*); *communément*, commonly (from *commun*); *conformément*, conformingly (from *conforme*); *énormément*, enormously (from *énorme*); *expressément*, expressly (from *exprès*); *importunément*, importunely (from *importun*); *obscurément*, obscurely (from *obscur*); *opiniâtrément*, obstinately (from *opiniâtre*); *précisément*, precisely (from *précis*); *profondément*, profoundly (from *profond*); *profusément*, profusely (from *profus*); *impunément*, with impunity (from *impuni*).

2.—*Bien*, well, *mal*, badly, *pis*, worse, *mieux*, better, must also be considered as adverbs of manner.

address, *adresse f.*
advice, *conseil m.*
attentive, *attentif*
cheapness, *bon marché m.*
to counsel, *conseiller*
desert, *désert m.*
despatch, *dépêche f.*
to forward, *expédier*
full, *plein*

to hang, *suspendre*
to hide, *cacher*
immediate, *immédiat*
legible, *lisible*
march, *marche f.*
name, *nom m.*
other, *autre*
to pass, *passer*
pole, *poteau m.*

to recommence, *recommencer*
to refresh, *rafraîchir*
road, *route f.*
sand, *sable m.*
suffering, *souffrance f.*
telegraph, *télégraphe m.*
wire, *fil (de fer) m.*
way, *moyen m.*

Exercise No. 23.

Form the Adverbs from the following Adjectives.

1. Facile—petit—diligent—savant—fou—triste—haut—vrai—profond—commun—lent—énorme—hardi—unique—délicat—franc—large—précis—impérieux—apparent—gentil—beau—raisonnable—démesuré—élégant—importun—chaud—innocent—aveugle—présent—mou—exprès—loyal—timide—remarquable—malheureux—gai—galant—délicieux—nouveau—fréquent—proportionné—imprudent—opiniâtre—religieux—nécessaire—égal—comique—intelligent—ingénu—propre—décent—clair—mortel—véhément—impuni.

(*) Would he sell ?—I should hear—should we wait ?—he would sell—they would not wait—they (*m.*) would hear—should I sell ?—they (*m.*) would sell—would he not sell ?—we should sell—should I not sell ?—should we sell ?—thou wouldst sell—you would hear—would they (*f.*) sell ?—you would wait—would they (*m.*) sell ?—he would hear—I should sell—would you not sell ?—we should hear—would I wait ?—would you sell ?—wouldst thou sell ?—you would sell—would she sell ?—should we not sell ?

2. Vous travaillez laborieusement. Il travaille bien et ses parents sont contents de[1] sa conduite. Il parle très éloquemment et tout le monde l'écoute[2] attentivement. Il parlait très froidement. Il apprend[3] aisément cette langue. Le temps passe rapidement. Je le vois[4] rarement. Ils sont[5] arrivés en ville et j'attends impatiemment le[6] résultat de leur visite. Nous l'aimons sincèrement. Il parle parfaitement la langue française. On trouve principalement cette fleur dans les pays froids.

The postman rarely comes[7] at eight o'clock. I wait (for) his answer impatiently. I am greatly astonished. That page is badly written,[8] you will recommence it immediately. I shall pass rapidly to the principal rules; I think that you will easily understand[9] them. That would certainly happen. He imitates his friend very well.

---

1 *de*, with 2 *l'écoute*, listens to him 3 *apprend*, learns 4 *vois*, see 5 *sont*, have 6 *le*, for the 7 comes, *vient* 8 written, *écrite* 9 will understand, *comprendrez*.
* See the conditional of *rendre*.

Questions on Grammar.

1. What is an adverb?
2. What is the place of adverbs in French?
3. How many classes of adverbs are there? what are they?
4. How do adverbs of manner end in French?
5. How are adverbs derived from adjectives ending with a vowel?
6. How are adverbs derived from adjectives ending with a consonant?
7. How are adverbs of manner derived from adjectives ending in *ant* or *ent*?
8. Give some adjectives ending with vowels which do not follow this rule?
9. Give some adverbs which take an acute accent on the *e* before *ment*?
10. Give some adverbs of manner which do not end in *ment*?

Conversation.

Who (*qui est-ce qui*) spoke so elegantly?	Qui est-ce qui a parlé si élégamment?
It (*is*) was the deputy who has been elected (*élu*) lately.	C'est le député qui a été élu dernièrement.
He speaks very slowly and distinctly. Do you hear him frequently?	Il parle très lentement et très distinctement. L'entendez-vous fréquemment?
No, I go to the house [of parliament] (*chambre*) very rarely.	Non, je vais très rarement à la chambre.
Did you arrive (*êtes vous arrivé*) safely at the end of your journey?	Etes-vous arrivé sain et sauf au terme de votre voyage?
Yes, thank you (*merci*); unhappily I found my sister dangerously ill, and I had only (the) time to run immediately to the doctor's.	Oui, merci; malheureusement j'ai trouvé ma sœur dangereusement malade, et je n'ai eu que le temps de courir immédiatement chez le docteur.
Does he come (*vient*) exactly at the time you expect him?	Vient-il exactement à l'heure à laquelle vous l'attendez?
Usually he comes very punctually.	Ordinairement il vient très ponctuellement.
Do you pay him regularly every week?	Le payez vous régulièrement chaque semaine?
Yes, I generally pay him every Saturday evening.	Oui, je le paie généralement chaque samedi soir.
Do you think really that he is in want of money?	Croyez-vous réellement qu'il ait besoin d'argent?
I think so.	Je le crois.

Reading Exercise No. 23.

On raconte qu'un paysan, dont le fils servait[1] dans un régiment en garnison[2] en Algérie,[3] reçut[4] un jour de lui une lettre dans laquelle il lui disait,[5] entre[6] autres choses, que ses souliers avaient été brûlés par le sable pendant les longues marches qu'il avait faites[7] dans le désert ; il finissait sa lettre en priant[8] son père de lui en envoyer une autre paire le plus tôt possible.[9] Nicolas,[10] c'était le nom du paysan, plein de compassion pour les fatigues et les souffrances de son fils, commanda[11] immédiatement une paire de souliers au cordonnier de son village. Mais quand ils furent faits,[12] il ne savait[13] de[14] quelle manière les lui envoyer, et il demandait conseil à tous ses amis. L'un d'eux, voulant[15] se moquer de[16] sa simplicité, lui conseilla de les lui expédier par le télégraphe, lui disant[17] qu'il n'aurait qu'[18]à les pendre au fil de fer qu'il voyait[19] soutenu[20] par des poteaux tout le long de[21] la route, et que la première dépêche, qui passerait à destination de l'Algérie, les transporterait[22] jusqu'à[23] Constantine, où se trouvait[24] alors son fils. La simplicité et le bon marché de ce moyen séduisirent[25] le paysan. Il mit[26] une adresse bien lisible, qu'avait écrite[27] le maître d'école,[28] sur les souliers ; y cacha deux pièces de cinq francs, pour que[29] son fils pût[30] se rafraîchir à sa santé et, étant sorti[31] du village, suspendit[32] les souliers au fil télégraphique, puis[33] retourna à son travail.

(To be continued.)

1 *servait*, served, 2 *garnison*, garrison, 3 *Algérie*, Algeria, 4 *reçut*, received, 5 *disait*, said, 6 *entre*, among, 7 *faites*, made, 8 *priant*, begging, 9 *le plus tôt possible*, as soon as possible, 10 *Nicolas*, Nicholas, 11 *commanda*, ordered, 12 *furent faits*, were made, 13 *savait*, knew, 14 *de*, in, 15 *voulant*, wishing, 16 *se moquer de*, laugh at, 17 *disant*, saying, 18 *ne...que*, only, 19 *voyait*, saw, 20 *soutenu*, supported, 21 *tout le long de*, all along, 22 *transporterait*, would transport them, 23 *jusqu'à*, as far as, 24 *se trouvait*, was, 25 *séduisirent*, seduced, 26 *mit*, put, 27 *écrite*, written, 28 *maître d'école*, school-master, 29 *pour que*, in order that, 30 *pût*, could, 31 *étant sorti*, having gone out, 32 *suspendit*, hung, 33 *puis*, then.

Twenty-fourth Lesson.　　　　　　*Vingt-quatrième Leçon.*

Adverbs of Time.

These adverbs are:
for the present:—*aujourd'hui*, to-day; *maintenant*, now; *à présent*, now; for the future:—*demain*, to-morrow; *après-demain*, the day after tomorrow; *bientôt*, soon; *avant peu*, shortly; *désormais*, henceforth; for the past:—*hier*, yesterday; *avant-hier*, the day before yesterday; *autrefois*, formerly; *jadis*, formerly; *depuis peu*, lately.

Other adverbs of time do not refer to any special time; as, *de bonne heure*, early; *tôt*, soon; *tard*, late; *déjà*, already; *encore*, still, yet; *souvent*, often; *longtemps*, for a long time; *toujours*, always; *jamais*, never; *tantôt*, sometimes; *quelquefois*, sometimes, &c.

Adverbs of Place.

The principal adverbs of place are:
où, where; *d'où*, from whence; *ici*, here; *là, y*, there; *devant*, before; *derrière*, behind; *dessus*, upon; *dessous*, underneath; *en haut*, above, upstairs; *en bas*, below, downstairs; *dedans, au dedans*, inside, within; *dehors, au dehors*, outside, without; *loin*, far; *près*, near; *partout*, everywhere; *auprès*, near; *ensemble*, together; *au dessus*, over; *au dessous*, beneath, &c.

Adverbs of Order.

They are generally formed from ordinal adjectives by adding *ment* to the feminine:
premièrement, firstly; *secondement*, secondly; *cinquièmement*, fifthly, &c.

There are also:—*d'abord*, at first; *auparavant*, before; *puis, ensuite*, then; *enfin*, at last; *alors*, then; *après*, after, &c.

Adverbs of Quantity.

The principal are:—*beaucoup*, much, many; *peu*, little; *un peu*, a little, rather; *assez*, enough; *trop*, too, too-much; *bien, fort, très*, very; *tout à fait*, quite; *au moins*, at least; *au plus*, at the most; *en outre*, besides; *cher*, dear; *bon marché*, cheap; *environ*, about; *seulement*, only; *ne.. que*, but, only, &c.

Adverbs of Comparison.

The principal are:—*plus*, more; *moins*, less; *aussi*, as; *comme*, as; *si*, so; *autant*, as much; *tant*, so much; *de même*, likewise; *davantage*, more; *le plus*, the most;. *le moins*, the least; *presque*, almost; *à peu près*, nearly; *que*, than, as, &c.

Adverbs of Affirmation, Negation and Doubt.

Adverbs of affirmation are:—*oui*, yes; *si*, yes (in answer to a negative question); *certes*, certainly; *vraiment*, indeed; *volontiers*, willingly; *assurément*, assuredly; *sans doute*, without doubt; *d'accord*, granted, &c.

Adverbs of negation are:—*non*, no; *ne...pas*, not; *point, pas du tout*, not at all; *nullement*, by no means; *cependant, toutefois*, however.

Adverbs of doubt are:—*peut-être*, perhaps; *probablement*, likely.

Adverbs of Interrogation.

The principal are:—*comment*, how; *combien*, how much; *combien de temps*, how long; *quand*, when; *pourquoi*, why; *où*, where, &c.

beggar, *mendiant m.*	to go out, *sortir*	to pay, *payer*
to communicate, *communiquer* [*buer*]	to grant, *accorder*	plant, *plante f.*
	hardly, *à peine*	prison, *prison f.*
to contribute, *contribuer*	idea, *idée f.*	to resist, *résister*
creditor, *créancier m.*	to lead, *conduire*	sad, *triste*
daily, *journalier*	to lock up, *enfermer*	to send back, *renvoyer*
debtor, *débiteur m.*	maintenance, *entretien m.* [*leux*]	sorrow, *chagrin m.*
to desire, *désirer*		tedious, *ennuyeux*
expense, *dépense f.*	marvellous, *merveilleux*	term, *terme m.*

Exercise No. 24.

1. My brother (has[1]) arrived the day before yesterday.—Formerly he was an officer.—I have seen[2] him very little lately.—It is still early, I thought that it was later.—I have been in France for a long time.—I was here and he was there.—Put[3] this (*m*,) before, and I shall put[4] that behind.—We were upstairs and they were downstairs.—It is very far.—You will find it everywhere.—He is outside.—They are together.—I did not like him at first.—You will speak before; I shall speak then.—He arrived[5] at last.—I like him (very) much.—It is rather dear.—You ask too much for it (of it).—This costs more.—It is nearly two o'clock.—Do you like it? Yes.—Do you not see[6] it? Yes.—I shall speak to him willingly.—I do not like him at all.—He will be here, perhaps, in two months.—How do you say[7] that?

(*)We loved—I punished—you received—we rendered—did I receive?—I loved—I did not love—he punished—did we not render?—they (*f.*) received—they (*m.*) rendered—he loved—thou renderedst—we punished—thou receivedst—I received—did you not love?—you loved—did you love?—I did not receive—you rendered—did I render?—They (*m.*) loved—he received—they (*m.*) punished—thou punishedst—we received—I rendered—we did not receive—thou lovedst—you punished.

2. Avez-vous déjà fini le livre que vous avez commencé avant-hier? Non; je le finirai demain. Etait-il dessus ou dessous? Il était dehors. Comment appelez-vous cette fleur? Aimez-vous cette plante? Non, je ne l'aime pas. Ce chapeau n'est-il pas à votre goût?—Si, je l'aime beaucoup. Pourquoi venez[8]-vous si tard. Il m'a été impossible de venir plus tôt. Trouvez-vous qu'ils vendent cela trop cher?—Un peu. Où irez[9]-vous d'abord?

Formerly he was very rich; now he is very poor. Sometimes he spoke to me. It is your cousin Charles who speaks best. He works more. My father will be here to-morrow, and we shall be there the day after to-morrow. I do not like him so much as his brother. He is very rich, and he is also very generous. I meet him sometimes in the park.

---

1 has, *est* 2 I have seen, *j'ai vu* 3 put, *mettez* 4 shall put, *mettrai* 5 arrived, *arriva* 6 do see, *voyez* 7 do say, *dites* 8 *venez*, come 9 *irez*, will go
(*) See the past definite of the four Conjugations (Supplement, p.p. 10 to 13).

Questions on Grammar.

1. Give the principal adverbs of time?
2. What are the principal adverbs of place?
3. How are adverbs of order generally formed?
4. Translate *much, as much, so much, how much.*
5. Give the adverbs of comparison mostly used.
6. What is the difference between *si* and *oui?*
7. Give some adverbs of negation?
8. Translate *how, enough, too, about.*

Conversation.

When will you be here?	Quand serez-vous ici?
I shall be here to-morrow early.	Je serai ici demain de bonne heure.
When will you start?	Quand partirez-vous?
(In) the evening as late as I can (*pourrai*).	Le soir, aussi tard que je pourrai.
How far will you go (*irez*)?	Jusqu'où irez-vous?
I shall go (*irai*) as far as the railway goes (*va*).	J'irai aussi loin que le chemin de fer va.
How long will you be absent?	Combien de temps serez-vous absent?
About two or three weeks, only.	Environ deux ou trois semaines, seulement.
How will you come back (*reviendrez*)?	Comment reviendrez-vous?
I do not know (*sais*) yet; but I think I shall come back by the steamboat.	Je ne sais pas encore; mais je pense que je reviendrai par le bateau à vapeur.
When will you write (*écrirez*) to me?	Quand m'écrirez-vous?
I shall write to you as soon as (*que*) I know (*saurai*) exactly the day of my return to London.	Je vous écrirai aussitôt que je saurai exactement le jour de mon retour à Londres.
Do you want me to do (*avez-vous besoin que je fasse*) anything for you here?	Avez-vous besoin que je fasse ici quelque chose pour vous?
I thank you (very) much indeed; I think I will accept your kind offer.	Je vous remercie beaucoup, vraiment; je pense que j'accepterai votre offre obligeante.
I shall do very willingly everything I can (*ce que je pourrai*).	Je ferai très volontiers tout ce que je pourrai.
Good bye.	Adieu!

Reading Exercise No. 24.
(continued from No. 23.)

Mais il était à peine parti,[1] qu'[2] un mendiant qui avait vu[3] de loin[4] ce qui se passait,[5] accourut,[6] s'empara[7] des souliers neufs et les remplaça par[8] les siens qui étaient dans la plus piteuse[9] condition. Une heure après, Nicolas, ne pouvant[10] résister au désir de savoir[11] si la dépêche était déjà passée[12], revint[13], et voyant[14] les vieux souliers à la place[15] des neufs : "Quelle merveilleuse rapidité," s'écria-t-il[16] ; et, décrochant[17] les vieux souliers, il alla les montrer à ses amis, disant[18] que c'étaient ceux que son fils lui avait renvoyés[19] par la même voie[20].

Un débiteur ayant été enfermé en prison pour dettes fit[21] un jour appeler son créancier. "Monsieur," lui dit-il[22], "sans vouloir[23] parler de la vie triste et ennuyeuse que je mène ici, je ne puis[24] penser sans un profond chagrin à[25] la dépense journalière que vous faites[26] ici inutilement à cause de moi[27], et j'ai voulu[28] vous communiquer une idée qui m'était venue[29]. Vous avez à payer deux francs par jour[30], pour ma détention dans cette prison. Faites[31] m'en sortir : donnez-moi ensuite un franc par jour et vous inscrirez[32] l'autre franc journellement[33] à mon avoir[34]. De[35] cette manière, vous me délivrerez[36] de ma captivité, vous contribuerez à mon entretien et vous arriverez[37] après un certain temps à éteindre[38] le capital que je vous dois." Le créancier comprit[39] que son débiteur avait raison[40], et le fit mettre[41] aussitôt en liberté : on ne sait pas[42] toutefois s'il lui accorda la pension qu'il lui demandait, ni combien de temps[43] il la lui paya.

1 était parti, *had gone*, 2 qu', *when*, 3 vu, *seen*, 4 de loin, *in the distance*, 5 se passait, *was passing*, 6 accourut, *ran*, 7 s'empara, *took possession*, 8 les remplaça par, *put in their place*, 9 piteuse, *pitiful*, 10 ne pouvant, *not being able*, 11 savoir, *knowing*, 12 passée, *passed*, 13 revint, *came back*, 14 voyant, *seeing*, 15 à la place, *in the place*, 16 s'écria-t-il, *he exclaimed*, 17 décrochant, *unhanging*, 18 disant, *saying*, 19 renvoyés, *sent back*, 20 voie, *conveyance*.
21 fit appeler, *sent for*, 22 dit-il, *he said*, 23 vouloir, *wishing*, 24 je ne puis, *I cannot*, 25 à, *of*, 26 faites, *make*, 27 à cause de moi, *on my account*, 28 voulu, *wished*, 29 était venue, *had come*, 30 par jour, *a day*, 31 faites, *cause*, 32 inscrirez, *will put down*, 33 journellement, *daily*, 34 avoir, *credit*, 35 de, *in*, 36 délivrerez, *will free*, 37 vous arriverez ... à, *you will succeed ... in*, 38 éteindre, *to pay off*, 39 comprit, *understood*, 40 avait raison, *was right*, 41 fit mettre, *caused to be put*, 42 on ne sait pas, *it is not known*, 43 combien de temps, *how long*.

TWENTY-FIFTH LESSON.   *Vingt-cinquième Leçon.*
PREPOSITIONS.

Prepositions are words placed before nouns, pronouns or verbs (in the Infinitive) to indicate the relations of these words with other words which precede. They can be divided into nine classes, viz: *place, order, union, separation, opposition, purpose, cause, means* and *specification*. (This division we give here for reference only).

Prepositions of place are: *dans*, into, in; *en*, in; *hors*, out; *devant*, before; *derrière*, behind; *sur*, on, upon; *sous*, under; *parmi*, among; *entre*, between; *vers*, towards.

Prepositions of order are: *avant*, before; *après*, after; *depuis*, since; *jusqu'à*, as far as, till.

Prepositions of union are: *avec*, with; *durant*, during; *pendant*, during, for; *outre*, besides; *selon*, according to; *suivant*, according to.

Prepositions of separation are: *sans*, without; *excepté*, except; *hormis*, save.

Prepositions of opposition are: *contre*, against; *malgré*, in spite of; *nonobstant*, notwithstanding.

Prepositions of purpose are: *envers*, towards; *touchant*, about; *pour*, for.

Prepositions of cause and means are: *par*, by; *moyennant*, by means of; *attendu*, considering.

Prepositions of specification are: *à*, to; *de*, of; *en*, in.

REMARKS 1.—Besides these prepositions, which may be called simple, there are many others, composed mostly with the preposition *à*, a noun or an adverb, and the preposition *de*.

This is a list of some of these expressions:

à cause de, on account of	*au dessous de*, under
à côté de, by	*au dessus de*, over
à fleur de, level with	*au devant de*, before
à force de, by dint of	*au derrière de*, behind
à l'égard de, with regard to, towards	*au lieu de*, instead of
à l'insu de, unknown to	*au milieu de*, amidst, in the middle of
à raison de, at the rate of	
à rebours de, contrary to	*au moyen de*, by means of
à travers de, through	*au niveau de*, even with
au delà de, on that side, beyond	*auprès de*, near
au dedans de, within	*autour de*, around
au dehors de, without	*au travers de*, through, &c.

2.—There are some other prepositions composed in a similar manner but without the preposition *à*; as,

en deçà de, on this side	*hors de*, out of	*vis à vis de*, opposite to, &c.
en dépit de, in spite of	*le long de*, along by	*tout près de*, close to
faute de, for want of	*près de*, near	*proche de*, near

3.—There are four prepositions which have *à* instead of *de;* viz: *jusqu'à*, as far as; *conformément à*, according to; *quant à*, as to; *par rapport à*, with regard to.

4.—Prepositions in French are always followed by the Infinitive.—*Je suis curieux* de *le voir.* I am curious *of* seeing it.

EXCEPTION.—The preposition *en* which before verbs generally translates *by*, is the only one which governs the present participle.

Vous l'apprendrez en *parlant.* You will learn it *by speaking.*

back, *dos m.*
ban, *ban m.*
bunch, *grappe f.*
church, *église f.*
consent, *consentement m.*
critical, *critique*
to cross, *traverser*
cupboard, *buffet m.*

fruit, *fruit m.*
grapes, *raisin m.*
impediment, *empêchement m.*
to live, *demeurer*
marriage, *mariage m.*
natural, *naturel*
nor, *ni*
to pardon, *pardonner*

to publish, *publier*
to relish, *savourer*
to resist, *résister*
to return, *retourner*
severe, *sévère*
to succeed, *réussir*
temptation, *tentation f.*
to travel, *voyager*
unhappy, *malheureux*

Exercise No. 25.

1. He is in the street.—She was before the door.—His house is between the church and your cousin's house.—We walked (*imperfect*(*)) towards Paris.—The cat is under the table.—The grapes are on the cupboard.—You will speak before him.—We shall walk as far as the town.—They were (*imp.*) with us.—I like them all, except your friend. They were(*imp.*)without money.—He has done[1] that in spite of me. This parcel is for your sister.—I have spoken to your aunt of this business. He was(*imp.*) by me.—The water was (*imp.*) nearly level with the street. He learns by dint of application.—We walked(*past definite*) at the rate of four miles an[2] hour.—His garden is on that side of the river.—I found (*p. d.*) him under a tree.—He will be here instead of his brother.—We shall walk around the garden.—The street was (*imp.*) built along the river.—He lives close to the church.—His house is opposite to ours.

(†)Receive (*s.*)—do not love—render (*p.*)—speak (*s.*)—let us render—let us sing—love (*s.*)—do not speak—let us walk—do not receive—love (*p.*)—let us cross—punish (*s.*)—let us finish—build (*s.*)—let us resist—do not punish—resist (*p.*)—render (*s.*)—do not sing—pardon (*s.*)—receive (*p.*)—finish (*s.*)—let us pardon—cross (*p.*)—let us receive—build (*p.*)—let us punish—do not render—punish (*p.*)—speak (*p.*)—let us love.

2. Mon oncle est venu au devant de[3] moi. Son mariage a été conclu[4] malgré mes objections. J'ai acheté ces fruits près de l'église. Il a chanté au lieu de son cousin. On ne peut[5] rien apprendre[6] sans travailler. Nous sommes venus[7] en marchant le long de la rivière. Ce village est situé en deçà de la montagne. Il a résisté en dépit de la tentation. Le buffet était entre les deux fenêtres.

My brother was (*imp.*) with me in the garden all the afternoon. He does not succeed for want of application. Sit down[8] close to me. Pay him that money at the rate of ten francs a[9] month. Walk about[10] two hours and you will arrive on that side of the mountain.

1 done, *fait* 2 an, *par* 3 *est venu au devant de*, has come to meet 4 *conclu*, concluded 5 *peut*, can 6 *apprendre*, to learn 7 *sommes venus*, have come 8 sit down, *asseyez-vous* 9 a, *par* 10 about, *environ*

(*) As the past definite has been given in the preceding lesson, we shall now indicate when the English past will have to be translated either by the past definite or by the Imperfect.

(†) See for the Imperative of the four conjugations (Supplement, p.p. 10 to 13).

Questions on Grammar.

1. What are prepositions?
2. Into how many classes can prepositions be divided?
3. Give the principal prepositions of place.
4. Translate *before* and *after* as prepositions of order.
5. What are the principal prepositions of union and separation?
6. Translate *against, in spite of*.
7. Give the principal prepositions of purpose, cause and means.
8. What are the prepositions of specification?
9. Translate *on account of, unknown to, contrary to*.
10. Give some compound prepositions, which do not begin with the preposition *à*.
11. What is the preposition which is the last word of nearly every compound preposition?
12. What are the four compound prepositions which end with *à* instead of *de*?
13. What mood do prepositions govern in French?
14. What is the only preposition which governs the present participle?

Conversation.

In what room do you live?	Dans quelle chambre demeurez-vous?
I live in the room of the second floor between yours and my brother's.	Je demeure dans la chambre du deuxième étage, entre la vôtre et celle de mon frère.
Can you see (*pouvez-vous voir*) far beyond the wall of the garden?	Pouvez-vous voir loin au delà du mur du jardin ?
I can see (*je peux voir*) the park and all the houses built along the river.	Je peux voir le parc et toutes les maisons bâties le long de la rivière.
How long will you stay with them?	Combien de temps resterez-vous avec eux?
Till the end of the month.	Jusqu'à la fin du mois.
How did you learn (*avez-vous appris*) French so well?	Comment avez-vous si bien appris le français ?
By dint of perseverance, by means of a good grammar and by taking advantage of every opportunity I found to speak it.	A force de persévérance, au moyen d'une bonne grammaire et en profitant de toutes les occasions que je trouvais de le parler.
How long did you learn it?	Combien de temps l'avez-vous appris?
I learned it (*ai appris*) for two years and a half?	Je l'ai appris pendant deux ans et demi.

Reading Exercise No. 25.

Un écolier[1] revenait[2] de l'église, où il avait entendu[3] publier des bans de mariage. En traversant le réfectoire il vit[4] sur le buffet des raisins magnifiques, et ne pouvant[5] résister à la tentation il en prit[6] un ; puis se rappelant[7] la manière dont[8] les bans avaient été publiés, et ne se croyant[9] vu[10], ni entendu[11] de personne, il dit : "Il y a[12] promesse de mariage entre cette grappe de raisin et ma bouche : toute personne qui connaîtrait[13] quelque empêchement à ce futur mariage est tenue[14] de le faire savoir[15] avant la célébration." Alors il savoura le fruit qui, très bon naturellement, avait en outre l'attrait[16] du fruit défendu[17]. Malheureusement le directeur l'avait aperçu[18] et entendu à travers une fenêtre entr'ouverte[19] et quelques instants après il le faisait venir[20] dans son cabinet[21], et sans autre préambule[22], il s'écriait[23] en brandissant[24] une verge[25] : "Il y a promesse de mariage entre cette verge et votre dos : toute personne qui connaîtrait quelque empêchement à ce futur mariage est tenue de le faire savoir avant la célébration." Toutefois, dans ce moment critique, l'écolier ne perdit[26] pas son sang-froid[27] et avant que le bras vengeur[28] ne fût retombé[29] sur lui : "Arrêtez, Monsieur le Directeur," s'écria-t-il, "je connais[30] un empêchement au mariage projeté[31] : c'est qu'une des deux parties intéressées[32] n'y donne pas son consentement." Cette repartie[33] désarma[34] la colère du maître, qui pardonna à l'écolier, après l'avoir cependant sévèrement admonesté[35].

1 *écolier*, school boy, 2 *revenait*, was coming back, 3 *entendu*, heard, 4 *vit*, saw, 5 *ne pouvant*, not being able, 6 *prit*, took, 7 *se rappelant*, remembering, 8 *dont*, in which, 9 *croyant*, believing, 10 *vu*, seen, 11 *entendu*, heard. 12 *il y a*, there is, 13 *connaîtrait*, would know, 14 *tenue*, bound, 15 *faire savoir*, make known, 16 *attrait*, attraction, 17 *défendu*, forbidden, 18 *aperçu*, perceived, 19 *entr'ouverte*, ajar, 20 *faisait venir*, made him come, 21 *cabinet*, study, 22 *préambule*, preamble, 23 *s'écriait*, exclaimed, 24 *brandissant*, brandishing, 25 *verge*, rod, 26 *perdit*, lost, 27 *sang-froid*, coolness, 28 *vengeur*, avenging, 29 *fût retombé*, had fallen, 30 *connais*, know, 31 *projeté*, projected, 32 *intéressées*, interested, 33 *repartie*, reply, 34 *désarma*, disarmed, 35 *admonesté*, admonished.

TWENTY-SIXTH LESSON. *Vingt-sixième Leçon.*

Conjunctions.

Conjunctions are so called because they join together sentences or the different parts of sentences.

There are two kinds of conjunctions : simple conjunctions, which consist of one word only, and compound conjunctions.

Government of Conjunctions.

Conjunctions govern either the infinitive, indicative or subjunctive. Those governing the infinitive are formed with the preposition *de*, as, *afin de*, in order to; *à moins de*, unless ; *avant de*, before ; *au lieu de*, instead of ; *de crainte de*, for fear that, &c.

Il vint me voir avant de *partir*. He came to see me *before* leaving.

In order to use an infinitive after a conjunction, it is necessary that this infinitive should refer to the subject of the principal sentence, as in the above example, which would not be correct if *partir* should refer to *me* instead of *il*.

As a rule, simple conjunctions all govern the indicative.

Je parlerai si vous voulez. I shall speak *if* you like.
Je pense, donc je suis. I think, *then* I exist.
Je viendrai quand il sera ici. I shall come *when* he is here.

The following conjunctions, all formed with the conjunction *que*, govern the subjunctive :

afin que, in order that	*loin que*, far from
à moins que, unless	*malgré que*, although
avant que, before	*non pas que*, not that
au cas que, in case that	*pour que*, in order that
bien que, though, although	*pourvu que*, provided that
de crainte que, lest	*quoique*, although
de peur que, for fear that	*sans que*, without
encore que, though	*soit que*, whether
jusqu'à ce que, till, until	*supposé que*, suppose that

The conjunction *que*, that, governs the subjunctive after verbs used negatively, and also verbs which imply an idea of fear, doubt, emotion, uncertainty, wish or command, and impersonal verbs. (*)

Je désire qu'il vienne. I wish *that he may come*.
Je ne veux pas qu'il parte. I do not wish *him to go*.
Il faut que vous parliez. You *must* speak.

A moins que, unless, *de crainte que*, *de peur que*, lest, for fear that, always require the verb that follows them to be preceded by the particle *ne*.

A moins qu'il ne vienne. Unless he should come.
De peur qu'il ne parte. For fear that he would leave.

After *Avant que* the verb may be preceded by *ne*.

Reviendra-t-il avant que je ne sorte ? Will he return before I go out ?

(*) Rules about the use of the Subjunctive are given in full in Lesson 74, page 294.

to answer, *répondre*	interval, *intervalle m.*	reign, *règne m.*
to assign, *assigner*	to inundate, *inonder*	to remain, *demeurer*
bet, *pari m.*	market, *marché m.*	to roll, *rouler*
to continue, *continuer*	mud, *boue f.*	to sell, *vendre*
definite, *défini*	pace, *pas m.*	soil, *sol m.*
to gain, *gagner*	praise, *éloge m.*	sonorous, *sonore*
gesture, *geste m.*	to pretend, *prétendre*	speech, *discours m.*
to increase, *accroître*	prey, *proie f.*	unbecoming, *malséant*
to indicate, *indiquer*		

Exercise No. 26.

1. In order to speak.—Before answering.—If you like.—When you sing.—In order that you may arrive(*).—Unless you pretend.—Before you continue.—In case that he may sell his horse.—Although you indicate to me his house.—Lest you fall.—For fear that you recommence.—Though you are very prudent.—Till he answers.—Although he has no fortune.—Although he speaks perfectly.—Not that I am satisfied.—In order that he may sell it.—Provided that we give him that.—Although it is late.—Without your buying anything.—Whether they are ill.—Suppose that he is absent.

(*)That you may love—that I might love—that he may not love—that we might not love—that I may sing—that we might love—that we may sing—that thou mightest love—that he may walk—that thou mayest love—that they *(m.)* might love—that you may not love—that we might continue—that he may love—that you might love—that they *(f.)* might not love—that he may sing—that we may love—that I may love—that he might love—that we may give—that he may not remain.

2. Je continuerai pourvu que vous me donniez votre opinion. Soit que vous soyez indiscret, ou que vous agissiez imprudemment il ne vous aime pas. Je viendrai[1] en cas que vous soyez à la maison[2]. Bien que vous ne l'aimiez pas, il parle toujours bien de vous. Je vous donnerai une lettre afin que vous la lui donniez. Il nous apporte toujours des fruits, quoique je ne les aime pas beaucoup. Je lui donne peu de travail, afin qu'il ait le temps d'aller vous voir[3]. Je pars[4] de peur qu'il ne m'attende.

Speak to him in order that he may give it *(m.)* to my brother. I like him although he speaks badly of me. I will remain until your uncle arrives. I refuse whether he is satisfied or not[5]. Send it immediately lest he will receive *(pres. subj.)* it too late. I lend it *(f.)* to you until I commence my lessons. I say[6] it to you in order that you may buy some in the[7] market. This coat is good although it is very cheap.

---

[1] *viendrai*, will come [2] *à la maison*, at home [3] *d'aller vous voir*, to go and see you [4] *pars*, leave [5] not, *non* [6] I say, *je dis* [7] in the, *au*

(*) See Supplt. for the Subjunctive of verbs Pages 6 to 13.

Questions on Grammar.

1. Why are conjunctions so called?
2. How many kinds of conjunctions are there?
3. What moods do conjunctions govern in French?
4. Which are the conjunctions which govern the Infinitive?
5. What is the condition required to use the Infinitive after conjunctions?
6. What are the conjunctions which govern the Indicative?
7. How are the conjunctions formed which govern the Subjunctive?
8. Give some of the conjunctions which govern the Subjunctive?
9. When does the conjunction *que* govern the Subjunctive?
10. What are the conjunctions which require the particle *ne* to be placed before the verb that follows *que*?

Conversation.

What will you do this morning before you go to your office?	Que ferez-vous ce matin, avant d'aller à votre bureau?
I shall write a letter in order to know if I must go and see my uncle this evening.	J'écrirai une lettre afin de savoir si je dois aller voir mon oncle dans la soirée.
Will you take me with you if you go?	Voulez-vous m'emmener avec vous si vous y allez?
With great pleasure, unless Mr X. should accompany me.	Avec grand plaisir, à moins que Monsieur X. ne m'accompagne.
Will you come back before I go to bed?	Reviendrez-vous avant que j'aille me coucher?
I do not know, although I shall do my best in order to be here as soon as possible.	Je ne sais pas, quoique je veuille faire de mon mieux pour être ici le plus tôt possible.
In case that I should go with you, could you tell me what train you intend to take in order that I might meet you at the station.	Au cas que j'aille avec vous, pourriez-vous me dire quel train vous avez l'intention de prendre afin que je puisse vous rencontrer à la station.
It will be six o'clock before I am able to leave the office; although I should like very much to leave earlier.	Il sera six heures avant que je puisse quitter le bureau; quoique je désire beaucoup le quitter plus tôt.
Then I shall be at the station at half past six.	Je serai donc à la station à six heures et demie.
Do you take much luggage with you?	Emportez-vous beaucoup de bagages?
No, I only take a very small portmanteau.	Non, je ne prends qu'un très petit porte-manteau.

Reading Exercise No. 26.

Le docteur Samuel Johnson fit[1] un jour un pari avec l'un de ses amis: il prétendait qu'il irait[2] au marché de poissons de Billingsgate et qu'il mettrait[3] une des marchandes[4] en colère, sans dire[5] un mot qu'elle pût[6] comprendre.[7] Il s'y rendit[8] en effet[9] et s'étant mis[10] à quelques pas d'une de ces dames, il se boucha[11] le nez avec affectation pour indiquer que le poisson qu'elle vendait n'était pas plus frais[12] qu'il ne fallait[13]. Le geste ne demeura pas inaperçu[14], et le docteur fut inondé d'épithètes[15] aussi sonores que malséantes, la dernière desquelles assignait à la mère du docteur une place bien définie dans le règne des quadrupèdes[16]. Le docteur lui répondit: "Vous êtes un article, Madame!" — "Pas plus article que vous-même[17], rustre mal élevé[18]." — "Madame vous êtes un substantif." — "Et vous ... vous ... vous," bégaya[19] la virago[20], à qui la colère de se voir insultée[21] en des termes inconnus[22] ôtait[23] déjà l'usage de la parole[24]. — "Vous êtes un pronom!" La marchande écuma de[25] rage, mais ne put proférer que[26] des sons inarticulés[27]. — "Vous êtes un verbe, un participe, un adverbe, un adjectif, une conjonction, une préposition, une interjection, continua Johnson en lançant[28] chacun de ces mots, par intervalle, de façon à[29] en accroître la portée[30]. L'énumération des dix parties du discours, n'avait jamais produit[31] un effet aussi formidable: à la dixième, la dame de Billingsgate se roulait dans la boue qui couvrait[32] le sol, en proie à de véritables convulsions: Johnson avait gagné son pari.

1 *fit*, made, 2 *irait*, would go, 3 *mettrait*, would put, 4 *marchandes*, stall-keepers, 5 *dire*, saying, 6 *pût*, could, 7 *comprendre*, understand, 8 *s'y rendit*, betook himself there, 9 *en effet*, in fact, 10 *s'étant mis*, having placed himself, 11 *boucha*, stopped, 12 *plus frais*, sweeter, 13 *qu'il ne fallait*, than it was necessary, 14 *inaperçu*, unperceived, 15 *d'épithètes*, with epithets, 16 *quadrupèdes*, quadrupeds, 17 *vous-même*, yourself, 18 *rustre mal élevé*, villanous scoundrel, 19 *bégaya*, stammered, 20 *virago*, virago, 21 *se voir insultée*, seeing herself abused, 22 *inconnus*, unknown, 23 *ôtait*, took away, 24 *l'usage de la parole*, the faculty of speaking, 25 *écuma de*, foamed with, 26 *ne put proférer que*, could only utter, 27 *inarticulés*, inarticulate, 28 *lançant*, casting, 29 *de façon à*, in such a manner as to, 30 *la portée*, the effect, 31 *produit*, produced, 32 *couvrait*, covered.

Twenty-seventh Lesson. *Vingt-septième Leçon.*

Conjunctions *(continued).*
(This lesson is for reference only.)

Besides their division into simple and compound, conjunctions are also divided into *copulative, augmentative, alternative, hypothetic, adversative, extensive, periodical, causative, conclusive, explicative, transitive* and *conductive.*

I.—*Copulative* conjunctions merely connect without adding anything to the idea; there are two of them: *et,* and, *ni,* neither, nor.

II.—*Augmentative* imply an idea of augmentation; they are the following: *de plus, bien plus, au surplus,* moreover; *d'ailleurs, outre que,* besides; *encore,* still.

III.—*Alternative* imply an idea of alternative or distinction they are as follow: *ou,* or; *ou bien,* either; *sinon,* if not; *tantôt,* sometimes.

IV.—*Hypothetic* or *conditional* conjunctions imply the idea of a condition without which what is meant by the principal sentence ceases to take place. The principal are the following: *si,* if, whether; *soit que,* whether; *pourvu que,* provided that; *à moins que,* unless; *quand,* when; *à condition que,* under the condition that; *en cas que,* in case that; *supposé que,* suppose that.

V.—*Adversative* conjunctions are those which indicate some difference, opposition or restriction between what precedes and what follows them, as, *mais,* but; *quoique,* although; *bien que,* though; *cependant,* however; *néanmoins,* nevertheless; *toutefois,* however; *de peur que, de crainte que,* lest, for fear that, &c.

VI.—*Extensive* conjunctions connect while enlarging the idea. They are: *jusqu'à ce que,* till; *encore,* still; *enfin,* at last; *aussi,* also; *même,* even; *tant,* so much.

VII.—*Periodical* conjunctions refer to a certain period or time, as: *quand, lorsque,* when; *dans le temps que,* at the time when; *pendant que, durant que,* while; *tandis que,* whilst; *tant que,* as long as; *aussitôt que,* as soon as; *dès que,* since; *avant que,* before; *depuis que,* since; *après que,* after; *à peine,* hardly, &c.

VIII.—*Causative* conjunctions imply an idea of cause or motive, as, *afin que,* in order that; *parce que,* because; *comme,* as; *car,* for; *puisque,* since; *d'autant que,* whereas; *aussi,* also; *attendu que,* considering that.

IX.—*Conclusive* conjunctions deduce a conclusion from a preceding sentence, as, *or,* now; *donc,* then; *par conséquent,* consequently; *c'est pourquoi,* therefore.

X.—*Explicative* conjunctions connect two sentences while conveying further explanations, as, *comme,* as; *en tant que,* as; *savoir, c'est-à-dire,* that is to say; *surtout,* above all; *de sorte que, de façon que,* so that; *si bien que,* so that.

XI.—*Transitive* conjunctions imply the idea of transition, as: *or,* now; *au reste,* besides; *du reste,* moreover; *après tout,* after all; *quant à,* as for, as to.

all at once, *tout de suite*
American, *américain*
to declare, *déclarer*
detail, *détail m.*
England, *Angleterre f.*
extraordinary, *extraordinaire*
fact, *fait m.*
feat, *prouesse f.*
journey, *voyage m.*

lie, *mensonge m.*
matter, *matière f.*
ocean, *océan m.*
once, *une fois*
passenger, *passager m.*
pigeon, *pigeon m.*
port, *port m.*
precise, *précis*
to relate, *raconter*
to remark, *remarquer*

to repeat, *répéter*
skill, *adresse f.*
steamboat, *bateau-à-vapeur m.*
story, *histoire f.*
to talk, *causer*
triumph, *triomphe m.*
turn, *tour m.*
United-States, *Etats-Unis m.*

Exercise No. 27.

1. The cat and the dog.—I remark and I repeat.—Neither you nor I. —Neither my brother nor my sister.—Moreover he has much skill. —Besides I have visited[1] all the ports of the Ocean.—Either you or I. —If not I shall go[2] to the United States.—If you like.—Whether you are satisfied or not.—Unless you repeat it.—When you would be here. —But he is an honest man.—Although you are my brother.—However you are discontented.—Lest he should be ill.—Till you are old.—When I was at Paris.—While he was young.—As soon as you come[3].—After he had finished.—Because it is extraordinary.—As you know[4].

(*)That we may punish—that I might punish—that you may receive —that he might not receive—that thou mightest not punish—that they *(m.)* might punish—that I may receive—that she may receive—that I might not receive—that he may punish—that we might punish—that you might receive—that we may receive—that they *(m.)* might not receive—that you may punish—that you might punish—that they *(f.)* may receive—that she may not receive—that thou mayest punish—that he might punish—that they *(f.)* may punish.

2. Je parlerai à votre ami et je lui dirai[5] de venir[6] demain matin. Je n'aime ni son frère ni sa sœur. Ou bien vous me donnerez celui-là, ou bien j'en achèterai un autre. Vous finirez votre travail, sinon vous serez puni. Tantôt il arrivait par le bateau à vapeur, tantôt il venait par le chemin de fer[7]. Je répèterai cette règle si vous le trouvez nécessaire. Quoique vous lui ayez raconté ce voyage extraordinaire il ne vous a pas cru[8]. Aussitôt que vous aurez fini de causer, je parlerai. Je dis[9] cela afin que vous soyez prudent.

We shall commence our journey all at once for fear that the weather might be[10] too bad if we should wait[11] till Saturday. If you repeat this extraordinary story, people will think that you are an impostor. He is very learned, however he is very modest. I shall punish him because he has talked during the lesson. I shall remain until he comes back[12] from his journey. Sometimes I find it easy, sometimes I find it difficult.

---

1 visited, *visité* 2 I shall go, *j'irai* 3 come, *viendrez* 4 know, *savez* 5 *dirai*, shall tell 6 *de venir*, to come 7 *chemin de fer*, railway 8 *cru*, believed 9 *dis*, say 10 would be, *ne soit* 11 should wait, *attendions* 12 comes back, *revienne*
(*) See Suppl. for the subjunctive of verbs of the 2nd and 3rd Conjugations (Pages 11 and 12)

Questions on Grammar.

1. How also can conjunctions be divided?
2. Is there any idea implied in *copulative* conjunctions? what are they?
3. What is the idea implied in *augmentative* conjunctions? give some.
4. What idea do *alternative* conjunctions imply? what are they?
5. What do *hypothetic* or *conditional* conjunctions imply? give some.
6. What are *adversative* conjunctions? give some.
7. What is the effect of *extensive* conjunctions? give some.
8. To what do *periodical* conjunctions refer? give some.
9. What is the idea implied in *causative* conjunctions? give some.
10. What is deduced by *conclusive* conjunctions? give some.
11. How do *explicative* conjunctions connect two sentences? give some.
12. What is the idea implied in *transitive* conjunctions? give some.

Conversation.

Did you bring your brother and sister with you?	Avez-vous amené votre frère et votre sœur avec vous?
I brought neither the one nor the other, but they will come this afternoon.	Je n'ai amené ni l'un ni l'autre, mais ils viendront cette après-midi.
When will you go to Paris?	Quand irez-vous à Paris?
I shall go there either in August or in September.	J'irai soit en août, soit en septembre.
Though you are very busy, I should like you to pay us a visit in the country. Could you come next Saturday?	Quoique vous soyez très occupé, je voudrais que vous nous fissiez une visite à la campagne. Pourriez-vous venir samedi prochain?
I cannot tell you until I have seen my partner, but I shall let you know before Friday.	Je ne puis vous le dire, jusqu'à ce que j'aie vu mon associé, mais je vous le ferai savoir avant vendredi.
Will you come and see my father while I am away?	Viendrez-vous voir mon père, tandis que je serai absent?
I shall come and see him every Sunday, if not twice a week.	Je viendrai le voir chaque dimanche, sinon deux fois par semaine.
I should like you also to write to me often.	J'aimerais aussi que vous m'écrivissiez souvent.
I shall do so under the condition that you will answer me immediately.	Je le ferai, à la condition que vous me répondiez immédiatement.
Have you bought a house since I saw you last week?	Avez-vous acheté une maison depuis que je vous ai vu la semaine dernière?
Yes, I bought one the day before yesterday.	Oui, j'en ai acheté une avant-hier.

Reading Exercise No. 27.

Pendant le dernier voyage d'un bateau à vapeur qui fait le service[1] entre l'Angleterre et les Etats-Unis, deux passagers, l'un Anglais et l'autre Américain, causaient de prouesses en matière de force et d'adresse. Tout-à-coup, et après avoir parlé des exploits[2] des autres, l'Américain déclara qu'il lui était arrivé[3] une fois de tirer[4] neuf cent-quatre-vingt-dix-neuf pigeons, l'un après l'autre. "Pourquoi pas mille?" remarqua son interlocuteur.—"J'ai dit[5] neuf cent-quatre-vingt-dix-neuf," répéta l'Américain d'un air vexé.[6] "Je ne ferais[7] certainement pas un mensonge pour un pigeon." Ce fut alors le tour de l'Anglais qui raconta avec des détails très circonstanciés,[8] le fait extraordinaire d'un homme qui avait nagé[9] tout le temps de Liverpool à Boston. "L'avez-vous vu[10]?" demanda l'Américain: "Si je l'ai vu? je faisais[11] précisément comme aujourd'hui la traversée[12] de l'Océan, et nous passâmes tout près de lui[13] à[14] quelques milles du port de Boston." —"Eh bien[15]! Monsieur," s'écria[16] l'Américain, d'un[17] air de triomphe "je suis bien heureux que vous l'ayez vu[18]: c'était moi; et, désormais[19], si quelqu'un a l'air[20] de douter[21] de la véracité de cette histoire, j'en appellerai[22] à votre témoignage[23], puisque vous avez été témoin oculaire[24] de mon exploit.

1 *fait le service*, plies, 2 *exploits*, exploits, 3 *était arrivé*, had happened 4 *tirer*, to shoot, 5 *j'ai dit*, I have said, 6 *vexé*, vexed, 7 *ferais*, would make, 8 *circonstanciés*, precise, 9 *nagé*, swum, 10 *vu*, seen, 11 *je faisais*, I was making, 12 *la traversée*, the (sea) voyage, 13 *tout près de lui*, close to him, 14 *à*, within, 15 *eh bien*, very well, 16 *s'écria*, exclaimed, 17 *d'*, with, 18 *ayez vu*, have seen, 19 *désormais*, henceforth, 20 *a l'air*, seems, 21 *de douter*, to suspect, 22 *j'en appellerai*, I shall appeal, 23 *témoignage*, testimony, 23 *témoin oculaire*, eye witness.

Twenty-eighth Lesson.   *Vingt-huitième Leçon*

Conjunctions *(concluded)*.

XII.—The *conductive* conjunction, which is so called because it conducts the sentence to its perfection, is the conjunction *que*, that. (See Lesson 26).

Que conjunction must not be confounded with *que* adverb and *que* relative or interrogative pronoun.

Que is an adverb at the beginning of the second term of a comparison, and translates *as, than*.

Il est plus riche que *moi*. He is richer *than* I. *Il est aussi savant* que *son frère*. He is as learned *as* his brother.

Que is also adverb, when joined to *ne*, in the meaning of *only, but*, or at the beginning of exclamative sentences in the meaning of *how*.

Il n'a que *quinze ans*. He is *but* fifteen years old.
Que *vous êtes bon! How* kind you are!

Que is a relative pronoun when it is preceded by a noun or pronoun, called its antecedent, and translates *whom* or *which*.

L'homme que *vous connaissez*. The man *whom* you know.
Le livre que *vous lisez*. The book *which* you read.
C'est le mien que *vous avez*. It is mine *which* you have.

Que is an interrogative pronoun, when at the beginning of an interrogative sentence and translates *what*.

Que *voulez-vous? What* do you wish!

Interjections,

Interjections are words used to express the sudden affections of the mind.

They are divided into:

1. Interjections of joy, as, *ah!* ah! *bon!* well!
2. grief: *ah!* ah! *hélas!* alas! *aïe! ouf!* dear me!
3. fear: *ah!* ah! *oh!* oh!
4. aversion: *fi! fi donc!* fie!
5. consent: *soit!* let it be so!
6. derision: *bah!* pshaw!
7. surprise: *eh! eh bien! hé!* ah! halloo!
8. to encourage: *allons! courage! ça!* come on! cheer up!
9. to warn: *gare!* beware! *holà!* hoa! hoy!
10. to call: *holà!* hoa! hoy! *hé!* eh!
11. to impose silence: *chut!* hush!
12. to applaud: *bravo!* bravo! hurrah!

Note.—*Oh* is spelled *ô* before nouns and pronouns:
ô *Dieu!* Oh God! ô *mon père!* Oh my father! ô *vous!* Oh you!

apartment, *appartement m.*	empire, *empire m.*	to open, *ouvrir*
ape, *singe m.*	to employ, *employer*	to oppose, *opposer*
blow, *coup m.*	to exasperate, *exaspérer*	philosopher, *philosophe m.*
cane, *canne f.*	extreme, *extrême*	to prepare, *préparer*
coach, *voiture f.*	face, *figure f.*	proceeding, *procédé m.*
comedy, *comédie f.*	German, *allemand*	to protest, *protester*
to consist, *consister*	to increase, *augmenter*	Prussia, *Prusse f.*
to dress, *habiller*	inn, *auberge f.*	to try, *essayer*
effort, *effort m.*	means, *moyen m.*	

Exercise No. 28.

1. I think that his face is very beautiful.—I do not think that the coach stops[1] at the inn.—He is more learned than his brother.—He has but one brother.—How patient you are!—The professor whom you know[2].—The news which he received *(past def.)*.—It is she whom he liked *(imp.)* best.—Well! I am very satisfied.—Alas! his father is dead. Fie! what have you done[3]?—Let it be so! I accept it.—Halloo! where are you?—Come on, my friends!—Beware, the passage is very dangerous. Hoa! come this way[4].—Hush! your mother sleeps[5].

(*)That we may return—that he might return—that they *(f.)* may return—that he might not return—that I may return—that we might return—that she may not return—that I might return—that he may not return—that you may return—that you might not return—that she may not return—that you might return—that we might not return—that they *(m.)* may return—that thou mayest return.

2. Je désire que vous alliez[6] voir[7] cette comédie. Je ne trouve pas que cette dame habille ses enfants avec beaucoup de goût. Les fleurs que vous avez dans votre jardin sont très belles. Les amis que vous avez sont très fidèles. Que vous êtes heureux! Je n'ai que deux heures à demeurer avec vous. Que désirez-vous? Je désire que vous soyez heureux. Hélas! il a perdu[8] toute sa fortune. Holà! votre père est dans la chambre et il désire que vous veniez[9]. Courage! vous aurez bientôt fini votre travail. Bravo! vos efforts seront récompensés. Silence! votre frère dort[10]. Fi donc! vous avez fait[11] une mauvaise action.

I believe[12] that he will be exasperated: he will protest against such[13] proceedings. Prussia is but one part of the German empire. H apartment consists of[14] four rooms rather[15] large than small. Ho beautiful those flowers are. Beware, the ape bites[16]. Let it be so, I shall give you ten francs for this cane. Hush! you will increase his grief if you speak to him of his misfortune.

* stops, *s'arrête* 2 know, *connaissez* 3 done, *fait* 4 come this way, *venez par ici* 5 sleeps, *dort* 6 *alliez*, may go 7 *voir*, to see 8 *perdu*, lost 9 *venez*, should come 10 *dort*, sleeps 11 *fait*, done 12 believe, *crois* 13 such, *de tels*, 14 of, *en* 15 rather, *plutôt* 16 bites, *mord*

(*) See Supplt. for the subjunctive of verbs of the 4th conjugation Page 1s.

Questions on Grammar.

1. What is the *conductive* conjunction?
2. Why is it so called?
3. What are the words with which *que* conjunction must not be confounded?
4. When is *que* an adverb?
5. When is *que* a relative pronoun?
6. When is *que* an interrogative pronoun?
7. What are interjections?
8. Give the interjections of *joy, grief, fear,* and *aversion.*
9. Give the interjections of *consent, derision, surprise, encouragement.*
10. What are the interjections used *to warn, to call, to silence, to applaud?*

Conversation.

What do you require?	Que voulez-vous?
I wish you to go to the bank to bring that money.	Je désire que vous alliez à la banque pour porter cet argent.
My brother has more time than I; would you allow him to go there instead of me?	Mon frère a plus de temps que moi; voulez-vous lui permettre d'y aller à ma place?
Let it be so! but tell him to go at once.	Soit! mais dites-lui d'y aller tout de suite.
Come on! be quick and do not remain too long away. When do you think you will be back?	Allons! dépêchez-vous et ne restez pas trop longtemps absent. Quand pensez-vous que vous serez de retour?
I do not think that I shall be away more than three quarters of an hour.	Je ne pense pas que je sois absent plus de trois quarts d'heure.
Take care! there is a cab: did you not see it?	Gare! voilà un fiacre: ne l'aviez-vous pas vu?
Yes, but I did not think that there was the slightest danger.	Si, mais je ne pensais pas qu'il y eût le moindre danger.
Halloo! where are you going?	Holà! où allez-vous?
I am going to the printing office.	Je vais à l'imprimerie.
Ah! have you anything to do there?	Ah! avez-vous quelque chose à y faire?
Certainly: I must go and correct some proofs.	Certainement: il faut que j'aille corriger quelques épreuves.
Will you remain there for a long time?	Y resterez-vous longtemps?
Oh no! I shall only be there a few minutes.	Oh non! je n'y resterai que quelques minutes.
Hush! somebody is speaking to me and I cannot hear what he says.	Chut! quelqu'un me parle et je ne peux pas entendre ce qu'il me dit.

Reading Exercise No. 28.

Lorsque Frédéric le Grand, roi de Prusse, allait faire[1] de petites excursions, il emmenait[2] souvent Voltaire avec lui. Il arriva[3] donc qu'une fois[4] le roi s'étant conformé[5] à cette habitude, que le philosophe le suivait[6] seul dans une voiture. Or un jeune page, que Voltaire avait fait punir[7] sévèrement, quelques jours auparavant, avait résolu[8] de se venger,[9] et comme le service[10] du jeune homme consistait à précéder[11] le roi, et à voir[12] si les relais[13] avaient été préparés, il raconta à tous les maîtres-de-poste[14] que le roi avait un vieux singe qu'il aimait beaucoup, qu'il habillait comme un gentilhomme[15] et qu'il emmenait dans ses voyages. "L'animal," disait-il[16], "ne connaît que[17] Sa Majesté; il est très-méchant[18], et s'il voulait[19] essayer de sortir[20] de sa voiture, il faudrait[21] employer tous les moyens pour l'en empêcher[22]." Chaque fois donc que[23] Voltaire arrivait à une maison de poste[24] et voulait[25] descendre[26] de voiture, les gens[27] de l'auberge s'opposaient à ses efforts: plusieurs fois même[28], comme il sortait[29] la main pour ouvrir la portière[30], il reçut sur les doigts de bons coups de canne, à la risée[31] des assistants. Voltaire ne savait[32] pas un mot d'Allemand et ne pouvait[33] protester contre de pareils[34] procédés: sa rage en était extrême et les contorsions de sa figure augmentaient encore l'hilarité générale: La nouvelle se répandit[35] de village en village et tout le monde accourait[36] pour voir[37] le singe du roi. Cette comédie se renouvela[38] tout le long de la route, et pour exaspérer encore la colère de Voltaire, le roi trouva le tour[39] si bon qu'il ne voulut[40] pas que l'auteur en fût puni.

1 *allait faire*, went to make, 2 *emmenait*, took, 3 *il arriva*, it happened, 4 *une fois*, once, 5 *s'étant conformé à*, having complied with, 6 *suivait*, followed, 7 *avait fait punir*, had caused to be punished, 8 *résolu*, resolved, 9 *de se venger*, to revenge himself, 10 *service*, duty, 11 *à précéder*, in preceding, 12 *à voir*, seeing, 13 *relais*, relays, 14 *maîtres-de-poste*, post-masters, 15 *gentilhomme*, nobleman, 16 *disait-il*, he said, 17 *ne connaît que*, knows nobody but, 18 *très-méchant*, very vicious, 19 *s'il voulait*, if it wished, 20 *de sortir*, to come out, 21 *il faudrait*, it would be necessary, 22 *l'en empêcher*, to prevent it from doing so, 23 *que*, when, 24 *maison de poste*, post house, 25 *voulait*, wished, 26 *descendre*, alight, 27 *les gens*, the servants, 28 *même*, even, 29 *sortait*, put out, 30 *la portière*, the carriage door, 31 *risée*, laughing, 32 *savait*, knew, 33 *pouvait*, could, 34 *de pareils*, such, 35 *se répandit*, spread, 36 *accourait*, ran 37 *voir*, to see, 38 *se renouvela*, was renewed, 39 *tour*, joke, 40 *voulut*, wished.

TWENTY-NINTH LESSON. *Vingt-neuvième Leçon*

Remarks on Verbs.(*)

There are certain verbs which, without being irregular, present certain peculiarities in their conjugation.

Verbs of the 1st Conjugation.

I.—Verbs ending in *cer*, take the cedilla under the *c* before *a* and *o*.—*Nous perçons* (from *percer*), we pierce; *je perçais*, I pierced.

II.—Verbs ending in *ger* take an *e* after the *g* before *a* and *o*.

Nous mangeons (from *manger*), we eat; *je mangeais*, I ate.

III.—Verbs ending in *eler* and *eter* double the *l* or the *t* before an *e* mute.

J'appelle (from *appeler*), I call; *j'appellerai*, I shall call.

Il jette (from *jeter*), he throws; *nous jetterions*, we should throw.

EXCEPTIONS.—*Acheter*, to buy; *harceler*, to harass; *peler*, to peel; *déceler*, to disclose; *bourreler*, to torment; *geler*, to freeze; *épeler*, to spell; *becqueter*, to peck, take the grave accent on the *e* instead of doubling the consonant.

IV.—Verbs having in the infinitive an *é* in the last syllable but one, change that *é* into *è* before an *e* mute.

J'espère (from *espérer*), I hope; *il espèrera*, he will hope.

Verbs having in the infinitive an *e* unaccented in the last syllable but one, change that *e* into *è* before an *e* mute.

Je pèse (from *peser*), I weigh; *nous mènerons* (from *mener*), we shall lead.

V.—Verbs ending in *yant* in the present participle change *y* into *i* before an *e* mute.

Je paie (from *payer*), I pay; *ils essuient* (from *essuyer*), they wipe; *vous emploierez* (from *employer*), they will employ.

Some writers, however, keep the *y* in verbs in *ayer*, as *payer*, and spell *je paye*.

Verbs of the 2nd Conjugation.

Haïr, to hate, drops the diæresis in the three persons singular of the Present Indicative: *je hais, tu hais, il hait,* and in the 2nd person singular of the Imperative *hais*.

Haïr is the only verb in French which takes no circumflex accent in the 3rd person singular of the Imperfect of the Subjunctive.

Fleurir, to bloom, to flourish, has two present Participles, *fleurissant*, blooming, and *florissant*, flourishing, and also two forms for the Imperfect Indicative.

Bénir has two past participles; *bénit*, consecrated; *béni*, blessed.

De l'eau bénite, holy water; *il fut béni par son père,* he was blessed by his father.

Verbs of the 3rd Conjugation.

Verbs in *cevoir*, like *recevoir*, take the cedilla under *c* before *u*: *je déçus, que je conçusse*.

The past participle of *devoir* is *dû* to distinguish it from *du*, of the. The feminine is spelt *due*.

(*) See for verbs, the Supplement.

to accompany, *accompagner*	to degenerate, *dégénérer*	heroine, *héroïne f.*
annal, *annale f.*	devoted, *dévoué*	love, *amour m.*
astonishment, *étonnement m.*	discreet, *discret*	nightly, *nocturne*
chief, *chef m.*	esteem, *estime f.*	order, *ordre m.*
combat, *combat m.*	exploit, *exploit m.*	report, *rapport m.*
consent, *consentement m.*	to expose, *exposer*	republic, *république f.*
danger, *danger m.*	to form, *former*	touching, *touchant*
	to fulfil, *remplir*	troop, *troupe f.*
	function, *fonction f.*	uniform, *uniforme m.*
	guard, *garde f.*	volunteer, *volontaire m.*

Exercise No. 29.

1. I announce—we announce—I announced *(imp.)*—we announced *(p. d.)*—he eats—I ate *(imp.)*—we eat—he ate *(p. d.)*—that we might eat—thou callest—we call—they call—we shall call—we should call—that I may call—that we might call—I have called—he buys—we buy—I bought *(imp.)*—I shall buy—we should buy—that I may buy—that we might buy—we had bought—he degenerates—you degenerate—I degenerated *(imp.)*—he would degenerate—we should degenerate—that he may degenerate—that you may degenerate—I lead—we lead—I led *(imp.)*—he led *(p. d.)*—I shall lead—we should lead—that he may lead—that you may lead—that he might lead—they had led—I pay—we pay—they pay—I paid *(imp.)*—they paid *(p. d.)*—I shall pay—we should pay—that I may pay—that you may pay—that I might pay—I hate—they hate—I hated *(imp.)*—they *(m.)* hated *(p. d.)*—hate (thou)—do not hate—I shall hate—we should hate—that I may hate—that we might hate—The trees were blooming (bloomed).—Fine arts[1] were flourishing.—His father has blessed him.—The church was consecrated.—I deceive—we deceive—he received *(p. d.)*—you received *(imp.)*—This is due to me.

2. Nous ne mangeons pas de viande. Ils mangeaient trop de fruits. Où menez-vous cet enfant. Je le mène dans le jardin. Combien pèse cela? Nous ne haïssons personne. Il hait cet homme. C'est une nation dégénérée. Ils dégénèrent chaque jour davantage. Il paierait ses dettes, s'il avait de l'argent. Vous l'emploierez si vous voulez[2] me faire[3] un plaisir. Les arbres fleurissaient dans tous les jardins. Les beaux arts florissaient à cette époque[4]. Ils ont reçu une lettre de leurs amis.

They ate much meat. We begin to speak French. He calls you. We shall buy new dresses this afternoon. Do they hope that we shall accompany them? We announce his death to his parents. They exasperate all their friends by their bad conduct. He leads the armies of the Republic to the combat. They call you: go (and) see what they desire. They announced that they would be here this morning.

---

[1] fine arts, *les beaux arts* [2] *voulez*, wish [3] *faire*, to do [4] *époque*, epoch [5] go and see, *allez voir*

Questions on Grammar.

1. When do verbs ending in *cer* take the cedilla under the *c*?
2. When do verbs ending in *ger* take *e* between the root and the ending?
3. When do verbs ending in *eler* and *eter* double the *l* or the *t*?
4. What are the principal exceptions to the preceding rule?
5. What becomes of the *é* of the penultimate syllable before an *e* mute?
6. What becomes of the *e* of the penultimate syllable before an *e* mute?
7. What becomes of the *y* in verbs ending in *yant* in the present participles, before an *e* mute?
8. What irregularity does the verb *hair* present?
9. What are the two present participles of *fleurir*?
10. What are the two past participles of *bénir*?
11. When do verbs ending in *cevoir* take the cedilla?
12. What is the spelling of the past participle of *devoir*?

Conversation.

Do you hope to be successful in this enterprise?	Espérez-vous réussir dans cette entreprise?
I hope so.	Je l'espère.
When do you commence?	Quand commencez-vous?
We commence in a few days.	Nous commençons dans quelques jours.
What will you have for your breakfast?	Que voulez-vous pour votre déjeuner?
A little bread and butter and a cup of tea will be sufficient.	Un peu de pain et de beurre et une tasse de thé suffiront.
How much does this fish weigh?	Combien pèse ce poisson?
It weighs two pounds and a half.	Il pèse deux livres et demie.
Where do you take your brother?	Où menez-vous votre frère?
I take him to his grandfather's.	Je le mène chez son grand père.
How much do you pay for his railway fare?	Combien payez-vous pour lui en chemin de fer?
I only pay ten pence.	Je ne paie que dix pence.
Were the trees blooming when you were in the country?	Les arbres fleurissaient-ils quand vous étiez à la campagne?
Yes, they were covered with flowers.	Oui, ils étaient couverts de fleurs.
Is your cousin in a flourishing position?	Votre cousin est-il dans une position florissante?
I do not know; but I think he is very successful in his business.	Je ne sais pas; mais je pense qu'il réussit très bien dans ses affaires.

Reading Exercise No. 29.

On trouve dans les annales des guerres de la première république française un exemple touchant de patriotisme et d'amour filial. Filles d'un ancien officier[1] qui, à la tête de la garde nationale de son village, faisait de fréquentes reconnaissances[2] pendant la nuit, Félicité et Théophile de Fernig, craignant[3] pour leur père le danger au quel il était exposé dans ces petites expéditions, qui dégénéraient souvent en escarmouches,[4] formèrent le projet de l'accompagner, sans qu'il le sût,[5] revêtues d'[6] habillements d'hommes,[7] que leur avait prêtés quelques amis dévoués et discrets. Elles mirent[8] leur projet à[9] exécution et pendant[10] quelque temps, prirent part aux[11] marches et aux combats nocturnes sans que leur père s'aperçût[12] de rien. Mais le général Beurnonville, ayant rencontré la petite troupe dont les exploits lui étaient connus[13], voulut[14] lui témoigner[15] son estime en la passant en revue[16]. Quel ne fut pas son étonnement en remarquant que deux des volontaires essayaient de changer de rang[17] pour échapper à ses regards[18]: il donna l'ordre à Monsieur de Fernig de les faire sortir[19] des rangs, et se voyant[20] découvertes[21], les deux jeune filles tombèrent aux genoux de leur père et lui demandèrent pardon[22]. Sur[23] le rapport du général en chef, la Convention envoya aux deux héroïnes des armes et des chevaux d'honneur. Elles continuèrent ensuite à accompagner leur père, avec son consentement, et on les retrouve[24] aux batailles de Valmy et de Jemmapes, remplissant les fonctions d'aides-de-camp du[25] général Dumouriez, et revêtues de[26] l'uniforme de cet emploi.

1 *ancien officier*, ex-officer, 2 *faisait des reconnaissances*, made reconnoitrings, 3 *craignant*, fearing, 4 *escarmouches*, skirmishes, 5 *sût*, knew, 6 *revêtues de*, clothed in, 7 *habillements d'homme*, men's garments, 8 *mirent*, put, 9 *à*, in, 10 *pendant*, for, 11 *prirent part aux*, took part in, 12 *s'aperçût de rien*, discovered anything, 13 *connus*, known, 14 *voulut*, wished, 15 *témoigner*, to show, 16 *en la passant en revue*, by reviewing it, 17 *changer de rang*, to change their ranks, 18 *à ses regards*, his attention, 19 *les faire sortir*, to make them come out of, 20 *se voyant*, seeing themselves, 21 *découvertes*, discovered, 22 *lui demandèrent pardon*, asked for his pardon, 23 *sur*, on, 24 *on les retrouve*, they are found again, 25 *aides-de-camp du*, aides-de-camp to, 26 *revêtues de*, dressed in the.

THIRTIETH LESSON. *Trentième Leçon.*

Words with aspirated H.

The rules which have been given for articles, demonstrative and possessive adjectives, show the necessity of knowing whether the *h* found at the beginning of words be aspirated (see lessons 1, 2, 4, 12 and 13).

This knowledge is also necessary to ascertain if the final *e* of monosyllabic words must be elided and if the linking of words has to take place.

The following is a list of the words in which the *h* is aspirated :

(*)hâbler, *to brag*
hache (f.), *axe*
hagard, *haggard*
hachis (m.), *hash*
haie (f.), *hedge*
haillon (m.), *rag*
haine (f.), *hatred*
haïr, *to hate*
haire (f.), *hair-shirt*
hâle, *drying wind*
hâlé, *sunburnt*
hâler, *to tow*
haleter, *to pant*
halle (f.), *market-hall*
hallebarde (f.), *halberd*
hallier (m.), *thicket*
halo (m.), *halo*
halte (f.), *halt*
hamac (m.), *hammock*
hameau (m.), *hamlet*
hampe (f.), *staff*
hanche (f.), *hip*
hangar (m.), *shed*
hanneton (m.), *cockchafer*
hanter, *to haunt* [nag
haquenée (f.), *ambling*
haquet (m.), *dray*
happer, *to snap*
harangue(f.), *harangue*
haras (m.), *breedingstud*
harasser, *to harass*
harceler, *to torment*
hardes (f. p.), *clothes*

hardi, *bold*
harem (m.), *harem*
hareng (m.), *herring*
hargneux, *quarrelsome*
haricot (m.), *Frenchbean*
haridelle (f.), *hack*
harnacher, *to harness*
harnais (m.), *harness*
harpe (f.), *harp*
harpie (f.), *harpy*
harpon (m.), *harpoon*
hart (f.), *withe*
hasard (m.), *hazard*
hase (f.), *doe-hare*
hâte (f.), *haste*
haubans(m.p.),*shrouds*
haubert (m.), *coat-of-mails*
hausser, *to raise*
haut, *high*
hautain, *haughty*
hautbois (m.), *oboe*
hâve, *emaciated*
hâvre (m.), *harbour*
havresac(m.), *knapsack*
heaume (m.), *helmet*
hennir, *to neigh*
héraut (m.), *herald*
hérisser, *to bristle*
hernie (f.), *hernia*
héron (m.), *heron*
héros(†) (m.), *hero*
herse (f.), *harrow, portcullis*

hêtre (m.), *beech-tree*
heurter, *to clash*
hibou (m.), *owl*
hideux, *hideous*
hiérarchie(f.),*hierarchy*
hisser, *to hoist*
hocher, *to toss*
homard (m.), *lobster*
honte (f.), *shame*
hoquet (m.), *hiccough*
horde (f.), *horde*
hotte (f.), *dorsel*
houblon (m.), *hop*
houe (f.), *hoe*
houille (f.), *coal*
houle (f.), *billow*
houlette (f.), *crook*
houppe (f.), *tuft*
houppelande (f.), *a sort of great coat*
houspiller, *to pull about*
housses (f. p.), *housings*
houx (m.), *holly*
huche (f.), *kneadingtrough*
huée (f.), *hooting*
huit, *eight*
huguenot (m.), *huguenot*
humer, *to inhale*
hune (f.), *top (marine)*
huppe (f.), *pewet*
hure (f.), *wild boar head*
hurler, *to howl*
hussard (m.), *hussar*

(*) Words very seldom used and words derived from those given in this list have been omitted.

(†) The *h* is mute in *héroïne, héroïsme* and *héroïque.*

accomplice, *complice m.*	henceforth, *dorénavant*	to rehabilitate, *réhabiliter*
affair, *affaire f.*	instead of, *au lieu de*	
arrival, *arrivée f.*	to live, *demeurer*	reprimand, *réprimande f.*
to assist, *aider*	miserly, *avare*	
to avoid, *éviter*	moon, *lune f.*	ripe, *mûr*
to claim for, *réclamer*	occasion, *occasion f.*	scandal, *scandale m.*
to contract, *contracter*	to order, *ordonner*	shrub, *arbuste m.*
disorder, *désordre m.*	orgy, *orgie f.*	since, *puisque*
enemy, *ennemi m.*	to present, *présenter*	spendthrift, *dissipateur m.*
to execute, *exécuter*	pretext, *prétexte m.*	
to facilitate, *faciliter*	prodigal, *prodigue*	to strike, *frapper*
heavy, *lourd*	rain, *pluie f.*	study, *étude f.*

Exercise No. 30.

(The words beginning with an h aspirated must be looked for in the list on the opposite page.)

1. J'ordonnerai (à) cet homme de réclamer sa hache. La haie est couverte de¹ fleurs. La houille est très chère cette année. L'habit de mon père est très bien fait². Mon ami craignait³ la haine de son ennemi. Il doit sa fortune au hasard. Le hautbois est un instrument très difficile Il n'y a plus⁴ de houille sous le hangar. Ce hameau est très joli. Les houblons ne sont pas encore mûrs. Le hérault se tenait⁵ devant la porte. Le soldat le frappa avec sa hallebarde. Le mendiant était couvert de haillons. Le havresac du soldat français est très lourd. Les chiens ont pénétré dans le hallier. Sa harangue a été très éloquente. Ce hamac est très commode. Je ne le hais pas. Ma hotte est dans le jardin. Le houx est un joli arbuste. Je n'en ai que huit. Le halo que l'on voit⁶ autour de la lune est généralement un signe de pluie. Avez-vous vu⁷ la harpe que mon père m'a achetée.

2. The herald announced the arrival of the hero. This man's dog is there. The shed is full of rags. I do not hate my enemies. The river is bordered with⁸ beech-trees. They have no housings. Do not strike this poor cat. The dishes are on the kneading-trough. My brother plays the⁹ oboe. Do not harness the horses now. He held a branch of holly in his¹⁰ hand. The hoe is in the garden. He was received with hootings by the multitude. He has some*a* very curious*a* helmets and coats-of-mail*b* in his collection. I inhale the cool air¹¹ of the morning. He lives in the hamlet. This child is very much¹² incommoded¹³ by the hiccough. Do you play the harp? She was (the) mother of eight children. This great coat belonged to¹⁴ my grandfather. The merchant who has sold you this coal has deceived you. The owl sleeps¹⁵ during the day.

---

1 *couverte de*, covered with 2 *fait*, made 3 *craignait*, feared 4 *il n'y a plus*, there is no more 5 *se tenait*, stood 6 *voit*, sees 7 *vu*, seen 8 bordered with, *bordée de* 9 to play an instrument, *jouer d'un instrument* 10 in his, *à la* 11 cool air, *air frais* 12 very much, *très* 13 incommoded, *incommodé* 14 belonged to, *était à* 15 sleeps. *dort*

Questions on Grammar.

1. How are the articles *the* and *some* translated before a noun beginning with a mute *h*?
2. How are the articles *the* and *some* translated before a noun beginning with an aspirated *h*?
3. How is the demonstrative adjective *this* translated before a singular masculine noun beginning with a mute *h*?
4. How is the demonstrative adjective *this* translated before a singular masculine noun beginning with an aspirated *h*?
5. How are the possessive adjectives *my, thy, his, hers, its* translated before a singular feminine noun beginning with a mute *h*?
6. How are the possessive adjectives *my, thy, his, hers, its* translated before a singular feminine noun beginning with an aspirated *h*?
7. How will you write *je, me, te, se, ne, que, &c.* before a mute *h*?

Conversation.

Where does this man live?	Où demeure cet homme?
He lives in the hamlet which you see on the top of the hill.	Il demeure dans le hameau que vous voyez sur le haut de la colline.
Where did you meet him?	Où l'avez-vous rencontré?
I met him at the market-hall.	Je l'ai rencontré à la halle.
Where did he put his clothes?	Où a-t-il mis ses (*)hardes?
He put them under the shed.	Il les a mises sous le hangar.
Tell him to bring the harness.	Dites-lui d'apporter les harnais.
He is gone to fetch the harrow.	Il est allé chercher la herse.
Do you hear your neighbour's hack? it has been neighing for some minutes.	Entendez-vous la haridelle de votre voisin? elle hennit depuis quelques minutes.
The flies torment it very probably.	Les mouches la harassent très probablement.
Where is the owl which we heard last night?	Où est le hibou que nous avons entendu la nuit dernière?
I think it is on the beech-tree which is on the other side of the river.	Je pense qu'il est sur le hêtre qui est de l'autre côté de la rivière.
What bird is that?	Quel oiseau est-ce?
It is a heron.	C'est un héron.
Where did you shoot it?	Où l'avez-vous tué?
On the banks of the pond which is between the hedge and the thicket.	Sur les bords de l'étang qui est entre la haie et le hallier.
Why has the dog been howling all the morning?	Pourquoi le chien a-t-il hurlé toute la matinée?
I do not know; it is very quarrelsome.	Je ne sais pas; il est très hargneux.

(*) The student will remember that no linking takes place before an aspirated *h*.

Reading Exercise No. 30.

Un marchand, très riche mais très avare, avait un fils qui était, comme cela arrive très souvent en pareil cas,[1] d'une extrême prodigalité. Envoyé par son père dans une ville d'université,[2] au lieu de consacrer[3] son temps à l'étude, il le passait[4] en plaisirs et en orgies, et il eut bientôt contracté des dettes considérables. Après avoir pourvu[5] pendant[6] quelque temps à ses dépenses, non sans accompagner chaque envoi[7] d'argent d'[8] une sévère réprimande, le marchand déclara à son fils que dorénavant il ne devait[9] plus[10] compter[11] sur lui pour payer ses dettes: il lui ordonnait en même temps de revenir[12] au foyer paternel[13]. En effet[14] l'enfant prodigue se présenta le jour suivant[15]: mais il n'était pas seul, il était accompagné de[16] deux hommes qui s'annoncèrent comme étant envoyés par un créancier pour conduire[17] le jeune homme à la prison pour dettes. Ils avaient espéré, disaient-ils[18], que son père se laisserait fléchir[19] encore une fois[20] et qu'ils ne seraient pas obligés d'exécuter l'ordre qu'ils avaient reçu. Le marchand, voulant[21] éviter le scandale, et se disant[22] que son fils n'aurait plus l'occasion de faire de dépenses à l'avenir[23], puisqu'il demeurerait avec lui et l'aiderait dans ses affaires, paya la somme qu'on lui[24] réclamait. Mais, hélas! son fils étant sorti[25] de la maison deux heures après sous un prétexte quelconque ne revint[26] pas: les deux records[27] étaient ses complices, et l'argent qui aurait dû[28] réhabiliter le dissipateur, ne servit qu'à[29] faciliter de nouveaux désordres.

1 *en pareil cas*, in such a case, 2 *ville d'université*, university town, 3 *consacrer*, devoting, 4 *passait*, spent, 5 *pourvu ... à*, provided ... for, 6 *pendant*, for, 7 *envoi*, remittance, 8 *d'*, with, 9 *devait*, ought, 10 *ne ... plus*, no .. more, 11 *compter*, rely, 12 *revenir*, to come back, 13 *foyer paternel*, father's home, 14 *en effet*, indeed, 15 *suivant*, following, 16 *de*, by, 17 *conduire*, to conduct, 18 *disaient-ils*, they said, 19 *se laisserait fléchir*, would allow himself to be softened, 20 *encore une fois*, once again, 21 *voulant*, wishing, 22 *se disant*, saying to himself, 23 *à l'avenir*, in the future, 24 *lui*, from him, 25 *étant sorti*, having gone out, 26 *revint*, came back, 27 *records*, bailiff's assistants, 28 *aurait dû*, ought to have, 29 *ne servit que*, only served.

TWENTY DIALOGUES

on subjects of everyday life.

(Vingt dialogues sur des sujets de la vie journalière.)

INDEX.
(Table des matières.)

A meeting	141	Une rencontre.
About the way, or road	142	Au sujet du chemin.
Visit	143	Visite.
Railway Journey	144	Voyage en chemin de fer.
do. do.	145	do. do.
Sea Journey	146	Traversée.
At a Town	147	Dans une ville.
Letting Apartments	148	Location d'appartements
With a servant	149	Avec un domestique.
Meals	150	Repas.
To write a letter	151	Pour écrire une lettre.
At a money changer's	152	Chez un changeur.
Buying	153	Achats.
Carriages	154	Voitures.
At table	155	A table.
A walk	156	Une promenade.
With a doctor	157	Avec un docteur.
Paris Museums	158	Musées de Paris.
The Streets of Paris	159	Les rues de Paris.
How to progress in French	160	Comment faire des progrès en Français.

A Meeting.	Une Rencontre.
Good morning, Mr. X..., how do you do?	Bonjour, Monsieur X..., comment vous portez-vous?
Quite well, thank you; how are you?	Très bien, merci; comment allez-vous?
Not very well, I had a bad cold last week and have not yet quite recovered from it.	Pas très bien; j'ai eu un mauvais rhume la semaine dernière, et je m'en suis pas encore tout-à-fait remis.
I am very sorry to hear that, but hope it will have no serious consequences. Is your family in good health?	Je suis très fâché d'apprendre cela; mais j'espère qu'il n'aura pas de sérieuses conséquences. Votre famille est-elle en bonne santé?
I have not seen any of them since the beginning of the week, as they have gone to the seaside.	Je n'ai vu aucun d'entre eux depuis le commencement de la semaine, vu qu'ils sont allés aux bains de mer.
Shall you not go and spend a few days with them?	Irez-vous passer quelques jours avec eux?
I should like it very much; but I am very busy.	Je le voudrais bien; mais je suis très occupé.
Did you see our friend, Mr. White the day before yesterday?	Avez-vous vu notre ami, Mr. White avant-hier?
Yes; I had an appointment with him, and saw him in the afternoon.	Oui; j'avais un rendez-vous avec lui, et je l'ai vu dans l'après-midi.
Is it true that he is not very successful in business?	Est-il vrai qu'il ne réussisse pas dans les affaires?
I cannot tell you precisely: but I think he has been rather unfortunate lately in his transactions.	Je ne peux pas vous le dire exactement; mais je crois qu'il a été un peu malheureux dernièrement dans ses transactions.
Did you buy anything at the auction yesterday?	Avez-vous acheté quelque chose hier aux enchères?
Yes, I bought several pieces of furniture, two oil-paintings and a few bottles of old port-wine.	Oui; j'ai acheté quelques meubles, deux tableaux à l'huile et quelques bouteilles de vieux vin de Porto.
Were many buyers there?	Y avait-il beaucoup d'acheteurs?
Not very many: the weather was rather bad, and I suppose that prevented many people from coming.	Pas beaucoup: le temps était un peu mauvais et je suppose que cela a empêché beaucoup de monde de venir.
Are you going to the Italian Opera to-night?	Allez-vous ce soir aux Italiens?
No; I do not understand a word of Italian, and besides the prices are rather too high for me.	Non; je ne comprends pas un mot d'Italien; et de plus les prix sont un peu trop élevés pour moi.
Where are you going?	Où allez-vous?
I must be at my office by two o'clock, and have just time to catch the train.	Je dois être à mon bureau vers deux heures et j'ai juste le temps de prendre le train.
Good bye!	Adieu.

About the way, or road.

Will you kindly tell me which is the shortest way to the Exchange?

With much pleasure. Go straight on until you arrive at the church which you see down there; then take the first street on the right and the second on the left.

Thank you. How long will it take me to go there?

About twenty minutes, if you do not stop on the way.

Can you tell me if I shall find a good restaurant before arriving at the Exchange?

You will find some in this street and many others near the Exchange; but the latter are rather expensive and I should advise you to go to one in this street, where you will be sure to find anything you require.

Is there any foreign money changer in the neighbourhood?

There is one opposite the church; but I should advise you to go to the goldsmith whose shop is just at the corner of the street which leads to the Exchange.

Is there any tramcar going in that direction?

There is one just coming; but it will not take you further than the church.

oes it stop there?

No; but, you would arrive at the river if you remained in it as far as it goes.

Can you direct me to the nearest post-office?

You will find it on the right, about two hundred paces from here.

Is the telegraph office at the same place?

No; you will find it on the other side, just opposite the fountain.

I thank you very much for your kindness, Sir.

Do not mention it.

Au sujet du chemin.

Voulez-vous avoir la bonté de me dire quel est le plus court chemin pour aller à la Bourse?

Avec beaucoup de plaisir. Allez tout droit jusqu'à ce que vous arriviez à l'église que vous voyez là-bas; prenez alors la première rue à droite et la seconde à gauche.

Je vous remercie. Combien de temps me faudra-t-il pour y aller?

Environ vingt minutes, si vous ne vous arrêtez pas en route.

Pouvez-vous me dire si je trouverai un bon restaurant avant d'arriver à la Bourse?

Vous en trouverez quelques uns dans cette rue et beaucoup d'autres près de la Bourse; mais ces derniers sont un peu chers, et je vous conseillerais d'aller dans un de ceux de cette rue, où vous seriez sûr de trouver tout ce dont vous avez besoin

Y a-t-il un changeur dans le voisinage?

Il y en a un en face de l'église; mais je vous conseillerais d'aller chez l'orfèvre dont le magasin est juste au coin de la rue qui conduit à la Bourse.

Y a-t-il un tramway qui aille dans cette direction?

En voilà justement un qui vient maintenant; mais il ne vous conduira pas plus loin que l'église.

S'arrête-t-il là?

Non; mais vous arriveriez à la rivière, si vous y restiez aussi longtemps qu'il marche.

Pouvez-vous m'indiquer le bureau de poste le plus prochain?

Vous le trouverez sur la droite, à environ deux cents pas d'ici.

Le bureau du télégraphe est-il au même endroit?

Non; vous le trouverez de l'autre côté, juste vis-à-vis de la fontaine.

Monsieur, je vous remercie beaucoup de votre obligeance.

Ne parlez pas de cela.

Visit.

Good morning, Madam; how do you do?

Very well, sir; and how is Mrs. X...?

Thank you very much, madam: Mrs X. is quite well, and she would certainly have accompanied me if her sister had not come from Paris to pay her a short visit.

I am very sorry she did not accompany you: I should have been very pleased to make Miss S...'s acquaintance.

Miss S... was very tired with her journey; but she will not leave London without coming to see you.

Tell her how pleased I shall be to see her: I am generally at home every day after 4 o'clock except Thursdays, and never go out in the evening. Have you been in the country with your family?

Yes, madam; we only returned a fortnight ago.

How was the weather while you were there?

We were rather fortunate; during the three weeks we remained at X... the weather was extremely fine.

Have you heard from your brother lately?

Yes, I had a letter from him yesterday.

Have you seen the last number of the "Monde Illustré?"

Yes, Madam; I am a subscriber to that illustrated paper.

Is there anything specially interesting in this number?

There are very good sketches from the correspondent at the seat of war.

Are you going already?

I am very sorry I cannot stay any longer, but must meet Mr. Z... at half past four.

Visite.

Bonjour, Madame; comment vous portez-vous?

Très bien, Monsieur; et comment va Madame X...?

Je vous remercie beaucoup, Madame: Madame X. va très bien et elle m'aurait certainement accompagné, si sa sœur n'était pas venue de Paris pour lui faire une courte visite.

Je suis très fâchée qu'elle ne vous ait pas accompagné: j'aurais été très heureuse de faire la connaissance de Mademoiselle S....

Mademoiselle S... était très fatiguée de son voyage; mais elle ne quittera pas Londres sans venir vous voir.

Dites-lui combien je serai heureuse de la voir: je suis généralement chez moi tous les jours après quatre heures, excepté les Jeudis, et je ne sors jamais dans la soirée. Avez-vous été à la campagne avec votre famille?

Oui, madame; nous ne sommes revenus qu'il y a quinze jours.

Quel temps faisait-il pendant que vous y étiez?

Nous avons été vraiment heureux: pendant les trois semaines que nous sommes restés à X... le temps a été extrêmement beau.

Avez-vous reçu dernièrement des nouvelles de votre frère?

Oui, j'ai reçu hier une lettre de lui.

Avez-vous vu le dernier numéro du Monde Illustré?

Oui, madame; je suis abonné à ce journal illustré.

Y a-t-il quelque chose de spécialement intéressant dans ce numéro?

Il y a de très bons croquis du correspondant du théâtre de la guerre.

Vous en allez-vous déjà?

Je regrette beaucoup de ne pas pouvoir rester plus longtemps mais je dois me rencontrer à quatre heures et demie avec Mr. Z.

Railway Journey.

Two tickets to Paris, please.
What class?
Second class.
Would you not like to have first class tickets for the sea journey.
What would be the difference in the price?
Two shillings.
When does the train leave?
At 10 o'clock.
How long will it take us to go to Dover?
About two-hours.
Where shall I have my luggage registered?
Next door.
Is there any smoking carriage in the train?
Yes, sir; there is also a Pulman car which any passenger can enter by paying a small additional sum.
Is there any special carriage for ladies?
No; it is not the custom in this country.
Is there any great difference between single and return tickets?
There is generally a difference of a quarter on the total amount.
Please weigh my luggage; handle the trunks carefully.
Take your seats, gentlemen.
Please allow my friends to remain on the platform until the train starts.
Your tickets, gentlemen.
Here they are.
You are in the wrong train, sir.
Where is my train, then? I was told to enter this carriage.
You very probably misunderstood the guard; you will have to go to the carriages which are opposite the clock: this train only goes to ....
Have I time to go and have some refreshments?
You have just five minutes.

Voyage en chemin de fer.

Deux billets pour Paris, s'il v. pl.
Quelle classe?
Deuxième classe.
Ne voudriez-vous pas avoir des billets de première classe pour la traversée?
Quelle serait la différence de prix?
Deux shellings.
Quand part le train?
A dix heures.
Combien de temps nous faut-il pour aller à Douvres?
Environ deux heures.
Où dois-je faire enregistrer mes bagages?
A la porte d'à côté.
Y a-t-il dans le train une voiture pour les fumeurs?
Oui, monsieur; il y a aussi une voiture Pulman où peut entrer chaque voyageur, en payant un petit supplément.
Y a-t-il des wagons spéciaux pour les Dames?
Non; ce n'est pas l'habitude dans ce pays-ci.
Y a-t-il une grande différence entre le prix des billets simples et celui des billets d'aller et retour?
Il y a généralement une différence d'un quart de la somme totale.
Veuillez peser mes bagages: maniez soigneusement les malles.
En voiture, messieurs.
Veuillez permettre à mes amis de rester sur le quai jusqu'à ce que le train parte.
Vos billets, messieurs.
Les voici.
Monsieur, vous êtes dans le mauvais train.
Où donc est mon train: on m'a dit d'entrer dans cette voiture.
Vous avez probablement mal compris le chef de train; vous aurez à aller jusqu'aux voitures qui sont en face de l'horloge; ce train-ci ne va qu'à ....
Ai-je le temps d'aller prendre quelque rafraîchissements?
Vous avez juste cinq minutes.

Railway Journey
(concluded).

Do you not think the train does not run very fast?

They are just repairing this part of the road and they must move over it very cautiously.

What is the name of the village we just saw on our right?

I do not know; it is the first time I have travelled this way.

Will you kindly shut the window; I have a bad cold and feel rather afraid of the draught.

Would you prefer to sit with your back towards the engine?

I will not trespass on your kindness.

It makes no difference to me.

When does the train arrive at our destination?

At five minutes past four.

Your tickets, gentleman.

Have we arrived?

You will be at Paris in two minutes, but the tickets are always collected before reaching the station.

Where have I to go to get my luggage?

Pass this way and you will see the custom officers standing at the entrance of the room where your luggage will be searched and then delivered to you.

Shall we have to wait a long time?

I do not think so: about a quarter of an hour or twenty minutes.

Do you want me to open this trunk? I have nothing in it but clothes.

We are bound to examine every trunk.

I have only a pound of tobacco for personal use.

You can close your portmanteau.

Voyage en chemin de fer
(fin).

Ne croyez-vous pas que le train ne marche pas très rapidement.

Ils sont en train de réparer cette partie de la voie, et on doit en cet endroit-ci marcher avec beaucoup de précautions.

Quel est le nom du village que nous venons de voir sur notre droite?

Je ne sais pas; c'est la première fois que je voyage par cette route.

Voudriez-vous avoir la bonté de fermer la portière; j'ai un mauvais rhume et je crains beaucoup les courants d'air.

Préféreriez-vous vous asseoir le dos tourné à la machine?

Je n'abuserai pas de votre bonté.

Cela m'est indifférent.

Quand le train arrive-t-il à notre destination?

A quatre heures cinq minutes.

Vos billets, messieurs.

Sommes-nous arrivés?

Vous serez à Paris dans deux minutes, mais on prend toujours les billets avant d'arriver à la gare.

Où dois-je aller pour avoir mes bagages?

Passez par ici et vous verrez les douaniers debout à l'entrée de la salle où vos bagages seront visités et ensuite vous seront remis.

Aurons-nous longtemps à attendre?

Je ne pense pas: environ un quart d'heure ou vingt minutes.

Voulez-vous que j'ouvre cette malle; je n'y ai que des effets.

Nous sommes forcés de visiter chaque malle.

Je n'ai qu'une livre de tabac pour mon usage personnel.

Vous pouvez fermer votre portemanteau.

Sea Journey.

Which is the steamer for Dieppe?

The one you see there alongside the quay.

When will she start?

At high water—at two thirty five

The steamer appears to me to be very small.

Oh, no; she is a very good size: she has been plying between Newhaven and Dieppe the last two years, and although the sea is often rough, has never required any important repairs.

Will you show me the way to the second class cabins?

Come this way, sir.

Steward, I am looking for a berth and cannot find any disengaged.

Here is an unoccupied berth, sir; do you wish to take anything?

Yes, please; bring me some tea.

The sea is now very calm: would you not like to go on deck? there are few passengers there, and the air is cool and bracing.

What is the light-house we see there, on the horizon?

It is the light-house at the entrance of the harbour.

What is that boat, which is coming to meet us?

I believe it is a pilot.

I think we are stopping.

Yes, we must wait until the tide will allow us to enter the port.

Is it not possible to hire a boat to take us ashore?

The sea is rather rough this morning: which I suppose is the reason I do not see any boats.

What is the signal they are just hoisting at the end of the pier?

The signal that there is enough water now to enter the harbour.

Traversée.

Quel est le bateau à vapeur de Dieppe?

C'est celui que vous voyez là le long du quai.

Quand partira-t-il?

A la marée haute, à deux heures trente-cinq.

Le bateau à vapeur me paraît très petit.

Oh, non; il est de bonne grandeur il y a deux ans qu'il fait le service entre Newhaven et Dieppe et quoique la mer soit souvent mauvaise, il n'a jamais eu besoin d'importantes réparations.

Voudriez-vous me montrer le chemin pour aller aux cabines de deuxième classe?

Venez par ici, Monsieur.

Maître d'hôtel, je cherche une place et je n'en puis trouver de vacante.

Voici une place vacante, Monsieur; désirez-vous prendre quelque-chose?

Oui, s'il vous plaît; apportez-moi du thé.

La mer est très calme maintenant: n'aimeriez-vous pas à aller sur le pont, il y a là peu de passagers et l'air est frais et vif.

Qu'est-ce que c'est que le phare que nous voyons là-bas à l'horizon?

C'est le phare de l'entrée du port.

Qu'est-ce que c'est que le bateau qui vient au devant de nous?

Je crois que c'est un pilote.

Je crois que nous nous arrêtons.

Oui, nous devons attendre que la marée nous permette d'entrer dans le port.

N'est il pas possible de louer un bateau pour aller à terre?

La mer est un peu houleuse, ce matin; c'est ce qui fait, je suppose, que je ne vois aucun bateau.

Quel est le signal qu'on hisse à l'extrémité de la jetée?

C'est le signal qu'il y a assez d'eau pour entrer dans le port.

At a Town.

Is there any omnibus which will take me to the Continental Hotel?

Any omnibus will take you there.

What are the edifices worthy of interest on account of their historical connections?

You ought to visit the Cathedral, the Town Hall, the Law courts, the bridges, and the old gates, the only remains of the ramparts of the city.

Is the cathedral a very ancient building?

It is one of the oldest specimens of gothic architecture in our country.

Is ...... an industrial town?

It is renowned for its cotton mills and also for its cloth manufactories.

What is the population of the city?

There were about two hundred and fifty three thousand inhabitants at the last census which took place at the end of last year.

Is there anything to be seen in the surrounding country?

There are the ruins of an old abbey, the modern castle of the Earl of ......, and a beautiful forest of oaks and beech-trees.

Will you be able to come with me to-morrow.

Yes; with much pleasure.

What is the width of the river?

About two hundred yards.

Is the current very rapid?

Not very.

What is the little chapel which I see there, on the top of the hill?

It is the cemetery chapel.

Are there any remarkable monuments in it?

Hardly any: it was only built ten years ago.

Dans une ville.

Y a-t-il un omnibus qui me conduise à l'Hôtel Continental?

N'importe quel omnibus vous y conduira.

Quels sont les édifices qui sont dignes d'intérêt, à cause des souvenirs historiques qui s'y rattachent?

Vous devriez visiter la cathédrale, l'hôtel de ville, le palais de justice, les ponts, et les vieilles portes, seuls vestiges des remparts de la cité.

La cathédrale est-elle un édifice très ancien?

C'est un des plus vieux spécimens d'architecture gothique de notre pays.

Est-ce que ...... est une ville industrielle?

Elle est renommée pour ses filatures de coton et aussi pour ses manufactures de drap.

Quelle est la population de cette ville?

Il y avait environ deux cent-cinquante-trois mille habitants au dernier recensement qui a eu lieu à la fin de l'année dernière.

Y a-t-il quelque chose a voir dans le pays environnant?

Il y a les ruines d'une vieille abbaye, le château moderne du comte de ......, et une belle forêt de de chênes et de hêtres.

Pourrez-vous venir avec moi demain?

Oui; avec beaucoup de plaisir.

Quelle est la largeur de la rivière?

Environ deux cents yards.

Le courant est-il très-rapide?

Non, il ne l'est pas.

Quelle est la petite chapelle que je vois là, sur le sommet de la colline?

C'est la chapelle du cimetière.

Y a-t-il quelques remarquables monuments?

Il n'y en a pour ainsi dire pas: il n'y a que dix ans qu'elle est bâtie.

Letting Apartments.

I should like to have a suite of rooms composed of a drawing-room, a dining room, three bedrooms, a kitchen, and two rooms for servants.

What floor would suit you best?

The first or second floor.

We have no apartments vacant on either of these floors, but we have just what you want on the third story.

I am afraid it would be too high.

I do not think it would inconvenience you at all, as there is a lift in the house.

Are there any stables belonging to the mansion?

No, sir; but the mews are situated within two minutes walk, and you can see them very well from the back windows of your apartment.

Is there any post and telegraph office in the street?

Yes, sir; there is a post office at the end of the street, and a letter box at the next house.

What is the rent which was paid by the preceding occupier?

One hundred and twenty pounds.

Is that sum inclusive of water and gas?

No, sir; that you have to pay separately.

Are the apartments to be let by the month or year?

They have always been let by the month, but the terms of a new arrangement can be submitted to the landlord.

Then could I see him?

the course of next week; leave me your address, I will let you know.

am quite willing to take the rooms, on condition I can have them by the year; I do not like removing every month.

Location d'appartements.

Je voudrais avoir un appartement composé d'un salon, d'une salle à manger, de trois chambres à coucher, d'une cuisine et de deux chambres de domestiques.

Quel est l'étage qui vous conviendrait le mieux?

Le premier ou le second étage.

Nous n'avons d'appartements vacants à aucun de ces étages, mais nous avons juste ce que vous désirez au troisième étage.

Je crains que cela ne soit trop haut.

Je ne pense pas que cela vous gêne du tout, vu qu'il y a un ascenseur dans la maison.

Y a-t-il des écuries qui appartiennent à la maison?

Non, monsieur; mais les écuries sont situées à deux minutes de marche, et vous pouvez les voir des fenêtres de derrière de votre appartement.

Y a-t-il un bureau de poste et de télégraphe dans la rue?

Oui, monsieur; il y a un bureau de poste au bout de la rue et une boîte aux lettres à la maison voisine.

Quel est le loyer que payait le locataire précédent?

Cent-vingt livres sterling.

Cette somme comprend elle l'eau et le gaz?

Non, monsieur; vous avez à les payer séparément.

Ces appartements peuvent-ils être loués au mois ou à l'année?

Ils ont toujours été loués au mois, mais les conditions d'un nouvel arrangement peuvent être soumises au propriétaire.

Quand pourrais-je le voir?

Dans le courant de la semaine prochaine; laissez-moi votre adresse, je vous le ferai savoir.

Je suis tout disposé à prendre les chambres, à la condition que je puisse les avoir à l'année; je n'aime pas à déménager chaque mois.

With a Servant.

What time do you get up every morning?

I generally rise between seven and half past.

Will you then call me every morning as soon as you are dressed?

Yes, sir; you may rely upon me, and should anything happen to prevent me, I shall not forget to tell another servant to knock at your door at the proper time.

Take my boots, please, and bring them back into my room as soon as they are cleaned.

The left boot is unsewed: shall I take it to the shoemaker to have it repaired?

Yes; but tell him that I want it this evening.

There are two letters for you, sir.

When did the postman bring them?

He brought them just now.

I found no water on my toilet table, last night; will you fetch me some, that I may dress myself; it is getting late.

Do you want anything else?

Yes; I should like to have two clean towels: do not forget to change them twice a week.

Somebody brought this note for you and waits for an answer.

Say that I am engaged and shall call this afternoon.

Mr. X...... asks if you can receive him.

Show him in.

Shall you want your supper this evening?

Yes; put it on my table, but do not wait for me; it is quite possible that I may be rather late, and I do not wish to disturb anybody in the house.

Here is a key which the landlord asked me to give you, in order that you may come in at any time you like.

Avec un Domestique.

A quelle heure vous levez-vous les matins?

Je me lève généralement entre sept heures et sept heures et demie.

Voulez-vous alors m'appeler tous les matins, aussi-tôt que vous serez habillé?

Oui, mons.; vous pouvez compter sur moi; et s'il arrivait quelque chose qui m'en empêchât, je n'oublierais pas de dire à un autre domestique de frapper à votre porte à l'heure convenable.

Prenez mes bottines, s'il vous plaît, et rapportez les dans ma chambre aussitôt qu'elles seront nettoyées.

La bottine gauche est décousue; dois-je la porter au cordonnier pour qu'il la répare?

Oui; mais dites-lui que j'en ai besoin ce soir.

Voici deux lettres pour vous, monsieur.

Quand le facteur les a-t-il apportées?

Il vient de les apporter.

Je n'ai pas trouvé d'eau sur ma table de toilette, hier soir; voulez-vous aller m'en chercher, que je m'habille; il se fait tard.

Avez-vous besoin de quelque autre chose?

Oui; je voudrais avoir deux essuie-mains propres; n'oubliez pas de les changer deux fois par semaine.

Quelqu'un a apporté cette lettre pour vous et attend une réponse.

Dites que je suis occupé et que je passerai cette après-midi.

M. X...... demande si vous pouvez le recevoir.

Faites le entrer.

Aurez-vous besoin de votre souper ce soir?

Oui; mettez-le sur ma table, mais ne m'attendez pas; il est possible que je rentre un peu tard et je ne veux déranger personne dans la maison.

Voici une clef que le propriétaire m'a chargé de vous donner, afin que vous puissiez rentrer à l'heure qui vous conviendra.

Meals.	Repas.
What do you wish to have for your breakfast?	Que désirez-vous avoir pour votre déjeuner?
Two boiled eggs, rather underdone, and a rasher of bacon.	Deux œufs à la coque, peu cuits, et une tranche de lard.
Would you like tea, coffee, or cocoa?	Voulez-vous du thé, du café ou du cacao?
Give me some tea, with two pieces of toasted bread.	Donnez-moi du thé, avec deux morceaux de pain grillé.
What will you have for your lunch?	Que voulez-vous pour votre déjeuner à la fourchette?
Some cold roast beef and salad, some cheese, and a bottle of beer.	Du bœuf rôti froid et de la salade, du fromage et une bouteille de bière.
We have some very nice cold roast chicken, and a leg of mutton; would you not like some instead of roast beef? I am afraid it is rather overdone for you.	Nous avons de très bon poulet rôti froid, et un gigot de mouton; en voudriez-vous au lieu de bœuf rôti? Je crains qu'il ne soit trop cuit pour vous.
Well, let me have some chicken.	Eh bien! faites-moi donner du poulet.
Will you dine with us this evening? we expect Mrs. X...... and her two daughters, and Mr. S......'s cousins.	Dînerez-vous avec nous ce soir? nous attendons madame X...... et ses deux filles, et les cousins de Mr. S.......
I am not sure I shall be able to come, but will do my best to be here. At what time do you dine?	Je ne suis pas sûr que je puisse venir, mais je ferai de mon mieux pour être ici. A quelle heure dînez-vous?
At seven o'clock.	A sept heures.
What shall we have for dinner.	Qu'aurons nous pour dîner?
Ox tail soup, salmon, a roasted turkey with ham, and a haunch of venison, asparagus and potatoes.	De la soupe à la queue de bœuf, du saumon, un dindon rôti avec du jambon et un gigot de venaison, des asperges et des pommes-de-terre.
Do not forget to have some supper ready for me.	N'oubliez pas de me préparer à souper.
Will you have cold meat?	Voulez-vous de la viande froide?
Yes; a small piece of cold veal will do very well, with some Roquefort cheese and a glass of claret.	Oui; un petit morceau de veau froid fera très bien mon affaire, avec du fromage de Roquefort et un verre de Bordeaux.
Will you kindly ask the landlady if she would mind my buying everything I require; of course she would charge me for cooking and attendance.	Voulez-vous avoir la bonté de demander à la propriétaire si cela lui ferait quelque chose que j'achetasse tout ce qu'il me faut; naturellement elle me ferait payer la cuisine et le service.
I will ask madam; but I know she does not much like that way of managing.	Je demanderai à madame; mais je sais qu'elle n'aime pas beaucoup cette manière de faire.

To write a Letter.

Be good enough to bring me some note paper, envelopes, ink, pens and sealing wax.

Here they are, sir, will you require any stamps?

I shall want a shilling's worth of halfpenny stamps to send some circular letters to my friends on the Continent; twelve penny ones, and four two pence halfpenny ones, as I must write to my brothers in France.

Are some of your letters ready? if so, I can take them to the post office when I go out.

When does the mail start?

The letters must be posted before half past five if you want to forward them by the evening mail.

I shall feel much obliged if you will post these two letters for France. I do not think I shall have time to finish the other three.

Do you not think that this letter is too heavy?

I do not think so; but they will weigh it for you at the post office, if you ask them.

Do not forget to bring me some post cards and two envelopes for registered letters.

Shall I procure the Post-office order for you, which you mentioned last night?

Yes, please.

What amount do you intend to send?

Two hundred and thirty-two francs, twenty-five centimes: I am just going out and shall get the money at my banker's.

Do not forget that no Post-office orders are issued after five o'clock.

I shall certainly be back before that time.

Pour écrire une Lettre.

Ayez la bonté de m'apporter du papier à lettre, des enveloppes, de l'encre, des plumes et de la cire à cacheter.

Voici, monsieur; aurez-vous besoin de timbres-poste?

J'aurai besoin d'un shelling de timbres de cinq centimes pour envoyer des lettres de faire-part à mes amis du Continent; de douze timbres de dix centimes, et de quatre timbres de vingt-cinq centimes, vu qu'il faut que j'écrive en France à mes frères.

Quelques unes de vos lettres sont elles prêtes? s'il en est ainsi, je pourrai les porter à la poste, quand je sortirai.

Quand part le courrier?

Les lettres doivent être mises à la poste avant cinq heures et demie si vous voulez les envoyer par le courrier du soir.

Je vous serai très obligé de bien vouloir mettre à la poste ces deux lettres pour France. Je ne pense pas que j'aie le temps de finir les trois autres.

Ne pensez-vous pas que cette lettre soit trop lourde?

Je ne pense pas; mais on vous la pèsera au bureau de poste si vous le demandez.

N'oubliez pas de m'apporter des cartes postales et deux enveloppes pour lettres chargées.

Vous prendrai-je le mandat sur la poste dont vous faisiez mention hier soir?

Oui, s'il vous plaît.

Quelle somme avez-vous l'intention d'envoyer?

Deux cent-trente-deux francs, vingt-cinq centimes: je vais sortir et j'irai chercher l'argent chez mon banquier.

N'oubliez pas qu'on ne délivre pas de mandats sur la poste après cinq heures.

Je serai certainement de retour avant cette heure.

At a Money Changer's.

Will you kindly change this hundred franc note and these twenty franc pieces for me?
Would you like to have gold or notes?
I will take a five-pound note, four pounds in gold and the rest in silver and copper.
What is the exchange for twenty franc pieces?
Fifteen shillings and eight pence.
I expected to lose only three pence on every piece?
I think, on the contrary, I am very reasonable in charging you four pence only.
Can you discount this draft?
I am sorry I cannot do that for you; we only discount drafts when the drawer and the bearer are personally known to us.

Can you direct me to any bank which would discount it?
I am afraid you will find the same difficulty everywhere, unless you are introduced by a friend.
Where could I sell these stocks?
I will take them of you at market prices.
Can you tell me how to invest a small capital?
I would advise you to buy Government bonds or some shares in our great Railway Companies. The interest is not very high, but you have not the slightest risk to run.
I am leaving town for a month: could I deposit these stocks with you?
We will certainly take them to oblige you; but should prefer your depositing them with your banker.
Will you advance me some money on these deeds?
No, sir; we are money changers, but never lend any money.

Chez un Changeur.

Voulez-vous avoir la bonté de me changer ce billet de cent francs et ces pièces de vingt francs?
Voulez-vous avoir de l'or ou des billets de banque?
Je prendrai un billet de banque de cinq livres, quatre livres en or, et le reste en argent et en billon.
Quel est le change pour les pièces de vingt francs?
Quinze shellings et huit pence.
Je ne pensais perdre que trois pence sur chaque pièce?
Je crois au contraire que je suis très raisonnable en ne vous prenant que quatre pence.
Pouvez-vous escompter cette traite?
Je suis fâché de ne pouvoir faire cela pour vous: nous n'escomptons de traites que quand le tireur et le porteur nous sont connus personnellement.

Pourriez-vous m'indiquer une banque qui l'escompterait?
J'ai peur que vous ne trouviez partout la même difficulté; à moins que vous ne soyez présenté par un ami.
Où pourrais-je vendre ces valeurs?
Je vous les prendrai aux prix du cours.
Pourriez-vous me dire comment placer un petit capital?
Je vous conseillerais d'acheter des fonds sur l'état ou quelques actions de nos grandes compagnies de chemins de fer. L'intérêt n'est pas très élevé, mais vous n'avez pas le moindre risque à courir.
Je quitte la ville pour un mois: pourrais-je déposer ces valeurs chez vous?
Nous les prendrons certainement pour vous obliger; mais nous préférerions que vous les dépossassiez chez votre banquier.
Voudriez-vous m'avancer de l'argent sur ces titres?
Non, monsieur; nous sommes changeurs, mais nous ne prêtons jamais d'argent.

Buying.	Achats.
How do you sell this?	Combien vendez-vous ceci?
At the price you see marked; all our goods have the prices marked in plain figures.	Au prix que vous voyez marqué; toutes nos marchandises portent leur prix marqué en chiffres connus.
Is that the lowest price?	Est-ce le plus bas prix?
Yes, we fix our prices as low as possible, and cannot reduce them.	Oui, nous faisons nos prix aussi bas que possible, et nous ne pouvons les réduire.
Give me five yards of this?	Donnez-moi cinq yards de ceci.
Do you think it will be enough?	Pensez-vous que ce soit assez; je crains que vous n'ayez de la peine à vous procurer la même étoffe dans quelques semaines.
I am afraid you will have some trouble in procuring the same material in a few weeks time.	
I am not satisfied with the cloth you sold me the other day. I had a good mind to return it to you.	Je ne suis pas contente du drap que vous m'avez vendu l'autre jour. J'avais bien envie de vous le renvoyer.
We are very sorry you did not do so, as we always do our best to satisfy all our customers.	Nous sommes très fâchés que vous ne l'ayez pas fait, vu que nous faisons toujours de notre mieux pour satisfaire tous nos clients.
Have you still any of the black velvet which you sold to my friend two days ago?	Avez-vous encore du velours noir que vous avez vendu à mon amie il y a deux jours?
I think so; yes, here it is; how much will you take: you can have it a little cheaper than Mrs. ...... if you take the whole, as it is a remnant.	Je pense que oui; le voici; combien en prendrez-vous? vous pouvez l'avoir à un peu meilleur marché que madame ......, si vous prenez le tout, vu que c'est un coupon.
I will take it then: whatever may be the fashion, velvet is always rich and elegant.	Je le prendrai donc: quelle que soit la mode, le velours est toujours riche et élégant.
Shall I show you anything else?	Vous montrerai-je quelque chose d'autre?
I am just considering if I am in want of anything more.	Je me demandais justement si j'avais besoin d'autre chose.
We have very nice sunshades which we could sell you at exceptionally low prices.	Nous avons de très jolies ombrelles que nous pourrions vous vendre à des prix exceptionnellement bas.
The season is rather advanced: I should prefer to have a cheap silk umbrella.	La saison est un peu avancée: je préférerais avoir un parapluie de soie à bon marché.
This is a very good article: I do not think you could buy it cheaper anywhere else.	Voici un très bon article: je ne pense pas que vous puissiez l'acheter autre part meilleur marché.
I will have this one. Please send it to my address, 65, Bessborough Street.	Je prendrai celui-ci. Veuillez me l'envoyer à mon adresse, rue de Bessborough, numéro 65.

Carriages.

Cabman, how much will you charge me to go to the Northern Railway station?

Two francs and fifty centimes, sir.

It is too much: I will give you two francs.

Very well, sir; what train do you want to catch?

I want to leave by the express.

Then we shall have no time to lose.

Where does this omnibus go?

It follows the whole line of the "Boulevards."

What is the fare?

Three pence inside and three half pence outside.

Is there any difference according to the distance?

No, it is the same fare any distance-

Will that omnibus take me to the Southern Railway Station?

No, you will have to take a transfer ticket.

Is there anything to pay for it?

No, the conductor is obliged to give it to anybody who asks for it, without any extra charge.

Where can I find a decent carriage at a reasonable charge?

At the next livery stables.

Are there any regular fares?

Yes, you can have carriages by the drive or by the hour at very moderate charges.

Are the fares the same at all times?

No; they are higher from half past twelve at night till six o'clock in the morning during the summer, and seven during the winter.

Is there anything to pay for the luggage?

Yes; you have to pay an extra charge of twenty-five centimes for every parcel.

Voitures.

Cocher, combien me prendrez-vous pour aller à la gare du Nord?

Deux francs cinquante centimes, monsieur.

C'est trop: je vous donnerai deux francs.

Très bien, monsieur; quel train voulez-vous prendre?

Je veux partir par l'"express."

Alors nous n'avons pas de temps à perdre.

Où va cet omnibus?

Il suit toute la ligne des Boulevards.

Quel est le tarif?

Trente centimes à l'intérieur et quinze centimes sur l'Impériale.

Y a-t-il quelque différence, d'après la distance?

Non, c'est le même tarif pour toutes les distances.

Cet omnibus me conduira-t-il à la Gare du Midi?

Non; vous aurez à prendre une correspondance.

Y a-t-il quelque chose à payer pour ce billet?

Non, le conducteur est obligé de le donner à tous ceux qui le demandent, sans aucune augmentation.

Où puis-je trouver une voiture convenable à un prix raisonnable.

A la première remise.

Existe-t-il un tarif réglementaire?

Oui; vous pouvez avoir des voitures à la course ou à l'heure à des prix très modérés.

Les prix sont-ils les mêmes à toute heure?

Non; ils sont plus élevés depuis minuit et demi jusqu'à six heures du matin, pendant l'été et sept heures pendant l'hiver.

Y a-t-il quelque chose à payer pour les bagages?

Oui; vous avez à payer un supplément de vingt-cinq centimes par colis.

At table.

Where shall I sit?
Take a chair near Mrs. X.......

Shall I help you to some soup?
Yes, thank you.
Mr. X......, will you kindly pass me a piece of bread?
With the greatest pleasure: do you prefer stale or new bread?

As a matter of taste I prefer new bread, but stale bread is more digestible.
Will you take a slice of this beef? it is very nicely done.
Give me a very small piece, please; I do not feel very hungry.

Do you wish to have some gravy?
No, thank you.
Have some potatoes and some haricot beans.
I would rather have some cauliflowers.
Will you kindly carve this fowl? I burnt my right hand the other day, and can hardly do anything with it.
Do you wish to have some more meat?
No, thank you, I have done very nicely.
Shall I help you to some salad? I must tell you that it is seasoned after the French fashion, that is to say, with olive oil and vinegar.
Thank you, I shall like very much to have some, I am rather fond of it.
Will you have some of this apple tart?
No, thank you: I prefer some jelly.
What would you like to drink?
I will take a glass of claret: beer causes me to feel sleepy, and I do not care for heavy wines.
I think you will like this wine: we buy it directly from the grower, to be sure that it has not undergone any adulteration.

A table.

Où m'asseierai-je?
Prenez une chaise près de madame X.......

Vous servirai-je de la soupe?
Oui, merci.
M. X... voulez-vous avoir la bonté de me passer un morceau de pain?
Avec le plus grand plaisir: préférez-vous le pain rassis ou le pain frais?

Comme affaire de goût, je préfère le pain frais, mais le pain rassis est plus facile à digérer.
Prendrez-vous une tranche de ce bœuf? il est très bien cuit.
Donnez m'en un tout petit morceau, je vous prie: je ne me sens pas très faim.

Voulez-vous un peu de jus?
Non, merci.
Prenez des pommes de terre et des haricots.
Je prendrais plutôt des choux-fleurs.
Voulez-vous avoir la bonté de découper cette volaille? je me suis brûlé la main droite l'autre jour et je peux à peine m'en servir.
Désirez-vous encore un peu de viande?
Non, merci; j'ai très bien dîné.

Désirez-vous de la salade? je dois vous dire qu'elle est assaisonnée à la Française, c'est-à-dire à l'huile d'olive et au vinaigre.

Merci, j'en prendrai avec beaucoup de plaisir, je l'aime beaucoup.

Voulez-vous un peu de cette tarte aux pommes?
Non, merci: je préfère de la gelée.
Que désirez-vous boire?
Je prendrai un verre de Bordeaux; la bière m'endort et je n'aime pas les vins capiteux.
Je pense que vous aimerez ce vin-ci: nous l'achetons directement au propriétaire, afin d'être sûr qu'il n'a subi aucun frelatage.

A Walk.

Will you come and take a walk with me? I have nothing to do this afternoon.

Where do you intend going?

I intend going to the "Tuileries," the garden is beautiful; flowers are now in full bloom; the fountains temper the heat of the day; orange trees are covered with blossom, and the chestnut trees invite visitors to sit in their cool and agreeable shade.

How late will it be when we come back?

I do not know: from the "Tuileries" I intend crossing the Concord Square, the most magnificent square in the world, with its perspective of palaces, public buildings, and gardens; then walking along the "Champs Elysees" as far as the "Triumphal arch of the Star.

Do you not think we should do better to take an open carriage and extend our excursion as far as the Boulogne Wood and Acclimatation Garden?

No; I feel I require some exercise and I think I shall enjoy my walk very much.

Very well; I will accompany you: shall we take umbrellas?

I believe it quite unnecessary; the barometer has risen since the beginning of the week, and there is no probability of rain this afternoon.

The clock has just struck nine; let us go, if we do not want to lose the most agreeable part of the day.

Do you not feel tired, and would you not like to sit down a few minutes?

I should like it very much: there is an empty bench, let us sit down.

Une promenade.

Voulez-vous venir faire une promenade avec moi? je n'ai rien à faire cette après-midi.

Où avez-vous l'intention d'aller?

J'ai l'intention d'aller aux Tuileries : le jardin en est beau ; les fleurs sont maintenant en pleine fleur ; les jets d'eau tempèrent la chaleur du jour ; les orangers sont couverts de fleurs et les châtaigniers invitent les visiteurs à s'asseoir à leur ombre fraîche et agréable.

Quelle heure sera-t-il quand nous reviendrons?

Je ne sais pas : en quittant les Tuileries, j'ai l'intention de traverser la place de la Concorde, la place la plus magnifique qu'il y ait au monde, avec sa perspective de palais, d'édifices publics et de jardins ; et alors de marcher le long de Champs Elysées, jusqu'à l'arc de triomphe de l'Etoile.

Ne pensez-vous pas que nous ferions mieux de prendre une voiture découverte et de pousser notre excursion jusqu'au bois de Boulogne et au jardin d'acclimatation?

Non ; j'ai besoin d'exercice et je pense que je prendrai beaucoup de plaisir à ma promenade.

Très bien ; je vous accompagnerai : emporterons-nous des parapluies?

Je crois que c'est tout-à-fait inutile ; le baromètre a monté depuis le commencement de la semaine. et il n'y a aucune probabilité qu'il pleuve cette après-midi.

L'horloge vient de sonner neuf heures ; partons si nous ne voulons pas perdre la partie la plus agréable de la journée.

Ne vous sentez-vous pas fatigué ; n'aimeriez-vous pas à vous asseoir quelques minutes?

J'aimerais beaucoup cela voilà un banc vide, asseyons-nous.

With a Doctor.

I was very unwell the day before yesterday; still worse yesterday, and I felt so bad this morning that I understood I was in want of a doctor's attendance.

What ails you?

I have a violent head-ache; I feel a pain in my limbs, and am not inclined to eat.

Allow me to feel your pulse: it is rather quick. Please show me your tongue. Did you sleep well last night?

Not well at all; I could not go to sleep before one o'clock in the morning.

Do you feel thirsty?

Very: I had some lemonade yesterday, but it did not quench my thirst.

Have you coughed at all lately?

Yes, I had two violent attacks of cough during the night.

You caught a cold very probably: the weather has been rather changeable, and many persons suffer from bronchitis. I shall write a prescription for you.

What do you advise me to eat this afternoon?

I think it will be best to abstain from having anything to-day: I hope you will have a good night's rest and to-morrow morning, I shall call again hoping to find you a great deal better.

Do you expect I shall be confined to my room for a long time?

Oh no! you only require a little rest, and take great care not to catch cold. If you follow exactly all my prescriptions, I have no doubt you will soon recover from this slight indisposition.

Do you think smoking would do me any harm?

I do not think it would do you any good.

Avec un Docteur.

J'ai été très indisposé avant-hier; encore plus hier; et je me suis senti si mal ce matin que j'ai compris que j'avais besoin de l'assistance d'un docteur.

Qu'avez-vous?

J'ai un violent mal de tête; je ressens une douleur dans les membres et je n'ai pas envie de manger.

Permettez-moi de vous tâter le pouls; il est un peu accéléré. Veuillez me montrer votre langue. Avez-vous bien dormi la nuit dernière?

Pas bien du tout; je n'ai pu m'endormir avant une heure du matin.

Vous sentez-vous altéré?

Très altéré: hier j'ai bu de la limonade, mais elle n'a pas apaisé ma soif.

Avez-vous toussé dernièrement?

Oui, j'ai eu deux violentes quintes de toux pendant la nuit.

Vous vous êtes probablement refroidi: le temps a été très variable et beaucoup de personnes souffrent de bronchites. Je vais vous écrire une ordonnance.

Que me conseillez-vous de manger cette après-midi?

Je pense qu'il vaudra mieux vous abstenir de rien prendre aujourd'hui: j'espère que vous aurez un bon repos pendant la nuit, et demain matin je reviendrai avec l'espoir de vous trouver en bien meilleure santé.

Pensez-vous que je sois longtemps consigné dans ma chambre?

Oh non! vous n'avez besoin que d'un peu de repos, et prenez grand soin de ne pas attraper un autre refroidissement. Si vous suivez exactement mes prescriptions, je ne doute pas que vous vous remettiez bientôt de cette légère indisposition.

Pensez-vous que fumer me fasse du mal?

Je ne pense pas que cela vous fasse de bien.

Paris Museums.

Which are the principal museums I ought to visit in this city.

There are the Louvre and the Luxembourg Museums, where are the most celebrated paintings of the ancient masters, and many of living artists.

Does the Louvre Museum contain anything else but paintings?

It includes a splendid collection of statues of the Grecian school, and antiques; also statues of more modern times, and of contemporary sculptors.

Are there any other museums worthy of a visit?

I should advise you to go to the Cluny museum, which contains very interesting collections of furniture and other objects or works of art of the mediæval epoch.

Is it free to the public?

Yes, like all the Museums I mentioned to you: there are, however, days when the public are only admitted with tickets.

Are these three the only museums in Paris?

There are several others less important: I shall only mention the Artillery Museum of St. Thomas d'Aquin, where you will see modern arms of all kinds in large numbers, arranged with much taste; and a beautiful and complete collection of ancient arms and armour.

Is it open every day?

It is only opened to the general public on Sundays, Thursdays and holidays.

Where are the paintings representing the principal episodes of French history?

In the Versailles museum.

When was the palace of Versailles transformed into picture galleries?

In the reign of Louis Philippe.

Musées de Paris.

Quels sont les principaux musées que je devrais visiter dans cette ville?

Il y a les musées du Louvre et du Luxembourg, où sont les plus célèbres tableaux des anciens maîtres et beaucoup de tableaux d'artistes vivants.

Le musée du Louvre contient-il autre chose que des peintures?

Il renferme une splendide collection de statues de l'école Grecque et d'antiques; et aussi des statues de temps plus modernes et de sculpteurs contemporains.

Y a-t-il d'autres musées qui méritent une visite?

Je vous conseillerais d'aller au musée de Cluny, qui contient des collections très-intéressantes de meubles et d'autres objets ou d'œuvres d'art du Moyen âge.

Est-il ouvert au public?

Oui, comme tous les musées que je vous ai mentionnés; il y a cependant des jours où le public n'est admis qu'avec des billets.

Ces trois musées sont-ils les seuls musées de Paris?

Il y en a plusieurs autres moins importants: je mentionnerai seulement le musée d'artillerie de St Thomas d'Aquin, où vous verrez des armes modernes de toute sorte, en grand nombre, arrangées avec beaucoup de goût; et une belle et complète collection d'armes anciennes et d'armures.

Est-il ouvert tous les jours?

Il n'est ouvert à tout le monde que les Dimanches, les Jeudis et les jours de fête.

Où sont les tableaux qui représentent les principaux épisodes de l'histoire de France?

Au musée de Versailles.

Quand le palais de Versailles fut-il transformé en galeries de peinture?

Sous le règne de Louis Philippe.

The Streets of Paris.

I am going to Paris next week; can you give me some information about the streets of that beautiful city?

It would take too long to enumerate the principal streets of Paris: Paris has greatly changed these last fifty years, and principally during the second empire. However I will mention the "Grands Boulevards" which run from "La Madeleine" to "La Place de la Bastille."

Are there any other streets which bear the name of Boulevards?

Yes, there are the Boulevards de Sébastopol and Strasbourg which run in a straight line from the Seine to the Eastern railway station and are prolonged on the other side of the river by the Boulevard St. Michel; the Boulevard Hausmann and many others.

Which is the longest street in Paris?

The Rue Lafayette which with its prolongation, the Rue d'Allemagne, is more than 5 kilometres long and starts from the new Opera House.

What do you call the street which runs round Paris, along the ramparts?

It has different names, generally those of the Generals of the first empire, like Victor, Brune, Bessière, Lannes, Mortier, &c., but bears the general name of Boulevards Extérieurs.

Which street do you consider as the finest in Paris?

The Rue de Rivoli, with its arcades and the splendid buildings which are in it. It is more than three kilometres long.

Are there any embankments in Paris?

On each side the river Seine is embanked, and its banks planted with rows of trees.

Les Rues de Paris.

Je vais à Paris la semaine prochaine; pouvez-vous me donner quelques renseignements sur les rues de cette belle ville?

Il me faudrait trop longtemps pour énumérer les principales rues de Paris : Paris a beaucoup changé depuis cinquante ans, et principalement pendant le second empire. Cependant je mentionnerai les grands boulevards qui s'étendent de la Madeleine à la place de la Bastille.

Y a-t-il d'autres rues qui portent le nom de Boulevards?

Oui, il y a les Boulevards de Sébastopol et de Strasbourg qui vont en droite ligne de la Seine à la gare du chemin de fer de l'Est et se prolongent de l'autre côté du fleuve par le Boulevard St-Michel; le Boulevard Hausmann et beaucoup d'autres.

Quelle est la plus longue rue de Paris?

La rue Lafayette qui, avec sa prolongation, la rue d'Allemagne, a plus de cinq kilomètres de long et part du nouvel Opéra.

Comment appelez-vous la rue qui fait le tour de Paris, le long des remparts?

Elle a différents noms: généralements ceux des généraux du premier empire, comme Victor, Brune, Bessières, Lannes, Mortier, &c.; mais elle porte le nom général de Boulevards Extérieurs.

Quelle rue considérez-vous comme la plus belle rue de Paris?

La rue de Rivoli, avec ses arcades et les splendides édifices qui s'y trouvent. Elle a plus de trois kilomètres de longueur.

Y a-t-il des quais à Paris?

De chaque côté la Seine est bordée de quais, et ses bords sont plantés de rangées d'arbres.

How to Progress in French.	Comment faire des progrès en Français.
I have learnt French at school; I took many lessons, in classes and privately: I know my grammar pretty well, and understand nearly everything I read, but cannot say two words in an intelligible manner. What should I do?	J'ai appris le Français à l'école; j'ai pris beaucoup de leçons dans des classes et de leçons particulières; je sais assez bien ma grammaire et je comprends presque tout ce que je lis; mais je ne sais pas dire deux mots d'une manière intelligible. Que devrais-je faire?
Hear French spoken; have a master that speaks to you in French, very slowly at first, and then more quickly, on the subjects which are familiar to you	Entendre parler français; avoir un maître qui vous parle Français, très lentement d'abord, et ensuite plus vite, sur les sujets qui vous sont familiers.
Is it, then, more useful to listen and to try to understand what is said in a language than trying to speak it one's self?	Est-il donc plus utile d'écouter et d'essayer de comprendre ce que l'on dit dans une langue, que d'essayer de la parler soi-même?
Both are useful and necessary; but you will never pronounce well yourself, if you do not train your ear by hearing that language spoken as frequently as you can.	Les deux choses sont utiles et nécessaires; mais vous ne prononcerez jamais bien vous-même, si vous ne dressez pas votre oreille en entendant parler cette langue aussi fréquemment que vous le pouvez.
When may I hope to be able to speak myself?	Quand puis-je espérer pouvoir parler moi-même?
When your ears can recognise a spoken word as quickly and as accurately as your eyes can read it when it is written or printed. Try to pronounce perfectly some words which contain the greatest difficulties of the French pronunciation, then refer to them for any other word of similar spelling. Read aloud as much as you can, as soon as you have acquired more facility in your pronunciation. Then try to speak and you will be astonished at your progress.	Quand votre oreille pourra reconnaître un mot parlé aussi vite et aussi exactement que vos yeux peuvent le lire quand il est écrit ou imprimé. Essayez de prononcer parfaitement quelques mots qui contiennent les plus grandes difficultés de la prononciation française, et rapportez-y, tout autre mot d'une orthographe analogue. Lisez à haute voix autant que vous le pouvez, aussitôt que vous avez acquis plus de facilité dans votre prononciation. Essayez alors de parler et vous serez étonné de vos progrès.
Can you tell me what is the cause of my not understanding French when spoken?	Pouvez-vous me dire quelle est la cause de ce que je ne comprends pas le Français quand on le parle?
It is because you are not particular enough about the word linking, when you speak yourself.	C'est parceque vous n'êtes pas assez minutieux au sujet de la liaison, quand vous parlez vous-même.

FRENCH VERBS.

REGULAR & IRREGULAR.

BY
A. P. HUGUENET.

CONTENTS.

	PAGE
Definitions	3
Formation of the Tenses	5
The auxiliary verb *avoir*, to have	8
The auxiliary verb *être*, to be	10
The verb *aimer*, to love (1st Conjugation)	12
The verb *punir*, to punish (2nd Conjugation)	13
The verb *recevoir*, to receive (3rd Conjugation)	14
The verb *rendre*, to render (4th Conjugation)	15
Compound tenses conjugated with *avoir*	16
Compound tenses conjugated with *être*	18
Transitive verbs used passively	20
Reflective verbs	21
Conjugation of verbs used negatively	22
Conjugation of verbs used interrogatively and interrogatively and negatively	23
Irregular and defective verbs—	
1st group	24
2nd group	26
Government of verbs	32
Table of the endings of French Verbs (Regular and Irregular)	35

THE VERB.

The verb (Latin, *verbum*, the word) is so called because it is the most important part of speech. There can be no sentence without a verb. Therefore a perfect knowledge of verbs is necessary for any one who wishes to write or to speak a language in a correct and intelligible manner.

The simplest definition of the verb is as follows:

The verb is the word which expresses the action performed by the subject, or the state of the subject.

je *travaille*, I *work;* il *dort,* he *sleeps;* je *suis* malade, I *am* ill.

1. Transitive Verbs in Active Voice.

Transitive verbs or active verbs are those which, not expressing by themselves any complete idea, require a word in the accusative case after them to complete the sense. That word answers the question *qui*, whom, or *que*, what?

j'*aime* mon père, I *love* my father; je *lis* le livre, I *read* the book.

2. Transitive Verbs in Passive Voice.

Verbs are in the Passive Voice when the action, instead of being performed by the subject, is performed on the subject.

      Mon père *est aimé*, my father is loved.
      Le verre *est cassé*, the glass is broken.

The passive voice is formed with the auxiliary *être*, to be, and the past participle of the transitive verb.

3. Intransitive or Neuter Verbs.

Intransitive or neuter verbs are those which generally express a complete sense by themselves. If any word be added to them it never answers the question *qui* or *que*, but one of the questions *à qui*, to whom, or *à quoi*, to what; *de qui*, of whom, or *de quoi*, of what, &c.

      L'enfant *dort*, the child *sleeps;* le livre *appartient* à mon père, the book *belongs* to my father.

4. Reflective, Pronominal, and Reciprocal Verbs.

Reflective and pronominal verbs are used when the action is performed by the subject on itself.

Il *se brûla*, he *burnt himself*; ils *se souviennent*, they *remember*.

Reflective verbs are transitive verbs which are conjugated with two personal pronouns of the same person, the one in the nominative case, as a subject, and the other in the accusative case, as an object or complement.

Pronominal verbs are verbs which can never be used without two pronouns, as *se repentir*, to repent; *se souvenir*, to remember; *se moquer*, to mock, &c.

Reciprocal verbs are those which, being identical in form to reflective and pronominal verbs, express that the action has been exchanged between two or more persons.

Ils *se saluent*, they *salute each other*.
Ils *se haïssent*, they *hate one another*.
Ils *s'écrivent*, they *write to one another*.

5. Impersonal Verbs.

Impersonal verbs are those which can only be used in the third person singular.

Il *pleut*, it *rains*; il *neige*, it *snows*; il *faut*, it *is necessary*.

6. Defective Verbs.

Defective verbs are those which are not used in all tenses as *gésir*, to lie; *ouïr*, to hear; *clore*, to close; *sourdre*, to spring; *tistre*, to weave, &c.

TENSES and MOODS.

Tenses.

Tenses are the inflexions of verbs by which they are made to signify that the action took place, takes place, or will take place at a certain time.

There are in reality only three tenses, *past*, *present*, and *future*; but a past action may have taken place at a more or less remote time, and a future action could take place sooner or later.

This is why there are different past and future tenses, while there is only one present tense.

Moods.

The moods are inflexions of the verb which indicate in what manner the assertion expressed by the verb is made.

There are five moods, as follows:

1. The *indicative*, which simply expresses an affirmation.
    Il *parle* français, he *speaks* French.
2. The *imperative* expresses an order or a prayer.
    Parlez, speak. *Donnez*-moi un morceau de pain, *give* me a piece of bread.
3. The *conditional* indicates that the action is subject to a condition.
    Je *chanterais* si vous le vouliez, I *would sing* if you liked it.
4. The *subjunctive* always depends on another verb which precedes it, and which generally expresses an idea of doubt, fear, uncertainty or negation.
    Je doute qu'il *vienne*, I doubt whether he *may come*.
    Je crains qu'il ne *soit* malade, I fear that he may *be* ill.
    Il n'est pas sûr qu'il *parle*, it is not sure that he *may speak*.
5. The *infinitive* expresses the affirmation in an indefinite manner, without referring to numbers or persons.
    Il est utile d'*étudier*, it is useful *to study*. C'est en *lisant* qu'on s'instruit, it is by *reading* that one becomes learned.

Formation of the Tenses of French Verbs.

Besides the division of the Verb into *simple* and *compound tenses*, which is common to languages in general, French Grammar divides the tenses into two categories :—*primitive* and *derivative tenses*.

The *primitive* tenses are those which serve to form the others; they are five in number:

> *The present of the infinitive;*
> *The present participle;*
> *The past participle;*
> *The present indicative;*
> *The past definite.*

The *derivative* tenses are, as their name indicates, those which are formed from the primitive tenses.

1. The INFINITIVE PRESENT forms two tenses:

   a. The *future absolute*, by the change of *r*, *oir*, or *re* into *rai*:

aimer : j'aime-*rai*.	to love : I shall love.
punir : je puni-*rai*.	to punish : I shall punish.
recevoir : je recev-*rai*.	to receive : I shall receive.
rendre : je rend-*rai*.	to render : I shall render.

   b. The *present conditional*, by the change of *r*, *oir*, or *re* into *rais*:

aimer : j'aime-*rais*.	to love : I should love.
punir : je puni-*rais*.	to punish : I should punish.
recevoir : je recev-*rais*.	to receive : I should receive.
rendre : je rend-*rais*.	to render : I should render.

---

2. The PRESENT PARTICIPLE forms three, or rather two and a half tenses:

   a. The three persons plural of the *present of the indicative*, by the change of *ant* into *ons, ez, ent*:

aimant : nous aim-*ons*, vous aim-*ez*, ils aim-*ent*.	loving : we love, you love, they love.
punissant : nous puniss-*ons*, vous puniss-*ez*, ils puniss-*ent*.	punishing : we punish, you punish, they punish.
rendant : nous rend-*ons*, vous rend-*ez*, ils rend-*ent*.	rendering : we render, you render, they render.

Exception.—Verbs in *oir* (third conjugation) end in the third person plural of the indicative in *oivent*, and not in *event*:

recevant : nous recev-*ons*, vous recev-*ez*, ils reç-*oivent*.	receiving : we receive, you receive, they receive.

   b. The *imperfect of the indicative*, by change of *ant* into *ais*.

aimant : j'aim-*ais*.	loving : I was loving.
punissant : je puniss-*ais*.	punishing : I was punishing.
recevant : je recev-*ais*.	receiving : I was receiving.
rendant : je rend-*ais*.	rendering : I was rendering.

   c. The *present of the subjunctive*, by the change of *ant* into *e*:

aimant : que j'aim-*e*.	loving : that I may love.
punissant : que je puniss-*e*.	punishing : that I may punish.
rendant : que je rend-*e*.	rendering : that I may render.

EXCEPTION.—Verbs in *oir* (third conjugation) change *evant* into *oive*, in the three persons singular and the 3rd person plural: recevant: que je reç-*oive*… ; qu'ils reç-*oivent*.

3. The PAST PARTICIPLE forms all the *compound tenses*, with the help of the auxiliaries *avoir* (to have) or *être* (to be). (*)

aimé : j'ai aimé, j'avais aimé, j'aurai aimé, &c.	loved ; I have loved, I had loved, I shall have loved.
puni: j'aurais puni, que j'aie puni, &c.	punished : I should have punished, that I may have punished, &c.
arrivé : je suis arrivé, j'étais arrivé, je serai arrivé, &c.	arrived : I have arrived, I had arrived, I shall have arrived.
tombé : je serai tombé, que je sois tombé, que je fusse tombé, &c.	fallen : I shall have fallen, that I may have fallen, that I might have fallen.

4. The PRESENT OF THE INDICATIVE forms the *Imperative* by the suppression of the pronouns subjects *je*, *nous* and *vous* :

j'aime : aime.	I love : love (thou).
nous aimons : aimons.	we love : let us love.
vous aimez : aimez.	you love : love (ye).
je punis : punis.	I punish : punish (thou).
nous punissons : punissons.	we punish : let us punish.
vous punissez : punissez.	you punish : punish (ye).

5. The PAST DEFINITIVE forms the *Imperfect of the Subjunctive* by the addition of *se* to the 2nd person singular.

tu aimas : que j'aimas-*se*.	I loved ; that I might love.
tu punis : que je punis-*se*.	I punished : that I might punish.
tu reçus : que je reçus-*se*.	I received : that I might receive.
tu rendis : que je rendis-*se*.	I rendered : that I might render.

(*) All active verbs have their compound tenses formed with the auxiliary *avoir*.
    Neuter verbs generally take *avoir*. The majority of those expressing *movement* take *être*.
    All reflective verbs take *être* in their compound tenses.

The Auxiliary Verb avoir, "to have."

Present INDICATIVE (*Indicatif Présent*).

j'ai, *I have.*
tu as, *thou hast.*
il (elle) a, *he (she, it) has.*

nous avons, *we have.*
vous avez, *you have.*
ils (elles) ont, *they have.*

Imperfect (*Imparfait*).

j'avais, *I had.*
tu avais, *thou hadst.*
il (elle) avait, *he (she, it) had.*

nous avions, *we had.*
vous aviez, *you had.*
ils (elles) avaient, *they had.*

Past Definite (*Passé défini*).

j'eus, *I had.*
tu eus, *thou hadst.*
il (elle) eut, *he (she, it) had.*

nous eûmes, *we had.*
vous eûtes, *you had.*
ils (elles) eurent, *they had.*

1st Future (*Futur absolu*).

j'aurai, *I shall or will have.*
tu auras, *thou wilt have.*
il (elle) aura, *he (she, it) will have.*

nous aurons, *we shall or will have.*
vous aurez, *you will have.*
ils (elles) auront, *they will have.*

1ST CONDITIONAL (*Conditionnel présent*).

j'aurais, *I should or would have.*
tu aurais, *thou wouldst have.*
il (elle) aurait, *he would have.*

nous aurions, *we should or would.*
vous auriez, *you would have[have.*
ils(elles) auraient, *they would have.*

IMPERATIVE (*Impératif*).

aie, *have (thou).*   ayons, *let us have.*   ayez, *have (ye).*

Present SUBJUNCTIVE (*Subjonctif présent*).

que j'aie, *that I may or should have, that I have.*
que tu aies, *that thou mayest have.*
qu'il ait, *that he may have.*

que nous ayons, *that we may have.*
que vous ayez, *that you may have.*
qu'ils aient, *that they may have.*

Imperfect (*Imparfait*).

que j'eusse, *that I might or should have, that I had.*
que tu eusses, *that thou mightest have.*
qu'il eût, *that he might have.*

que nous eussions, *that we might have.*
que vous eussiez, *that you might have.*
qu'ils eussent, *that they might have.*

Present INFINITIVE (*Infinitif présent*).
avoir, *to have.*

Present Participle (*Participe présent*).
ayant, *having.*

Past Participle (*Participe passé*).
eu, *had.*

COMPOUND TENSES.

Perfect (*Passé indéfini*).

j'ai eu, *I have had.*
tu as eu, *thou hast had.*
il a eu, *he has had.*
elle a eu, *she has had.*

nous avons eu, *we have had.*
vous avez eu, *you have had.*
ils ont eu, } *they have had.*
elles ont eu, }

Pluperfect (*Plus-que-parfait*).

j'avais eu, *I had had.*
tu avais eu, *thou hadst had.*
il avait eu, *he had had.*

nous avions eu, *we had had.*
vous aviez eu, *you had had.*
ils avaient eu, *they had had.*

2nd Pluperfect (*Passé antérieur*).

j'eus eu, *I had had.*
tu eus eu, *thou hadst had.*
il eut eu, *he had had.*

nous cûmes eu, *we had had.*
vous eûtes eu, *you had had.*
ils eurent eu, *they had had.*

2nd Future (*Futur antérieur*).

j'aurai eu, *I shall have had.*
tu auras eu, *thou wilt have had.*
il aura eu, *he will have had.*

nous aurons eu, *we shall have had.*
vous aurez eu, *you will have had.*
ils auront eu, *they will have had.*

2nd Conditional (*Conditionnel passé*).

j'aurais (*) eu, *I should have had.*
tu aurais eu, *thou wouldst have had.*
il aurait eu, *he would have had.*

nous aurions eu, *we should have had.*
vous auriez eu, *you would have had.*
ils auraient eu, *they would have had.*

Perfect SUBJUNCTIVE (*Subjonctif passé*).

que j'aie eu, *that I may have had.*
que tu aies eu, *that thou mayest have had.*
qu'il ait eu, *that he may have had.*

que nous ayons eu, *that we may have had.*
que vous ayez eu, *that you may have had.*
qu'ils aient eu, *that they may have had.*

Pluperfect (*Plus-que-parfait*).

que j'eusse eu, *that I might have had.*
que tu eusses eu, *that thou mightest have had.*
qu'il eût eu, *that he might have had.*

que nous eussions eu, *that we might have had.*
que vous eussiez eu, *that you might have had.*
qu'ils eussent eu, *that they might have had.*

Past Infinitive (*Infinitif passé*).

avoir eu, *to have had.*

Past Participle (*Participe passé*).

ayant eu, *having had.*

(*) The imperfect of the subjunctive is often used instead of the conditional of the auxiliary verb: *j'eusse eu, tu eusses eu, il eût eu, nous eussions eu, vous eussiez eu, ils eussent eu.*

The Auxiliary Verb être, "to be."

Present INDICATIVE (*Indicatif présent*).

je suis, *I am.*	nous sommes, *we are.*
tu es, *thou art.*	vous êtes, *you are.*
il (elle) est, *he (she, it) is.*	ils (elles) sont, *they are.*

Imperfect (*Imparfait*).

j'étais, *I was.*	nous étions, *we were.*
tu étais, *thou wast.*	vous étiez, *you were.*
il (elle) était, *he (she, it) was.*	ils (elles) étaient, *they were.*

Past Definite (*Passé défini*).

je fus, *I was.*	nous fûmes, *we were.*
tu fus, *thou wast.*	vous fûtes, *you were.*
il (elle) fut, *he (she, it) was.*	ils (elles) furent, *they were.*

1st Future (*Futur absolu*).

je serai, *I shall be.*	nous serons, *we shall be.*
tu seras, *thou wilt be.*	vous serez, *you will be.*
il (elle) sera, *he (she, it) will be.*	ils (elles) seront, *they will be.*

1st CONDITIONAL (*Conditionnel présent*).

je serais, *I should be.*	nous serions, *we should be.*
tu serais, *thou wouldst be.*	vous seriez, *you would be.*
il (elle) serait, *he (she, it) would be.*	ils (elles) seraient, *they would be.*

IMPERATIVE (*Impératif*).

sois, *be (thou).*   soyons, *let us be.*   soyez, *be (ye).*

Present SUBJUNCTIVE (*Subjonctif présent*).

que je sois, *that I may be, that I be.*	que nous soyons, *that we may be.*
que tu sois, *that thou mayest be.*	que vous soyez, *that you may be.*
qu'il soit, *that he may be.*	qu'ils soient, *that they may be.*

Imperfect (*Imparfait*).

que je fusse, *that I might or should be, that I were.*	que nous fussions, *that we might be.*
que tu fusses, *that thou mightest be.*	que vous fussiez, *that you might be.*
qu'il fût, *that he might be.*	qu'ils fussent, *that they might be.*

Present INFINITIVE (*Infinitif présent*).

être, *to be.*

Present Participle (*Participe présent*).

étant, *being.*

Past Participle (*Participe passé*).

été, *been.*

COMPOUND TENSES.

Perfect (*Passé indéfini*).

j'ai été, *I have been.*
tu as été, *thou hast been.*
il a été, *he has been.*
elle a été, *she has been*

nous avons été, *we have been.*
vous avez été, *you have been.*
ils ont été \} *they have been.*
elles ont été

Pluperfect (*Plus-que-parfait*).

j'avais été, *I had been.*
tu avais été, *thou hadst been.*
il avait été, *he had been.*

nous avions été, *we had been.*
vous aviez été, *you had been.*
ils avaient été, *they had been.*

2nd Pluperfect (*Passé antérieur*).

j'eus été, *I had been.*
tu eus été, *thou hadst been.*
il eut été, *he had been.*

nous eûmes été, *we had been.*
vous eûtes été, *you had been.*
ils eurent été, *they had been.*

2nd Future (*Futur antérieur*).

j'aurai été, *I shall have been.*
tu auras été, *thou wilt have been.*
il aura été, *he will have been.*

nous aurons été, *we shall have been.*
vous aurez été, *you will have been.*
ils auront été, *they will have been.*

2nd Conditional (*Conditionnel passé*).

j'aurais *or* j'eusse été, *I should or would have been.*
tu aurais *or* tu eusses été, *thou wouldst have been.*
il aurait *or* il eût été, *he would have been.*
nous aurions *or* nous eussions été, *we should have been.*
vous auriez *or* vous eussiez été, *you would have been.*
ils auraient *or* ils eussent été, *they would have been.*

Perfect Subjunctive (*Subjonctif passé*).

que j'aie été, *that I may have been.*
que tu aies été, *that thou mayest have been.*
qu'il ait été, *that he may have been.*

que nous ayons été, *that we may have been.*
que vous ayez été, *that you may have been.*
qu'ils aient été, *that they may have been.*

Pluperfect (*Plus-que-parfait*).

que j'eusse été, *that I might have been.*
que tu eusses été, *that thou mightest have been.*
qu'il eût été, *that he might have been.*

que nous eussions été, *that we might have been.*
que vous eussiez été, *that you might have been.*
qu'ils eussent été, *that they might have been.*

Past Infinitive (*Infinitif passé*).
avoir été, *to have been.*

Past Participle (*Participe passé*).
ayant été, *having been.*

The Four Regular Conjugations.

All French verbs end either in *er* (1st Conjugation), in *ir* (2nd Conj.) in *oir* (3rd Conj.), or in *re* (4th Conj.); thence four ways of conjugating regular verbs, or four regular Conjugations.

Simple Tenses of aim-*er*, to love.   *(First Conjugation.)*

(*) P 4 Present INDICATIVE *(Indicatif présent)*.

j'aim-e, *I love, I am loving.*	nous aim-ons, *we love.*
tu aim-es, *thou lovest.*	vous aim-ez, *you love.* } D2
il (elle) aim-e, *he (she, it) loves.*	ils (elles) aim-ent, *they love.*

(*) D 2   Imperfect *(Imparfait)*.

j'aim-ais, *I was loving.*	nous aim-ions, *we loved.*
tu aim-ais, *thou lovedst.*	vous aim-iez, *you loved.*
il (elle) aim-ait, *he (she, it) loved.*	ils (elles) aim-aient, *they loved.*

P 5   Past definite *(Passé défini)*.

j'aim-ai, *I loved.*	nous aim-âmes, *we loved.*
tu aim-as, *thou lovedst.*	vous aim-âtes, *you loved.*
il (elle) aim-a, *he (she, it) loved.*	ils (elles) aim-èrent, *they loved.*

D 1st Future *(Futur absolu)*.

j'aim-erai, *I shall or will love.*	nous aim-erons, *we shall love.*
tu aim-eras, *thou shalt love.*	vous aim-erez, *you shall love.*
il (elle) aim-era, *he (she, it) shall love.*	ils (elles) aim-eront, *they shall love.*

D 1   1st Conditional *(Conditionnel présent)*.

j'aim-erais, *I should or would love.*	nous aim-erions, *we should love.*
tu aim-erais, *thou wouldst love.*	vous aim-eriez, *you would love.*
il (elle) aim-erait, *he (she, it) would love.*	ils (elles) aim-eraient, *they would love.*

D 4   Imperative *(Impératif)*.

aim-e, *love (thou).*   aim-ons, *let us love.*   aim-ez, *love (ye).*

D 2   Present Subjunctive *(Subjonctif présent)*.

que j'aim-e, *that I may love.*	que nous aim-ions, *that we may love.*
que tu aim-es, *that thou mayest love.*	que vous aim-iez, *that you may love.*
qu'il (elle) aim-e, *that he (she, it) may love.*	qu'ils (elles) aim-ent, *that they may love.*

D 5   Imperfect *(Imparfait)*.

que j'aim-asse, *that I might love.*	que nous aim-assions, *that we might love.*
que tu aim-asses, *that thou mightest love.* *[it) might love.*	que vous aim-assiez, *that you might love.* *[might love.*
qu'il (elle) aim-ât, *that he (she,*	qu'ils (elles) aim-assent, *that they*

P 1   Present INFINITIVE *(Infinitif présent)*.   aim-er, *to love.*
P 2   Present participle *(Participe présent)*.   aim-ant, *loving.*
P 3   Past participle *(Participe passé)*.   aim-é, aimée, *loved.*

(*) P Primitive tenses.   D Derivative tenses.   Derivative tenses are marked with the same number as the primitive tenses from which they are derived.

SIMPLE TENSES of pun-*ir*, to punish (*Second Conjugation*).

P 4 Present INDICATIVE (*Indicatif présent*).

je pun-is, *I punish, I am punishing*	nous pun-issons, *we punish.*
tu pun-is, *thou punishest*	vous pun-issez, *you punish.*
il (elle) pun-it, *he (she, it) punishes*	ils (elles) pun-issent, *they punish.*

} D2

D 2 Imperfect (*Imparfait*).

je pun-issais, *I punished, I was punishing.*	nous pun-issions, *we punished.*
tu pun-issais, *thou punishedst.*	vous pun-issiez, *you punished.*
il (elle) pun-issait, *he (she, it) punished.*	ils (elles) pun-issaient, *they punished.*

P 5 Past definite (*Passé défini*).

je pun-is, *I punished.*	nous pun-îmes, *we punished.*
tu pun-is, *thou punishedst* [*ished.*	vous pun-îtes, *you punished.*
il (elle) pun-it, *he (she, it) pun-*	ils (elles) pun-irent, *they punished.*

D 1 1st Future (*Futur absolu*).

je pun-irai, *I shall punish.*	nous pun-irons, *we shall punish.*
tu pun-iras, *thou wilt punish.*	nous pun-irez, *you will punish.*
il (elle) pun-ira, *he (she, it) will punish.*	ils (elles) pun-iront, *they will punish.*

D 1 1st CONDITIONAL (*Conditionnel présent*).

je pun-irais, *I should punish.*	nous pun-irions, *we should punish*
tu pun-irais, *thou wouldst punish.*	vous pun-iriez, *you should punish.*
il (elle) pun-irait, *he (she, it) would punish.*	ils (elles) pun-iraient, *they should punish.*

D 2 IMPERATIVE (*Impératif*).

pun-is, *punish (thou).* pun-issons, *let us punish.* pun-issez, *punish (ye)*

D 2 Present SUBJUNCTIVE (*Subjonctif présent*).

que je pun-isse, *that I may punish.* [*punish.*	que nous pun-issions, *that we might punish.* [*punish*
que tu pun-isses, *that thou mayest*	que vous pun-issiez, *that you may*
qu'il (elle) pun-isse, *that he (she, it) may punish.*	qu'ils (elles) pun-issent, *that they may punish.*

D 4 Imperfect (*Imparfait*).

que je pun-isse, *that I might punish* [*est punish*	que nous pun-issions, *hat we might punish.* [*punish*
que tu pun-isses, *that thou might-*	que vous pun-issiez, *that you might*
qu'il (elle) pun-ît, *that he (she, it) might punish.*	qu'ils (elles) pun-issent, *that they might punish.*

P 1 Present INFINITIVE (*Infinitif présent*).
pun-ir, *to punish.*

P 2 Present participle (*Participe présent*).
pun-issant, *punishing,*

P 3 Past participle (*Participe passé*).
pun-i, pun-ie, *punished.*

SIMPLE TENSES of recev-*oir*, to receive (*Third Conjugation.*)

P 4 Present INDICATIVE (*Indicatif présent*).

je reç-ois, *I receive, I am receiving.*
tu reç-ois, *thou receivest.*
il (elle) reç-oit, *he (she, it) receives.*

nous rec-evons, *we receive.* ⎫ D2
vous rec-evez, *you receive.* ⎬
ils (elles) reç-oivent, *they receive.* ⎭

D 2 Imperfect (*Imparfait*).

je rec-evais, *I received, I was receiving.*
tu rec-evais, *thou receivedst [ceived.*
il (elle) rec-evait, *he (she, it) re-*

nous rec-evions, *we received.*
vous rec-eviez, *you received.*
ils (elles) rec-evaient, *they received.*

P 5 Past definite (*Passé défini*).

je reç-us, *I received.*
tu reç-us, *thou receivedst.*
il (elle) reç-ut, *he (she, it) received.*

nous reç-ûmes, *we received.*
vous reç-ûtes, *you received.*
ils (elles) reç-urent, *they received.*

D 1 1st Future (*Futur absolu*).

je rec-evrai, *I shall receive.*
tu rec-evras, *thou wilt receive.*
il (elle) rec-evra, *he (she, it) will receive.*

nous rec-evrons, *we shall receive.*
vous rec-evrez, *you will receive.*
ils (elles) rec-evront, *they will receive.*

D 1 1st CONDITIONAL (*Conditionnel présent*).

je rec-evrais, *I should receive.*
tu rec-evrais, *thou wouldst receive.*
il (elle) rec-evrait, *he (she, it) would receive.*

nous rec-evrions, *we should receive.*
vous rec-evriez, *you would receive.*
ils (elles) rec-evraient, *they would receive.*

D 4 IMPERATIVE (*Impératif*).

reç-ois, *receive (thou)*. rec-evons, *let us receive*. rec-evez, *receive (ye)*.

D 2 Present SUBJUNCTIVE (*Subjonctif présent*).

que je reç-oive, *that I may receive.*
que tu reç-oives, *that thou mayest receive.*
qu'il (elle) reç-oive, *that he (she, it) may receive.*

que nous rec-evions, *that we may receive* [*receive.*
que vous rec-eviez, *that you may*
qu'ils (elles) reç-oivent, *that they may receive.*

D 5 Imperfect (*Imparfait*).

que je reç-usse, *that I might receive.* [*est receive.*
que tu reç-usses, *that thou might-*
qu'il (elle) reç-ût, *that he (she, it), might receive.*

que nous reç-ussions, *that we might receive.* [*might receive.*
que vous reç-ussiez, *that you*
qu'ils (elles) reç-ussent, *that they might receive.*

P 1 Present INFINITIVE (*Infinitif présent*).
rec-evoir, *to receive.*

P 2 Present participle (*Participe présent*).
rec-evant, *receiving.*

P 3 Past participle (*Participe passé*).
reç-u, reç-ue, *received.*

SIMPLE TENSES of rend-*re*, to render (*Fourth Conjugation*),

P 4   Present INDICATIVE (*Indicatif présent*).

je rend-s, *I render, I am rendering.*	nous rend-ons, *we render.*
tu rend-s, *thou renderest.*	vous rend-ez, *you render.* } D 2
il (elle) rend, *he (she, it) renders.*	ils (elles) rend-ent, *they render.*

D 2   Imperfect (*Imparfait*).

je rend-ais, *I rendered, I was rendering.*	nous rend-ions, *we rendered.*
tu rend-ais, *thou renderest* [*dered.*	vous rend-iez, *you rendered.*
il (elle) rend-ait, *he (she, it) ren-*	ils (elles) rend-aient, *they rendered.*

P 5   Past Definite (*Passé défini*).

je rend-is, *I rendered.*	nous rend-îmes, *we rendered.*
tu rend-is, *thou renderest.*	vous rend-îtes, *you rendered.*
il(elle)rend-it, *he(she, it) rendered.*	ils (elles) rend-irent, *they rendered.*

D 1   1st Future (*Futur absolu*).

je rend-rai, *I shall render.*	nous rend-rons, *we shall render.*
tu rend-ras, *thou wilt render.*	vous rend-rez, *you will render.*
il (elle) rend-ra, *he (she, it) will render.*	ils (elles) rend-ront, *they will render.*

D 1   1st CONDITIONAL (*Conditionnel présent*).

je rend-rais, *I should render.*	nous rend-rions, *we should render.*
tu rend-rais, *thou wouldst render.*	vous rend-riez, *you would render.*
il (elle) rend-rait, *he (she, it) would render.*	ils (elles) rend-raient, *they would render.*

D 4   IMPERATIVE (*Impératif*).

rend-s, *render (thou).*   rend-ons, *let us render.*   rend-ez, *render (ye).*

D 2   Present SUBJUNCTIVE (*Subjonctif présent*).

que je rend-e, *that I may render.* [*render.*	que nous rend-ions, *that we may render.* [*render.*
que tu rend-es, *that thou mayest*	que vous rend-iez, *that you may*
qu'il (elle) rend-e, *that he (she, it) may render.*	qu'ils (elles) rend-ent, *that they may render.*

D 5   Imperfect (*Imparfait*).

que je rend-isse, *that I might render.* [*est render.*	que nous rend-issions, *that we might render* [*might render.*
que tu rend-isses, *that thou might-*	que vous rend-issiez, *that you*
qu'il (elle) rend-ît, *that he (she, it) might render.*	qu'ils (elles) rend-issent, *that they might render.*

P 1   Present INFINITIVE (*Infinitif présent*).
rend-re, *to render.*

P 2   Present Participle (*Participe présent*).
rend-ant, *rendering.*

P 3   Past Participle (*Participe passé*).
rend-u, rend-ue, *rendered.*

D3 COMPOUND TENSES
Conjugated with "avoir" (to have).

(To this Category belong all the *transitive* and the majority of the *intransitive verbs*).

The Verb AIMER (to love).
INDICATIVE MOOD.

Perfect *(Passé indéfini)*.
j'ai aimé, *I have loved.*
tu as aimé, *thou hast loved.*
il a aimé, *he has loved.*
nous avons aimé*, *we have loved.*
vous avez aimé, *you have loved.*
ils ont aimé, *they have loved.*

Pluperfect *(Plus-que-parfait)*.
j'avais aimé, *I had loved.*
tu avais aimé, *thou hadst loved.*
il avait aimé, *he had loved.*
nous avions aimé, *we had loved.*
vous aviez aimé, *you had loved.*
ils avaient aimé, *they have loved.*

2nd Pluperfect *(Passé antérieur)*.
j'eus aimé, *I had loved.*
tu eus aimé, *thou hadst loved.*
il eut aimé, *he had loved.*
nous eûmes aimé, *we had loved.*
vous eûtes aimé, *you had loved.*
ils eurent aimé, *they had loved.*

2nd Future *(Futur antérieur)*.
j'aurai aimé, *I shall have loved.*
tu auras aimé, *thou wilt have loved.*
il aura aimé, *he will have loved.*
nous aurons aimé, *we shall have loved.*
vous aurez aimé, *you will have loved.*
ils auront aimé, *they will have loved.*

---

* After *avoir*, the past participle never agrees with the subject, but agrees with the object when preceded by it.
    Ex. . Nous avons *aimé* nos parents, we have loved our parents.
        Les parents que nous avons *aimés*, the parents whom we have loved

CONDITIONAL MOOD.

2nd Conditional (*) (*Passé*).

j'aurais aimé, *I should have loved.*
tu aurais aimé, *thou wouldst have loved.*
il aurait aimé, *he would have loved.*
nous aurions aimé, *we should have loved.*
vous auriez aimé, *you would have loved.*
ils auraient aimé, *they would have loved.*

SUBJUNCTIVE MOOD.

Perfect (*Passé*).

que j'aie aimé, *that I may have loved.*
que tu aies aimé, *that thou mayest have loved.*
qu'il ait aimé, *that he may have loved.*
que nous ayons aimé, *that we may have loved.*
que vous ayez aimé, *that you may have loved.*
qu'ils aient aimé, *that they may have loved.*

Pluperfect (*Plus-que-parfait*).

que j'eusse aimé, *that I might have loved.*
que tu eusses aimé, *that thou mightest have loved.*
qu'il eût aimé, *that he might have loved.*
que nous eussions aimé, *that we might have loved.*
que vous eussiez aimé, *that you might have loved.*
qu'ils eussent aimé, *that they might have loved.*

INFINITIVE MOOD.

Past (*Passé*).

avoir aimé, *to have loved.*

Past Participle (*Participe passé*).

ayant aimé, *having loved.*

(*) The following forms are also used:—*J'eusse aimé, tu eusses aimé, il eût aimé, nous eussions aimé, vous eussiez aimé, ils eussent aimé.*

D 3 COMPOUND TENSES

Conjugated with "être" (to be).

(To this Category belong all the *reflective* and a few *intransitive* expressing movement.)

The Verb TOMBER (to fall):

INDICATIVE MOOD.

Perfect (*Passé indéfini*).

je suis tombé *or* tombée,(*) *I have fallen.*
tu es tombé *or* tombée, *thou hast fallen.*
il est tombé, *he (it) has fallen.*
elle est tombée, *she (it) has fallen.*
nous sommes tombés *or* tombées, *we have fallen.*
vous êtes tombés *or* tombées, *you have fallen.*
ils sont tombés   } *they have fallen.*
elles sont tombées }

Pluperfect (*Plus-que-parfait*).

j'étais tombé *or* tombée, *I had fallen.*
tu étais tombé *or* tombée, *thou hadst fallen.*
il était tombé, *he (it) had fallen.*
elle était tombée, *she (it) had fallen.*
nous étions tombés *or* tombées, *we had fallen.*
vous étiez tombés *or* tombées, *you had fallen.*
ils étaient tombés   } *they had fallen.*
elles étaient tombées }

2nd Pluperfect (*Passé antérieur*).

je fus tombé *or* tombée, *I had fallen.*
tu fus tombé *or* tombée, *thou hadst fallen.*
il fut tombé, *he (it) had fallen.*
elle fut tombée, *she (it) had fallen.*
nous fûmes tombés *or* tombées, *we had fallen.*
vous fûtes tombés *or* tombées, *you had fallen.*
il furent tombés   } *they had fallen.*
elles furent tombées }

2nd Future (*Futur antérieur*).

je serai tombé *or* tombée, *I shall have fallen.*
tu seras tombé *or* tombée, *thou wilt have fallen.*
il sera tombé, *he (it) will have fallen.*
elle sera tombée, *she (it) will have fallen.*
nous serons tombés *or* tombées, *we shall have fallen.*
vous serez tombés *or* tombées, *you shall have fallen.*
ils seront tombés   } *they will have fallen.*
elles seront tombées }

(*) After *être*, the past participle agrees with the subject.

CONDITIONAL MOOD.
2nd Conditional (*) *(Passé)*.

je serais tombé *or* tombée, *I should have fallen.*
tu serais tombé *or* tombée, *thou wouldst have fallen.*
il serait tombé, *he (it) would have fallen.*
elle serait tombée, *she (it) would have fallen.*
nous serions tombés *or* tombées, *we should have fallen.*
vous seriez tombés *or* tombées, *you would have fallen.*
ils seraient tombés } *they would have fallen.*
elles seraient tombées

SUBJUNCTIVE MOOD.
Perfect *(Passé)*.

que je sois tombé *or* tombée, *that I may have fallen*
que tu sois tombé *or* tombée, *that thou mayest have fallen.*
qu'il soit tombé, *that he (it) may have fallen.*
qu'elle soit tombée, *that she (it) may have fallen.*
que nous soyons tombés *or* tombées, *that we may have fallen.*
que vous soyez tombés *or* tombées, *that you may have fallen.*
qu'ils soient tombés } *that they may have fallen.*
qu'elles soient tombées

Pluperfect *(Plus-que-parfait)*.

que je fusse tombé *or* tombée, *that I might have fallen*
que tu fusses tombé *or* tombée, *that thou mightest have fallen.*
qu'il fût tombé, *that he (it) might have fallen.*
qu'elle fût tombée, *that she (it) might have fallen.*
que nous fussions tombés *or* tombées, *that we might have fallen.*
que vous fussiez tombés *or* tombées, *that you might have fallen.*
qu'ils fussent tombés } *that they might have fallen.*
qu'elles fussent tombées

INFINITIVE MOOD.
Past *(Passé)*.

être tombé *or* tombée, tombés *or* tombées, *to have fallen.*

Past Participle *(Participe passé)*.

étant tombé *or* tombée, tombés *or* tombées, *having fallen.*

(*) The following form is also used:—
    je fusse tombé *or* tombée.
    tu fusses tombé *or* tombée.
    il fût tombé, elle fût tombée.
    nous fussions tombés *or* tombées.
    vous fussiez tombés *or* tombées.
    ils fussent tombés, elles fussent tombées.

Conjugation of Transitive Verbs Used Passively.

Être aimé, *to be loved.*

Present INDICATIVE (*Indicatif présent*).

je suis aimé, *I am loved.*
tu es aimé, *thou art loved.*
il est aimé, *he is loved.*
elle est aimée, *she is loved.*

nous sommes aimés, *we are loved.*
vous êtes aimés, *you are loved.*
ils sont aimés   } *they are loved.*
elles sont aimées

Imperfect (*Imparfait*).

j'étais aimé, *I was loved.*
tu étais aimé, *thou wast loved.*
il était aimé, *he was loved.*

nous étions aimés, *we were loved.*
vous étiez aimés, *you were loved.*
ils étaient aimés, *they were loved.*

Past Definite (*Passé défini*).

je fus aimé, *I was loved.*
tu fus aimé, *thou wast loved.*
il fut aimé, *he was loved.*

nous fûmes aimés, *we were loved.*
vous fûtes aimés, *you were loved.*
ils furent aimés, *they were loved.*

1st Future (*Futur absolu*).

je serai aimé, *I shall be loved.*
tu seras aimé, *thou wilt be loved.*
il sera aimé, *he will be loved.*

nous serons aimés, *we shall be loved.*
vous serez aimés, *you will be loved.*
ils seront aimés, *they will be loved.*

1st CONDITIONAL (*Conditionnel présent*).

je serais aimé, *I should be loved.*

tu serais aimé, *thou wouldst be loved.*
il serait aimé, *he would be loved.*

nous serions aimés, *we should be loved.* [*loved.*
vous seriez aimés, *you would be*
ils seraient aimés, *they would be loved.*

IMPERATIVE (*Impératif*).

sois aimé, *be loved*, soyons aimés, *let us be loved*, soyez aimés, *be (ye) loved.*

Present SUBJUNCTIVE (*Subjonctif présent*).

que je sois aimé, *that I may be loved.* [*be loved.*
que tu sois aimé, *that thou mayest*
qu'il soit aimé, *that he may be loved.*

que nous soyons aimés, *that we may be loved.* [*may be loved.*
que vous soyez aimés, *that you*
qu'ils soient aimés, *that they may be loved.*

Imperfect (*Imparfait*).

que je fusse aimé, *that I might be loved.* [*est be loved.*
que tu fusses aimé, *that thou might-*
qu'il fût aimé, *that he might be loved.*

que nous fussions aimés, *that we might be loved.* [*might be loved.*
que vous fussiez aimés, *that you*
qu'ils fussent aimés, *that they might be loved.*

Present INFINITIVE : être aimé, *to be loved.*
Present Participle : étant aimé, *being loved.*
Past Participle : été aimé, *been loved.*

Conjugation of Reflective Verbs.
Se flatter, *to flatter one's self.*
Present Indicative (*Indicatif présent*).

je me flatte, *I flatter myself.* | nous nous flattons, *we flatter ourselves.*
tu te flattes, *thou flatterest thyself.* | vous vous flattez, *you flatter yourselves.*
il se flatte, *he flatters himself.* | ils se flattent, *they flatter themselves.*

Imperfect (*Imparfait*).

je me flattais, *I flattered myself.* | nous nous flattions, *we flattered ourselves.*
tu te flattais, *thou flatteredst thyself.* | vous vous flattiez, *you flattered yourselves.*
il se flattait, *he flattered himself.* | ils se flattaient, *they flattered themselves.*

Past Definite (*Passé défini*).

je me flattai, *I flattered myself.* | nous nous flattâmes, *we flattered ourselves.*
tu te flattas, *thou flatteredst thyself.* | vous vous flattâtes, *you flattered yourselves.*
il se flatta, *he flattered himself.* | ils se flattèrent, *they flattered themselves.*

1st Future (*Futur absolu*).

je me flatterai, *I shall flatter myself.* | nous nous flatterons, *we will flatter ourselves.*
tu te flatteras, *thou wilt flatter thyself.* | vous vous flatterez, *you will flatter yourselves.*
il se flattera, *he will flatter himself.* | ils se flatteront, *they will flatter themselves.*

1st Conditional (*Conditionnel présent*).

je me flatterais, *I should flatter myself.* | nous nous flatterions, *we should flatter ourselves.*
tu te flatterais, *thou wouldst flatter thyself.* | vous vous flatteriez, *you would flatter yourselves.*
il se flatterait, *he would flatter himself.* | ils se flatteraient, *they would flatter themselves.*

Imperative (*Impératif*).

flatte-toi, *flatter thyself.* | flattons-nous, *let us flatter ourselves.*
flattez-vous, *flatter yourselves.*

Present Subjunctive (*Subjonctif présent*).

que je me flatte, *that I may flatter myself.* | que nous nous flattions, *that we may flatter ourselves.*
que tu te flattes, *that thou mayest flatter thyself.* | que vous vous flattiez, *that you may flatter yourselves.*
qu'il se flatte, *that he may flatter himself.* | qu'ils se flattent, *that they may flatter themselves.*

Imperfect (*Imparfait*).

que je me flattasse, *that I might flatter myself.* | que nous nous flattassions, *that we might flatter ourselves.*
que tu te flattasses, *that thou mightest flatter thyself.* | que vous vous flattassiez, *that you might flatter yourselves.*
qu'il se flattât, *that he might flatter himself.* | qu'ils se flattassent, *that they might flatter themselves.*

Present Infinitive :   se flatter, *to flatter one's self.*
Present Participle :   se flattant, *flattering one's self.*
Past Participle :   flatté, *flattered.*

Verbs can be conjugated in four ways, viz. :—
- (a) **Affirmatively** : je suis, *I am.*
- (b) **Negatively** : je ne suis pas, *I am not.*
- (c) **Interrogatively** : suis-je, *am I?*
- (d) **Negatively & Interrogatively** : ne suis-je pas, *am I not?*

French Verbs Conjugated Negatively.

Ne pas aimer, *not to love.*

Present INDICATIVE (*Indicatif présent*).

je n'aime pas, *I do not love.* | nous n'aimons pas, *we do not love.*
tu n'aimes pas, *thou dost not love.* | vous n'aimez pas, *you do not love.*
il n'aime pas, *he does not love.* | ils n'aiment pas, *they do not love.*

Imperfect (*Imparfait*).

je n'aimais pas, *I do not love.* | nous n'aimions pas, *we did not love.*
tu n'aimais pas, *thou didst not love.* | vous n'aimiez pas, *you did not love.*
il n'aimait pas, *he did not love.* | ils n'aimaient pas, *they did not love.*

Past Definite (*Passé défini*).

je n'aimai pas, *I did not love.* | nous n'aimâmes pas, *we did not love.*
tu n'aimas pas, *thou didst not love.* | vous n'aimâtes pas, *you did not love.*
il n'aima pas, *he did not love.* | ils n'aimèrent pas, *they did not love.*

Future (*Futur*).

je n'aimerai pas, *I shall, will not love.* | nous n'aimerons pas, *we shall, will not love.*
tu n'aimeras pas, *thou shalt, wilt not love.* [*love.* | vous n'aimerez pas, *you shall, will not love.* [*not love.*
il n'aimera pas, *he shall, will not* | ils n'aimeront pas, *they shall, will*

1st CONDITIONAL (*Conditionnel présent*).

je n'aimerais pas, *I should, would not love.* [*wouldst not love.* | nous n'aimerions pas, *we should, would not love.* [*would not love.*
tu n'aimerais pas, *thou shouldst,* | vous n'aimeriez pas, *you should,*
il n'aimerait pas, *he should, would not love.* | ils n'aimeraient pas, *they should, would not love.*

IMPERATIVE (*Impératif*).

n'aime pas, *do not love,* n'aimons pas, *let us not love,*
n'aimez pas, *do not love.*

Present SUBJUNCTIVE (*Subjonctif présent*).

que je n'aime pas, *that I may not love.* [*mayest not love.* | que nous n'aimions pas, *that we may not love.* [*may not love.*
que tu n'aimes pas, *that thou* | que vous n'aimiez pas, *that you*
qu'il n'aime pas, *that he may not love.* | qu'ils n'aiment pas, *that they may not love.*

Imperfect (*Imparfait*).

que je n'aimasse pas, *that I might not love.* [*mightest not love.* | que nous n'aimassions pas, *that we might not love.* [*might not love.*
que tu n'aimasses pas, *that thou* | que vous n'aimassiez pas, *that you*
qu'il n'aimât pas, *that he might not love.* | qu'ils n'aimassent pas, *that they might not love.*

Present INFINITIVE (*Infinitif présent*) : ne pas aimer, *not to love.*
Present Participle (*Participe présent*) : n'aimant pas, *not loving.*
Past Participle (*Participe passé*) : ne...... pas aimé, *not loved.*

French Verbs conjugated Interrogatively.(*) | Interrogatively and Negatively.

Aimer, *to love.* | Ne pas aimer, *not to love.*

Present INDICATIVE (*Indicatif présent*).

aimé-je ? *do I love ?*	n'aimé-je pas ? *do I not love ?*
aimes-tu ? *dost thou love ?*	n'aimes-tu pas ? *dost thou not love ?*
aime-t-il ? *does he love ?*	n'aime-t-il pas ? *does he not love ?*
aimons-nous ? *do we love ?*	n'aimons-nous pas ? *do we not love ?*
aimez-vous ? *do you love ?*	n'aimez-vous pas ? *do you not love ?*
aiment-ils ? *do they love ?*	n'aiment-ils pas ? *do they not love ?*

Imperfect (*Imparfait*).

aimais-je ? *did I love ?*	n'aimais-je pas ? *did I not love ?*
aimais-tu ? *didst thou love ?*	n'aimais-tu pas ? *didst thou not love ?*
aimait-il ? *did he love ?*	n'aimait-il pas ? *did he not love ?*
aimions-nous ? *did we love ?*	n'aimions-nous pas? *did we not love ?*
aimiez-vous ? *did you love ?*	n'aimiez-vous pas? *did you not love ?*
aimaient-ils ? *did they love ?*	n'aimaient-ils pas? *did they not love ?*

Past Definite (*Passé défini*).

aimai-je ? *did I love ?*	n'aimai-je pas ? *did I not love ?*
aimas-tu ? *didst thou love ?*	n'aimas-tu pas? *didst thou not love ?*
aima-t-il ? *did he love ?*	n'aima-t-il pas ? *did he not love ?*
aimâmes-nous? *did we love ?*	n'aimâmes-nous pas ? *did we not love ?*
aimâtes-vous ? *did you love ?*	n'aimâtes-vous pas ? *did you not love ?*
aimèrent-ils ? *did they love ?*	n'aimèrent-ils pas ? *did they not love ?*

1st Future (*Futur absolu*).

aimerai-je ? *shall I love ?*	n'aimerai-je pas ? *shall I not love?*
aimeras-tu ? *wilt thou love ?*	n'aimeras-tu pas ? *wilt thou not love ?*
aimera-t-il ? *will he love ?*	n'aimera-t-il pas ? *will he not love?*
aimerons-nous ? *shall we love ?*	n'aimerons-nous pas ? *shall we not love ?*
aimerez-vous ? *will you love ?*	n'aimerez-vous pas ? *will you not love ?*
aimeront-ils? *will they love ?*	n'aimeront-ils pas ? *will they not love ?*

1st CONDITIONAL (*Conditionnel présent*).

aimerais-je ? *should I love ?*	n'aimerais-je pas ? *should I not love ?*
aimerais-tu ? *wouldst thou love ?*	n'aimerais-tu pas ? *wouldst thou not love ?*
aimerait-il ? *would he love ?*	n'aimerait-il pas ? *would he not love ?*
aimerions-nous ? *should we love ?*	n'aimerions-nous pas? *should we not love ?*
aimeriez-vous ? *would you love ?*	n'aimeriez-vous pas ? *would you not love ?*
aimeraient-ils ? *would they love ?*	n'aimeraient-ils pas ? *would they not love.*

(*) Verbs are never used Interrogatively in the Imperative nor in the Subjunctive, as an order could not be given under the form of a question, and a verb in the Subjunctive is always governed by another verb which expresses the Interrogation if the sentence be Interrogative.

Irregular and Defective Verbs.

FIRST GROUP.

This group consists of all irregular verbs which form their derivative tenses in accordance with the rules given for the formation of tenses. Verbs, compounds of others, are only given when they are not conjugated like them.

PRIMITIVE TENSES.

Present Infinitive.	Present Participle.	Past Participle.	Present Indicative	Past Definite.
bouillir, *to boil*	bouillant	bouilli	je bous	je bouillis
choir, *to fall*	......	chu	......	......
couvrir, *to cover*	couvrant	couvert	je couvre	je couvris
dormir, *to sleep*	dormant	dormi	je dors	je dormis
forfaire, *to forfeit*	......	forfait	......	......
fuir, *to shun, flee*	fuyant	fui	je fuis	je fuis
gésir, *to lie*	gisant	......	il gît	......
issir, *to issue*	......	issu	......	......
mentir, *to lie*	mentant	menti	je mens	je mentis
offrir, *to offer*	offrant	offert	j'offre	j'offris
ouïr, *to hear*	......	ouï	j'ouïs	......
ouvrir, *to open*	ouvrant	ouvert	j'ouvre	j'ouvris
partir, *to depart*	partant	parti	je pars	je partis
repentir (se), *to repent*	se repentant	repenti	je me repens	je me repentis
saillir(*), *to project*	saillant	sailli	il saille	il saillit
sentir, *to feel*	sentant	senti	je sens	je sentis
servir, *to serve*	servant	servi	je sers	je servis
sortir, *to go out*	sortant	sorti	je sors	je sortis
souffrir, *to suffer*	souffrant	souffert	je souffre	je souffris
tressaillir, *to start*	tressaillant	tressailli	je tresaille	je tressaillis
vêtir, *to clothe*	vêtant	vêtu	je vêts	je vêtis
pleuvoir, *to rain*	pleuvant	plu	il pleut	il plut
surseoir, *to reprieve*	sursoyant	sursis	je sursois	je sursis
absoudre, *to absolve*	absolvant	absous, (*f.*) absoute	j'absous	......
battre, *to beat*	battant	battu	je bats	je battis
braire, *to bray*	......	......	il brait	......
bruire, *to rustle*	......	......	il bruit	......
clore, *to close*	......	clos	je clos	......
conclure, *to conclude*	concluant	conclu	je conclus	je conclus

(*) *Saillir* in the sense of *to spring out, to stream* is regular.

PRIMITIVE TENSES.

Present Infinitive	Present Participle	Past Participle	Present Indicative	Past Definite
conduire (*), to con-duct	conduisant	conduit	je conduis	je conduisis
confire, to pickle, preserve	confisant	confit	je confis	je confis
connaître(†), to know	connaissant	connu	je connais	je connus
coudre, to sew.	cousant	cousu	je couds	je cousis
craindre(‡), to fear	craignant	craint	je crains	je craignis
croire, to believe	croyant	cru	je crois	je crus
croître, to grow	croissant	crû	je croîs	je crûs
écrire, to write	écrivant	écrit	j'écris	j'écrivis
exclure, to exclude	excluant	exclu	j'exclus	j'exclus
frire, to fry	......	frit	je fris	......
lire, to read	lisant	lu	je lis	je lus
luire, to shine	luisant	lui	je luis	......
maudire, to curse	maudissant	maudit	je maudis	je maudis
médire, to slander	médisant	médit	je médis	je médis
mettre, to put	mettant	mis	je mets	je mis
moudre, to grind	moulant	moulu	je mouds	je moulus
naître, to be born	naissant	né	je nais	je naquis
nuire, to hurt	nuisant	nui	je nuis	je nuisis
plaire, to please to	plaisant	plu	je plais	je plus
résoudre, to resolve	résolvant	résou, ré-solu	je résous	je résolus
rire, to laugh	riant	ri	je ris	je ris
rompre, to break	rompant	rompu	je romps	je rompis
sourdre, to spring	......	......	......	......
suffire, to suffice	suffisant	suffi	je suffis	je suffis
suivre, to follow	suivant	suivi	je suis	je suivis
taire (se), to be silent	se taisant	tu	je me tais	je me tus
tistre, to weave	......	tissu	......	......
traire, to milk	trayant	trait	je trais	......
vaincre, to conquer	vainquant	vaincu	je vaincs	je vainquis
vivre, to live	vivant	vécu	je vis	je vécus

(*) All verbs ending in *uire*, except *bruire*, *luire* and *nuire*, are conjugated like *conduire*.

(†) All verbs ending in *attre*, except *nattre*, are conjugated like *connaître*.

(‡) All verbs ending in *aindre*, *eindre* and *oindre*, are irregular, and must be conjugated like *craindre*.

IRREGULAR AND

SECOND

This group consists of the irregular verbs which do not form all

NOTES. I. All verbs form their Imperfect of the Subjunctive regularly from the Past Definite. *Savoir*, to know, and *avoir*, to have, are the only ones in which the Imperfects of the Indicative *je savais, j'avais* are not formed regularly from the Present Participle.

PRIMITIVE TENSES.

Present INFINITIVE.	Present PARTICIPLE	Past PARTICIPLE	Present INDICATIVE	Past DEFINITE.
aller, *to go*	allant	allé	je vais	j'allai
envoyer, *to send*	envoyant	envoyé	j'envoie	j'envoyai
acquérir, *to acquire*	acquérant	acquis	j'acquiers	j'acquis
courir, *to run*	courant	couru	je cours	je courus
cueillir, *to gather*	cueillant	cueilli	je cueille	je cueillis
faillir, *to fail*.	faillant	failli	{ je faux, *or* je faillis }	je faillis
mourir, *to die*	mourant	mort	je meurs	je mourus
tenir, *to hold*	tenant	tenu	je tiens	je tins
venir, *to come*	venant	venu	je viens	je vins

DEFECTIVE VERBS.

GROUP.

their derivative tenses in accordance with the rules of formation.

II. The persons of those tenses regularly formed from the primitive tenses are printed in italics.
III. Derivative tenses which are not given here are formed regularly.

DERIVATIVE TENSES,

of which the formation is irregular, either throughout or in certain persons only.

{ PRESENT INDICATIVE: *Je vais*, tu va, il va; *nous allons, vous allez*, ils vont.—FUTURE: J'irai, tu iras, &c.—CONDITIONAL: J'irais, tu irais, &c.—IMPERATIVE: Va, *allons, allez*.—PRESENT SUBJUNCTIVE: Que j'aille, que tu ailles, *que nous allions, que vous alliez*, qu'ils aillent.

{ FUTURE: J'enverrai, tu enverras, &c.—CONDITIONAL: J'enverrais, tu enverrais, &c.

{ PRESENT INDICATIVE: *J'acquiers, tu acquiers, il acquiert, nous acquérons, vous acquérez*, ils acquièrent.—FUTURE: J'acquerrai, tu acquerras, &c.—CONDITIONAL: J'acquerrais, tu acquerrais, &c.—PRESENT SUBJUNCTIVE: Que j'acquière, que tu acquières, qu'il acquière; *que nous acquérions, que vous acquériez*, qu'ils acquièrent.

{ FUTURE: Je courrai, tu courras, &c.—CONDITIONAL: Je courrais, tu courrais, &c.

{ FUTURE: Je cueillerai, tu cueilleras, &c.—CONDITIONAL: Je cueillerais, tu cueillerais, &c.

{ FUTURE: Je faudrai, or *je faillirai*, &c.—CONDITIONAL: Je faudrais, or *je faillirais*.

{ PRESENT INDICATIVE: *Je meurs, tu meurs, il meurt; nous mourons, vous mourez*, ils meurent.—FUTURE: Je mourrai, tu mourras, &c.—CONDITIONAL: Je mourrais, tu mourrais, &c.—PRESENT SUBJUNCTIVE: Que je meure, que tu meures, qu'il meure; *que nous mourions, que vous mouriez*, qu'ils meurent.

{ PRESENT INDICATIVE: *Je tiens, tu tiens, il tient, nous tenons, vous tenez*, ils tiennent.—FUTURE: Je tiendrai, tu tiendras, &c.—CONDITIONAL: Je tiendrais, tu tiendrais, &c.—PRESENT SUBJUNCTIVE: Que te tienne, que tu tiennes, qu'il tienne; *que nous tenions, que vous teniez*, qu'ils tiennent.

{ PRESENT INDICATIVE: *Je viens, tu viens, il vient; nous venons, vous venez*, ils viennent.—FUTURE: je viendrai, tu viendras, &c.—CONDITIONAL: Je viendrais, tu viendrais, &c.—PRESENT SUBJUNCTIVE: Que je vienne, que tu viennes, qu'il vienne: *que nous venions, que vous veniez*, qu'ils viennent.

SECOND

Present INFINITIVE.	Present PARTICIPLE	Past PARTICIPLE	Present INDICATIVE	Past DEFINITE.
déchoir, *to decay, to decline*	...	déchu	je déchois	je déchus
échoir, *to fall due*	échéant	échu	il échoit	il échut
falloir, *to be necessary*	...	fallu	il faut	il fallut
mouvoir, *to move*	mouvant	mu	je meus	je mus
pouvoir, *to be able*	pouvant	pu	je peux *or* puis	je pus
pourvoir, *to provide*	pourvoyant	pourvu	je pourvois	je pourvus
prévaloir, *to prevail*	prévalant	prévalu	je prévaux	je prévalus
prévoir, *to foresee*	prévoyant	prévu	je prévois	je prévis
*s'asseoir, *to sit*	s'asseyant	assis	je m'assieds	je m'assis
savoir, *to know*	sachant	su	je sais	je sus
seoir, *to fit*	séant	...	il sied	...

* *Asseoir* is also conjugated more regularly, its primitive tenses being *assoyant, assis, j'assois, j'assis*.

GROUP—*Continued.*

DERIVATIVE TENSES.

> **Present Indicative**: *Je déchois, tu déchois, il déchoit;* nous déchoyons, vous déchoyez, ils déchoient.—**Future**: Je décherrai, tu décherras, &c.—**Conditional**: Je décherrais, tu décherrais, &c.—**Present Subjunctive**: *Que je déchoie, que tu déchoies, qu'il déchoie, que vous déchoyions, que vous déchoyiez, qu'ils déchoient.*

> **Future**: Il écherra.—**Conditional**: Il écherrait.—**Present Subjunctive**: Qu'il échoie.

> **Future**: Il faudra.—**Conditional**: Il faudrait.—**Present Subjunctive**: Qu'il faille.

> **Present Indicative**: *Je meus, tu meus, il meut, nous mouvons, vous mouvez, ils meuvent.*—**Present Subjunctive**: Que je meuve, que tu meuves, qu'il meuve, *que nous mouvions, que vous mouviez,* qu'ils meuvent.

> **Present Indicative**: *Je peux* or *je puis, tu peux, il peut, nous pouvons, vous pouvez,* ils peuvent.—**Future**: Je pourrai, tu pourras, &c.—**Conditional**: Je pourrais, tu pourrais, &c.—**Present Subjunctive**: Que je puisse, que tu puisses, &c.

> **Future**: Je pourvoirai.—**Conditional**: Je pourvoirais.

> **Future**: Je prévaudrai.—**Conditional**: Je prévaudrais. No Imperative. **Present Subjunctive**: Que je prévale.

> **Future**: Je prévoirai.—**Conditional**: Je prévoirais.

> **Present Indicative**: *Je m'assieds, tu t'assieds, il s'assied; nous nous asseyons, vous vous asseyez, ils s'asseient.*—**Future**: Je m'assiérai, tu t'assiéras, &c., *also,* je m'asseierai, tu t'asseieras, &c.—**Conditional**: Je m'assiérais, tu t'assiérais, &c., *also,* je m'asseierais, tu t'asseierais, &c.

> **Present Indicative**: *Je sais, tu sais, il sait;* nous savons, vous savez, ils savent.—**Imperfect**: Je savais, tu savais, &c.—**Future**: Je saurai, tu sauras, &c.—**Conditional**: Je saurais, tu saurais, &c.—**Imperative**: Sache, sachons, sachez.

> **Present Indicative**: Il sied, ils siéent.—**Imperfect**: Il seyait, ils seyaient.—**Future**: Il siéra, ils siéront.—**Conditional**: Il siérait, ils siéraient.—**Present Subjunctive**: Qu'il siée, qu'ils siéent.

Present INFINITIVE.	Present PARTICIPLE.	Past PARTICIPLE.	Present INDICATIVE.	Past DEFINITE.
valoir *to be worth*	valant	valu	je vaux	je valus
voir, *to see*	voyant	vu	je vois	je vis
vouloir, *to be willing* or *to wish*	voulant	voulu	je veux	je voulus
boire, *to drink*	buvant	bu	je bois	je bus
dire, *to say*	disant	dit	je dis	je dis
faire, *to make*	faisant	fait	je fais	je fis
prendre, *to take*	prenant	pris	je prends	je pris

GROUP—*Continued.*

DERIVATIVE TENSES.

{ PRESENT INDICATIVE: *Je vaux, tu vaux, il vaut ; nous valons, vous valez, ils valent.*—FUTURE: Je vaudrai, tu vaudras, &c.—CONDITIONAL: Je vaudrais, tu vaudrais, &c.—*No* IMPERATIVE.—SUBJUNCTIVE: Que je vaille, que tu vailles, qu'il vaille: *que nous valions, que vous valiez,* qu'ils vaillent.

FUTURE : Je verrai, tu verras, &c.—CONDITIONAL : Je verrais, tu verrais, &c.

{ PRESENT INDICATIVE: *Je veux, tu veux, il veut : nous voulons, vous voulez,* ils veulent.—FUTURE: Je voudrai, tu voudras, &c.—CONDITIONAL: Je voudrais, &c.—IMPERATIVE: ... ... veuillez.—PRESENT SUBJUNCTIVE: Que je veuille, qu tu veuilles, qu'il veuille ; *que nous voulions, que vous vouliez,* qu'ils veuillent.

{ PRESENT INDICATIVE: *Je bois, tu bois, il boit ; nous buvons, vous buvez,* ils boivent.—PRESENT SUBJUNCTIVE: Que je boive, que tu boives, qu'il boive ; *que nous buvions, que vous buviez,* qu'ils boivent.

{ PRESENT INDICATIVE: *Je dis, tu dis, il dit : nous disons,* vous dites, *ils disent.*—NOTE. *Dédire* (to retract), *médire* (to slander), *prédire* (to predict), *interdire* (to interdict), *contredire* (to contradict), are written in the 2nd person plural of the PRESENT INDICATIVE : *vous dédisez, vous médisez, vous prédisez, vous interdisez, vous contredisez.* *Redire,* to say again, is the only compound of *dire,* which is entirely conjugated like it.

{ PRESENT INDICATIVE: *Je fais, tu fais, il fait ; nous faisons,* vous faites, ils font.—FUTURE: Je ferai, tu feras, &c.—CONDITIONAL: Je ferais, tu ferais, &c.—PRESENT SUBJUNCTIVE : Que je fasse, que tu fasses, &c.

{ PRESENT INDICATIVE: *Je prends, tu prends, il prend ; nous prenons, vous prenez,* ils prennent. PRESENT SUBJUNCTIVE : Que je prenne, que tu prennes, qu'il prenne, *que nous prenions, que vous preniez,* qu'ils prennent.

Government of Verbs.

LIST OF VERBS WHICH GOVERN THE PREPOSITION *de*.

absoudre, *to absolve.*
s'abstenir, *to abstain from*
accuser, *to accuse of*
achever, *to finish to*
affecter, *to affect to*
s'affliger, *to be grieved at*
ambitionner, *to be ambitious to*
appartenir, *to belong to*
appréhender, *to apprehend to*
avertir, *to warn to*
s'aviser, *to bethink one's self of*
avoir coutume, *to be used to*
blâmer, *to blame for*
brûler, *to long to*
cesser, *to cease to*
se chagriner, *to vex one's self*
charger, *to charge to*
commander, *to command*
conjurer, *to conjure to*
conseiller, *to advise to*
se contenter, *to be contented with*
convaincre, *to convince*
convenir, *to agree to*
craindre, *to fear to*
décider, *to decide*
décourager, *to discourage*
dédaigner, *to disdain*
défendre, *to forbid to*
défier, *to defy to*
dégoûter, *to disgust*
demander, *to ask to*
se dépêcher, *to hasten to*
se désaccoutumer, *to disaccustom one's self*
désespérer, *to despair of*
se déshabituer, *to lose the habit of*
se désister, *to desist*
détourner, *to deter*
différer, *to defer to*
dire, *to tell to*
discontinuer, *to discontinue to*
disconvenir, *to disagree to*
dispenser, *to dispense with*
dissuader, *to dissuade from*
écrire, *to write to*
s'efforcer, *to endeavour to*
s'effrayer, *to frighten at*
empêcher, *to prevent to*
s'empresser de, *to hasten to*
enjoindre, *to enjoin to*
s'ennuyer, *to get tired.*
entreprendre, *to undertake to*
essayer, *to try to*
s'étonner, *to wonder at*
être charmé, *to be delighted at*
être surpris, *to be surprised to*
être tenté, *to be tempted to*
éviter, *to avoid to*
excuser, *to excuse to*
exempter, *to exempt from*
feindre, *to feign to*
féliciter, *to congratulate upon*
finir, *to finish to*
se flatter, *to flatter one's self for*
frémir, *to shudder*
se garder, *to beware of*
gagner, *to gain*
se glorifier, *to glory in*
gronder, *to scold for*
se hâter, *to hasten to*
s'imaginer, *to imagine to*
s'impatienter, *to grow impatient*
jurer, *to swear*
s'indigner, *to grow indignant*
se lasser, *to grow tired*
manquer(*), *to fail to*
méditer, *to meditate*
se mêler, *to meddle with*
menacer, *to threaten to*
mériter, *to deserve to*
se moquer, *to laugh at*
négliger, *to neglect to*
offrir, *to offer to*
obliger, *to oblige to*
obtenir, *to obtain*
s'offenser, *to be offended at*
omettre, *to omit to*
ordonner, *to order to*
oublier, *to forget to*
pardonner, *to forgive for*

parier, *to bet*
parler, *to talk of*
permettre, *to allow*
persuader, *to persuade to*
se piquer de, *to pretend to*
plaindre, *to pity for*
prescrire, *to prescribe to*
presser, *to urge to*
prier, *to request to*
priver, *to deprive*
professer, *to profess*
projeter, *to project*
promettre, *to promise to*
proposer, *to propose to*
recommander, *to recommend to*
redouter, *to dread*
refuser, *to refuse to*
regretter, *to regret to*
se rappeler, *recollect*
se réjouir, *to rejoice to*

remercier, *to thank for*
se repentir, *to repent*
réprimander, *to reprove*
reprendre, *to chide*
reprocher, *to reproach for*
résoudre, *to resolve to*
rire, *to laugh at*
risquer, *to risk to*
rougir, *to blush to*
sommer, *to summon*
se soucier, *to care for*
souffrir, *to suffer*
soupçonner, *to suspect*
se souvenir, *to remember to*
suggérer, *to suggest to*
supplier, *to entreat to*
tâcher, *to endeavour to*
tenter, *to tempt*
trembler, *to tremble at*
se vanter, *to boast of*

Verbs which Govern the Preposition à.

s'abaisser, *to stoop to*
aboutir, *to lead to*   [*self to*
s'accoutumer, *to accustom one's*
admettre, *to admit to*
s'adonner, *to addict one's self to*
aider, *to help to*
aimer, *to like to*
s'amuser, *to amuse one's self with*
animer, *to animate to*
s'appliquer, *to apply one's self*
apprendre, *to learn to*
s'apprêter, *to prepare one's self to*
s'arrêter, *to stop at*
aspirer, *to aspire to*
s'attendre, *to expect to*
autoriser, *to authorise*
avoir, *to have to*
balancer, *to hesitate to*
se borner, *to limit one's self to*
chercher, *to seek to*
commencer, *to begin to*
condamner, *to condemn to*
consentir, *to consent to*
consister, *to consist to*
continuer(*), *to continue to*
contraindre, *to compel to*
contribuer, *to contribute to*
se décider à, *to make up one's mind to*
demander(*), *to ask to*

dépenser, *to spend at*
destiner, *to destine to*
se déterminer, *to determine on*
se dévouer, *to devote one's self to*
se disposer, *to dispose one's self to*
donner, *to give to*
employer, *to employ to*
encourager, *to encourage to*
engager, *to induce to*
enhardir, *to embolden to*
enseigner, *to teach*
s'étudier, *to prepare one's self to*
être, *to be*
s'évertuer, *to exert one's self to*
exceller, *to excel to*
exciter, *to excite to*
exercer, *to exercise to*
exhorter, *to exhort to*
exposer, *to expose to*
forcer, *to oblige to*
former, *to train up*
habituer, *to accustom to*
se hasarder, *to venture*
hésiter, *to hesitate to*
induire, *to induce*
inviter, *to invite to*
se mettre, *to set at*
montrer, *to show to*
obliger(*), *to oblige to*

s'obstiner, *to persist in*
s'occuper(*), *to occupy one's self*
parvenir, *to succeed in*
penser, *to think of*
perdre, *to lose to*
persévérer, *to persevere in*
persister, *to persist in*
se plaire, *to delight in*
porter, *to prompt*
pousser, *to excite to*
préparer, *to prepare to*
prétendre, *to aspire to*
provoquer, *to incite to*
recommencer, *to begin again to*
se refuser, *to refuse to*
renoncer, *to renounce to*
répugner, *to be repugnant at*
se résigner, *to be resigned to*
se résoudre, *to resolve to*
rester, *to remain to*
réussir, *to succeed in*
servir, *to serve to*
songer, *to think of*
se soumettre, *to submit to*
tarder(*), *to postpone, to long*
suffire(*), *to be sufficient*
travailler, *to work to*
tendre, *to tend to*
tenir, *to wish*
viser, *to aim at*

LIST OF VERBS WHICH REQUIRE NO PREPOSITION BEFORE THE INFINITIVE WHICH FOLLOWS THEM.

aimer mieux, *to like better*
aller(†), *to go*
avoir beau, *to be in vain*
avouer, *to own*
compter, *to intend*
confesser, *to confess*
daigner, *to deign*
déclarer, *to declare*
déposer, *to depose*
désirer, *to wish*
devoir, *to owe*
entendre, *to hear*
envoyer, *to send*
espérer, *to hope*
faillir, *to fail*
faire, *to cause*
falloir, *to be necessary*
s'imaginer, *to imagine*
laisser, *to let*
nier, *to deny*
oser, *to dare*
paraître, *to appear*
penser, *to expect*
pouvoir, *to be able*
préférer, *to prefer*
prétendre, *to pretend*
savoir, *to know*
sembler, *to seem*
souhaiter, *to wish*
soutenir, *to maintain*
valoir mieux, *to be worth more*
venir(‡), *to come*
voir, *to see*
voler, *to hasten*
vouloir, *to be willing*

In examining the preceding lists, the student will notice how frequently French verbs govern a preposition other than the one which is the translation of the preposition used in English. Therefore it will be necessary to study these lists very carefully, and to refer to them every time the least doubt arises on that very important subject.

(*) Verbs marked with an asterisk in these lists sometimes take *de*, and sometimes *à*, according to euphony: but *de* must be used in the passive.
  Ex.: Je suis obligé de faire cela, *I am obliged to do that.*

(†) In the meaning of *to be about to do something.* Ex.: je vais sortir, *I am going out.*

(‡) *Venir*, in the meaning of *to have just done*, governs the preposition *de*.
  Ex.: je viens de rentrer, *I have just returned.*

Table of the Endings of French Verbs (Regular and Irregular).

		1st Conjugation.	2nd, 3rd, and 4th Conjugations.
INDICATIVE	*Present*[A]	e, es, e, ons, ez, ent	s or z, s or x, t[1] (*), ons, ez, ent e, es, e, ons, ez, ent, only in *cueillir, couvrir, offrir, ouvrir, souffrir, tressaillir,* and their compounds
	Imperfect	ais, ais, ait, ions, iez, aient	like the 1st conjugation
	Past Definite	ai, as, a, âmes, âtes, èrent	is, is, it, îmes, îtes, irent us, us, ut, ûmes, ûtes, urent ins, ins, int, înmes, întes, inrent (*venir & tenir* only)
	Future	rai, ras, ra, rons, rez, ront	like the 1st conjugation
CONDITIONAL	*Present*	rais, rais, rait, rions, riez, raient	like the 1st conjugation
IMPERATIVE[3]		..., e, ..., ons, ez, ...	..., s, ..., ons, ez, ..., e, ..., ons, ez, ... only in *cueillir, couvrir, offrir, ouvrir, souffrir, tressaillir,* and their compounds
SUBJUNCTIVE	*Present*[4]	e, es, e, ions, iez, ent	like the 1st conjugation
	Imperfect	asse, asses, ât, assions, assiez, assent	isse, isses, ît, issions, issiez, issent usse, usses, ût, ussions, ussiez, ussent insse, insses, înt, inssions, inssiez, inssent (*venir & tenir* only)

(*) These figures refer to the Exceptions given on page 36.

Exceptions.*

1. **Verbs ending in *ds* and *es* in the First Person keep *d* and *s* in the Third Person without the addition of a *t*.**

2.
Avoir, to have:	j'ai,	tu as,	il a,	nous avons,	vous avez,	ils ont
Être, to be:	je suis,	tu es,	il est,	nous sommes,	vous êtes,	ils sont
Aller, to go:	je vais,	tu vas,	il va,	nous allons,	vous allez,	ils vont
Dire, to say:	...	...	...	...	vous dites,	...
Faire, to make:	...	...	...	...	vous faites	ils font

3.
Avoir:	...	aie,	...	ayons,	ayez	...
Être:	...	sois,	...	soyons,	soyez	...
Savoir:	...	sache,	...	sachons,	sachez	...
Vouloir:	...	...	...	...	veuillez	...
Aller:	...	va,	...	allons,	allez	...

4.
Avoir:	que je sois,	...	qu'il ait	...
Être:	que je sois,	que tu sois,	qu'il soit	...

(*) See page 35.

www.ingramcontent.com/pod-product-compliance
Lightning Source LLC
Chambersburg PA
CBHW020824230426
43666CB00007B/1091